Praise for *Straight Talk*

"Rick Brandon is like a Michelin Star Master Chef who serves wholesome food for the brain in a deliciously scrumptious package. He is one of the few authors who weaves the magic of an in-person workshop between the covers of his book. *Straight Talk* is another masterpiece in Brandon's indomitable style that combines powerful and practical insights with an engaging and enjoyable style."

—Kedar Vashi, Learning and Development Head,
Coca-Cola International

"Rick Brandon's relevant, practical, and engaging approach focuses on the exact skills needed for productive influence while recognizing that in the real world, conversations can be tough, emotional, and don't always go according to plan. *Straight Talk* truly gets it!"

—Kevin DeNoia, Global Head of Leadership and
Executive Development, Credit Suisse

"*Straight Talk* is *the* most unique and practical book I have read on influence management and interpersonal effectiveness. I feel like I just attended Rick Brandon's highly rated workshop in book form in the comfort of my own home . . . What an achievement! There are tips, tools, checklists, or models on practically every page. As a bonus, *Straight Talk* is just flat-out fun to read. Dr. Brandon has set the new gold standard."

—Ed Betof, Worldwide Vice President, Talent Management
& CLO, Becton, Dickinson and Company (Retired)

"*Straight Talk* is a fun read with a conversational tone—packed with real-world examples, relevant quotes, practical tips, and exercises. It's so engaging and action oriented that you'll feel like you're attending an interpersonal skills workshop while reading this book. Dr. Brandon also addresses the complexities of our virtual and hybrid world, giving us an influence savvy how-to manual for our time!"

—Janice Winstead, Director, Leadership Development, Anthem, Inc.

"*Straight Talk* is a spot-on, practical, and critical book for maximizing your interpersonal effectiveness, influence, and work results during this time of COVID. Just like his workshops at Autodesk were for years, Brandon's down-to-earth teaching is fun and easy to absorb . . . Brilliant!"

—Jan Becker, Chief Human Resources Officer, Autodesk (Retired)

"*Straight Talk* is a great, helpful, and practical handbook for understanding and building critical soft skills. Understanding communication dynamics in a mega-corporation in today's work world isn't easy . . . I've witnessed Rick Brandon's "go to" consulting to develop my Fortune 50 company's key talent, and now his *Straight Talk* is the go-to book for developing professional teams and early career executives in the 'real world.'"

—Martin Robatti, Global Human Resources Leader, Fortune 50 company

"*Straight Talk* is a communication skills handbook—a skills-building workshop in book form . . . Brandon packs each chapter with practical tips, simple how-to instruction, relevant quotes, real-world examples, metaphors, humor, and skill drills."
—Nicole Glasrud Haydon, Vice President Learning & Development, Fortune 500 Company

"I'm excited about this book! *Straight Talk* is an invaluable field guide for communication and influence skills in today's demanding, ever-changing, and increasingly virtual work environment. It takes special talent for an author to translate a wildly successful interpersonal skills workshop into book format in such a dynamic, fun, and practical way, and Dr. Brandon is at the top of his game."
—Lisa Goude-Vera, Senior Manager Talent Development, Lockheed Martin Space

"In a world where we're looking at our phones more than talking to one another, those who can pick up their heads and have meaningful conversations have an advantage. *Straight Talk* is a practical guidebook with clear, direct, actionable advice for anyone looking to build their communication skills into a superpower both at work and at home. Dr. Brandon's latest book builds readers' interpersonal savvy through engaging, humor-laced teaching; fun and practical drills; and insights about each skill's application in our modern world of remote work."
—Beth Loeb, Director of Learning & Development, TESLA (retired)

"Dr. Brandon has taught interpersonal influence savvy for decades and now he's made his workshop available in a fun, flowing, reader-friendly book form! Rick's dynamic delivery style in his workshops comes through loud and clear, complete with 'Humor Hits,' 'Demonstration' scripts, and 'Coaching Huddles' to help the readers grapple with their discomfort in learning skills. It's truly a comprehensive and inspiring read!"
—Meribeth Germino, Senior Leadership and Team Performance, Genentech

"Reading only the first few pages turns out to be addictive, like a Netflix series! In today's remote, hybrid, high-pressured, and depersonalized work world, everyone needs skills for re-connecting, achieving results, and excelling. Rick Brandon throws every worker a life preserver for navigating the influence waters with savvy, impact, empathy, and win-win outcomes."
—Doris Bisaro, Group Diversity and Inclusion Lead, Generali Global

"Rick Brandon first grounds readers in the fundamental interpersonal skills of assertive speaking and active listening for accuracy and empathy—skills that are critical to workplace effectiveness and productivity. Then he transitions the learners into step-by-step formats for optimizing essential conversations in gaining agreements, advising others, coaching, challenging ideas, and constructively confronting others to hold them accountable. These competencies help individuals master interpersonal communication with confidence."
—Lisa Welker-Finney, Vice President Human Resources, Boston Scientific Group

"Just in time! In today's stressful and emotion-laden business environment, where employees are blunt (saying whatever's on their mind) or fearful (saying nothing at all), Dr. Brandon's book is filled with practical how-tos for successfully handling any communication challenge that may arise. Thank you!"

—Deborrah Himsel, VP of Organizational Effectiveness, Avon Products (former) and University of Arizona's Eller College of Management's faculty

"Dr. Rick Brandon has knocked it out of the park again! His new book, *Straight Talk*, is an easy, entertaining, and potentially life-changing read. It cleverly transports readers into a workshop he's teaching, exposing them to tools and practices that can be immediately used. This "workshop in a book" is a must-read for anyone who wants to kick it up a notch to dramatically transform both their personal and business interactions and relationships."

—Delta Emerson, President, Global Shared Services, Ryan, LLC (former)

"*Straight Talk* is exactly what the title suggests—Dr. Brandon shares practical, common sense skills, delivered in a funny, easy-to-read format that sounds like he's talking right to you! He gives it to you straight and shares his own vulnerable moments while he encourages us to get better. I love this book—Brandon's examples, stories, and activities come to life in your mind, as if you were attending a live workshop with him!"

—Jen Crabb, Talent Development, Fortune 500 financial services company

"Having been fortunate enough to learn from Rick within his Institute for Management Studies workshops for many years, I was thrilled to learn that he finally decided to share all his insights, best practices, and proven techniques in book form, complete with insightful and clear explanations, dramatic scripted demonstrations, and rigorous practice exercises. This wonderful book is packed with actionable insights and tools to take your communication skills to the next level."

—Charles Good, President, Institute for Management Studies

"*Straight Talk* provides a "workshop" in a quick and easy-to-read format that teaches direct, assertive, empathic, and positive communication skills in a world that requires even more refined communications due to the global and cultural lines we need to reach across . . . *Straight Talk* is an easy-to-use guide that can be used to build and refresh skills . . . enhancing their ability to overcome obstacles and achieve their goals!"

—Stephen Shaffer, Vice President Human Resources, SNP Transformations, Inc.

"We have been bombarded lately with warnings that the 'soft' skills are critical for success today. The author has written a book about some of the most important ones, and he does a superb job of not only defining 'Straight Talk,' but also giving us a guidebook so that we can practice it immediately! And if the practice makes perfect saying is indeed true . . . this book can be a crucial aid. Take it to heart, apply the suggestions immediately, or share with your own team so that the real effect of this is multiplied."

—Beverly Kaye, coauthor of *Help Them Grow or Watch Them Go*, *Love 'Em or Lose 'Em*, *Up Is Not the Only Way*, & *Love It Don't Leave It*

"*Straight Talk* delivers dozens of practical skills, strategies, and tips for anyone whose job demands stellar communication skills. For me, the biggest impact will be in preventing and resolving conflicts, vital keys to collaboration, productive work relationships, and results-driven company cultures."

—Marty Seldman, coauthor of *Survival of the Savvy* and
Leading in the Global Matrix

"As the author of *Every Job Is a Sales Job*, I'd hoped that *Straight Talk* would increase readers' persuasiveness—in any job as well as official selling roles. Brandon's book delivers the goods. He's spot-on calling the book 'edu-tainment.' Like his workshops, he delivers practical, relevant, and robust teaching points and, many times, comedy!"

—Cindy McGovern, author of WSJ bestseller, *Every Job Is a Sales Job*

"Communicating well with those around us is so essential, personally and professionally, and can seem so challenging. Reading Rick Brandon's *Straight Talk* is like having a good friend who cares about you and wants you to be a great communicator—and who has the experience and insight to help you get there. Supportive, funny, and practical throughout, Brandon makes effective communication seem refreshingly doable."

—Erika Andersen, bestselling author of *Change from the Inside
Out* and Founding Partner of Proteus International

"With humor and ease, Rick Brandon brings practical, easy-to-remember skills and approaches to the toughest part of our work—the hundreds of in-person and remote interactions that make up our daily work experience. When one bad conversation can ruin your day, your relationship with your colleagues or your boss, or your ability to get work done, this proven collection of tools can save the day!"

—Lori Mazan, Cofounder and President, Sounding Board, Inc.

"In this engaging workshop-in-a-book, Rick Brandon expertly makes the case for the primary importance of impactful communication skills for success and gives us a no-nonsense action plan for stepping up to the next level of interpersonal power. You can have all the subject matter expertise in the world, but without effectively communicating your ideas, your expertise is useless. That's an oversight in training and education that Rick Brandon masterfully corrects in his new book."

—Gregory A. Ketchum, PhD, Principal, TalentPlanet, My Coach-on-
Demand Podcasts™ and author of *Trapped in the Big Easy: A Hurricane,
Leadership from the Heart, and the Quest for a Life of Purpose*

"In his new book, *Straight Talk*, Dr. Rick Brandon has taken his many years of experience teaching communication and influencing skills to some of the world's largest organizations and distilled them into a pragmatic 'how to' guide. It's a fun approach that puts the reader into the middle of one of Dr. Brandon's programs with a focus on application. *Straight Talk* is a wonderful resource for anyone, but it is critical for managers who need to influence others or have those difficult conversations."

—Jon Peters, Founder, AthenaOnline

"Organizations are waking up to an interpersonal imperative—and *Straight Talk* arrives in the nick of time, offering timely skills given the disconnected nature of work relationships these days due to COVID, hybrid/remote workplaces, and rampant pressures. Communication effectiveness is a mission-critical competency and Brandon ensures can-do readiness with a bottom-line focus rather than any 'touchy feely' purposes. The kicker is his skill set recipe for defusing volatility when others dump their emotional garbage on you!"

—David Pollay, author of *The Law of the Garbage Truck*

"*Straight Talk: Influence Skills for Collaboration and Commitment* is an essential set of abilities to cultivate for today's world. Organizational change and productivity flow through the relationships we cultivate at work. This requires all of us to 'level up' our emotional intelligence and interpersonal skills through active listening, conversations (difficult and building connection), and defusing emotional reactions. This book brings practical how-to skills that will enhance the professional competence of any individual—no matter where they sit in the organization."

—Dr. Kathleen E. Allen, author of *Leading from the Roots: Nature Inspired Leadership for Today's World*

Straight Talk

Also by Rick Brandon, PhD

Survival of the Savvy:
High-Integrity Political Tactics for Career and Company Success

Straight Talk

Influence Skills for Collaboration and Commitment

Rick Brandon, PhD

Matt Holt Books
An Imprint of BenBella Books, Inc.
Dallas, TX

Matt Holt Books is an imprint of BenBella Books, Inc.
10440 N. Central Expressway
Suite 800
Dallas, TX 75231
benbellabooks.com
Send feedback to feedback@benbellabooks.com.

Matt Holt and *BenBella* are federally registered trademarks.

Printed in the United States of America
10 9 8 7 6 5 4 3 2 1

Library of Congress Control Number: 2021040714
ISBN 9781637740651 (trade cloth)
ISBN 9781637740668 (ebook)

Editing by Katie Dickman
Copyediting by Michael Fedison
Proofreading by James Fraleigh and Marissa Wold Uhrina
Indexing by Amy Murphy
Text design and composition by PerfecType, Nashville, TN
Cover design by Brigid Pearson
Interior icons from the Noun Project: demonstration (Claire Jones), dumbbell (Travis J. Lee), comedy mask (b farias), human mind research (Vectors Point), clapperboard (Lona Muoi), whistle (ainul muttaqin), and networking (mynamepong)
Printed by Lake Book Manufacturing

To Bob and Dot . . . The many people whose lives they touched were forever enriched by their vision, wisdom, clarity, and heart

Contents

PART III:
ROUGH SAILING CONVERSATIONS

Introduction

A Workshop-in-a-Book

Life is what happens while you are busy making other plans.
—John Lennon

The above John Lennon quote reminds us to take a good hard look at how we navigate our lives—including our work and personal relationships. Life is too short to just drift along suffering what the founder of humanistic psychology, Abraham Maslow, called "the psychopathology of the average."

I wrote *Straight Talk: Influence Skills for Collaboration and Commitment* to give you my global training company's workshop in book form. Its mission is to help you to turn off autopilot and become more aware and accountable around how you're living and relating with others. Thank you for opening yourself to being more conscious and purposeful about your communication and influence efforts.

When friends and family heard I was writing again, some asked, "Rick, are you nuts? Aren't you afraid the book might hurt your Brandon Partners training company's sales?" Nah, I figured. Not all companies will be clients anyway, so why not share the concepts and skills? Besides, I've taught communication skills my entire career, and I get psychic goodies from making an impact. So, the thought of reaching more "participants" with this book is a high. OK, maybe I need to get out more!

I call what you're reading a "workshop-in-a-book," because it simulates the *Straight Talk* course's practical, down-to-earth, non-academic, and fun delivery style so that folks who can't attend the workshop can benefit. That's why the chapters are called "modules." I've tried to keep the book upbeat and amusing to keep you engaged and at ease as if you were in the workshop.

My Commitments to You

A Wellness Versus Fix-It Model. You don't have to be sick physically to get healthier. The same is true with your interpersonal influence health. I want to support you, building on what you *already* know about positive and impactful communication. I'm not here to criticize you.

No Guilt Trips. You'll discover some mistakes you've made in your interpersonal communication, perhaps even ways that you've been hurtful in your work or home relationships. Please do not judge yourself or beat yourself up. The purpose is *awareness* and improvement, not remorse or blame. This book is a NO GUILT ZONE. My mom was a travel agent for guilt trips. I'm not a big fan of it as a motivator.

No Panaceas. I'm not peddling naïve, quick-fix solutions. We're not talking miraculous overnight changes, but practical ones that gradually make a real impact. Hurricanes and tornadoes get all the publicity, but termites effect massive change with tiny bites. Small steps are significant over time.

Back to Basics. While many skills will be new or upgraded, others may seem like commonsense basics. But common sense isn't always common practice. True professionals get back to basics, whether it's an athlete at training camp or a master violinist practicing scales to become a virtuoso.

Expanding Potential Rather Than Diagnosing. I won't analyze why you communicate how you do. No psycho-archeological expeditions into your past! Just skill-building for the future. When I was a therapist, an acquaintance remarked with a smirk, "So, you're one of those 'shrinks,' huh?" I countered, "Actually, I'm a 'stretch.' I'm not into boiling down someone's whole being into some narrow label or telling them why they are how they are. I prefer to help people stretch their potential and expand their thinking."

Please Make a Commitment to Yourself

I invite you to get the most out of your reading by adopting the suggestions below. They will help you get the most from this workshop-in-a-book.

You Decide What Fits. I won't play know-it-all or claim to know what's right for you. Treat this book as a "*work-shop.*" Let's *work* hard with self-examination and experimentation, but you get to *shop.* Try on each skill. If it doesn't fit, put it back on the rack! Some skills will fit perfectly, others with a few alterations, and some not at all. All I ask is that you try them on.

Recognize Your Own Cultural Perspective. Our interpretations of people's behavior are colored by our own cultural lens. It's impossible to account here for every culture's communication norms, so I depend on you to apply your experience and sensitivity to adjust or even ignore some of my guidelines. Please adapt the skills to take into account national, generational, racial, gender, and sexual orientation considerations.

Look for the Donut, Not the Hole. I invite you to look for where the skills *will* work, not for where or why they won't. Otherwise, when you finish reading, all you'll have is a list of where you *can't* use these tools. Let's choose a healthier, optimistic outlook about the skills' value and applicability.

Be Optimistic. A joke Ronald Reagan would mention at press conferences is about two young boys—Jimmy the optimist and Timmy the pessimist. Five-year-old Jimmy is an optimist and his twin, Timmy, is a pessimist. For Christmas, their folks buy Timmy a new bicycle. He cries, whining that he might fall. They have no money left for good-natured Jimmy. They gather up some horse manure and wrap it for the optimist. Jimmy opens his box, screams with glee, and digs his hands into the poop. The dad is dumbfounded and asks, "Jimmy, how can you be so happy but Timmy is miserable with his shiny bike?" Little Jimmy cheerfully answers with a twinkle of wisdom in his eyes. "Well, Daddy, I just figured . . . with all this crap, there must be a pony in here!" In the same vein, I'll be throwing a lot of material at you, but I hope you'll look for the pony!

Discipline Yourself to Sharpen Your Axe. Taking time out of a busy life to hone interpersonal influence skills takes discipline. My definition of *discipline* is "doing what you don't want to do when you don't want to do it." Investing time and energy to "sharpen your axe" (getting your communication tools in good shape) pays off in the long run. Abe Lincoln said, "Give me six hours to chop down a tree and I will spend the first four sharpening the axe."

Don't Take It Personally . . . On Second Thought, DO! This is primarily a book on business communication. However, applying *Straight Talk* in your personal life will boost your happiness and help you to be more congruent with your values of caring, trust, and integrity. Your overall well-being will spill over into your work life success and satisfaction.

Special Features of This Workshop-in-a-Book

You can expect the following components, just like in my in-person and virtual courses:

 WORKSHOP TIME. Throughout the book, I'll ask you to imagine you are in a *Straight Talk* workshop. Please mentally transport yourself into these involvement scenarios so that you feel what it's like to be a participant.

 EXERCISE. Since this is a workshop-in-a-book, I've packed in many practice drills and other activities to make your learning action-oriented and practical. Please don't skip them. They will enhance your insights, bump up your enjoyment, and build and integrate your skills. You can write answers at www.BrandonPartners.com/StraightTalkBook, where you'll find a downloadable *Straight Talk Exercises Journal*. Please, please, please either use that fillable pdf document or at least create your own *Journal* for completing these engagement tasks.

 HUMOR HIT. I believe we learn best if we're having fun, so I've included occasional relevant joke jolts to keep the reading "edu-taining."

SELF-TALK SHIFT. In the movie *Yellow Submarine*, the Beatles say, "It's all in the mind, you know." Communicating effectively isn't just about how we interact with others, but also how we speak to ourselves. Therefore, I have embedded "Self-Talk Shifts" throughout the book, examples of how to adjust your internal mental chatter for optimal application of the skills.

 DEMONSTRATION. In addition to many shorter examples, at times I'll pull together teaching points with longer demonstrations. Please imagine that you are in a workshop watching a scripted role-play or videotaped demonstration.

 COACHING HUDDLE. In my programs, I stay attuned to participant struggles, possible misinterpretations of the content, and the need for encouragement. You are now my "participant," so I've inserted "Coaching Huddles" that are akin to my chatting with you at a coffee break to clarify a point, add supportive input to help you over a learning hump, or check in on how your learning is going. We're in this together!

VIRTUAL VARIATIONS. Our new work world involves rampant remote communication, so at the end of most chapters you'll find tips for adapting the module in question's *Straight Talk* skill set to virtual meetings, telephone calls, and emails.

Our Workshop Agenda: Module Flow

Instead of spewing out a fragmented potpourri of techniques, the content flow is visually organized from the inside out, as shown on the next page. After building the "Why" case for this book, we'll learn together from the inside out, starting with the *Straight Talk Mindset*, next learning Core Communication Skills, and then funneling them into various easier and tougher interactions you have from day to day.

Part I: Core Communication Skills

Your workshop-in-a-book first establishes the need for *Straight Talk* skills to survive in today's chaotic, challenging work world (module one). We'll next position the importance of your Self-Talk as the enabler of a "F.I.T." *Straight Talk Mindset* (module two), using this acronym:

- *Foster the Business Case* for positive communication,
- *Identify Your Communication Patterns*, and
- *Take the Straight Talk Challenge* to be accountable for constructive communication.

Next, we'll hone the core skills of *Assertive Speaking* (module three). Because they form the building blocks of firmly yet respectfully expressing yourself, we use an "A.B.C." acronym for these *Assertive Speaking* skills:

- *Assertive Delivery,*
- *Bias-Free Language,* and
- *Checking Reactions.*

You'll probably be surprised at all the benefits of empathic, accurate *Active Listening* (modules four and five). It costs us something to "pay attention" (e.g., our time, our energy, and our own agenda). That's why the acronym for this core skill is "F.E.E." and stands for:

- *Focusing,*
- *Exploring,* and
- *Empathizing.*

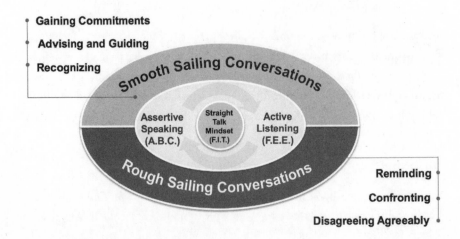

Introduction Diagram 1 | *The Straight Talk* Model

Part II: "Smooth Sailing" Conversations

The *Straight Talk Mindset, Assertive Speaking*, and *Active Listening* skills don't occur in a vacuum. We'll funnel them into Messages and Conversation Formats to efficiently and effectively conduct day-to-day workplace discussions. These less stressful *Straight Talk* situations are less demanding yet critical to master for reliable results, accountability, and optimal relationships:

- *Advising and Guiding* others who approach us with a problem (module six).
- *Gaining Commitments* as a key influence conversation to achieve buy-in (module seven).
- *Recognizing* helpful and positive actions (module eight).

Part III: "Rough Sailing" Conversations

You'll likely rate these tougher *Straight Talk* conversations right up there with walking on crushed glass because they often involve defensive, emotional, or resistant reactions that you'll learn to de-escalate—including yelling, crying, stomping out, threats, and stony silence. They demand clear Message Templates and step-by-step formats to avoid detonation. The "Rough Sailing" applications are:

- *Reminding* others when there is "slippage" or faltering results (module nine).
- *Confronting* problem behavior or a pattern of dropping the ball (module ten).
- *Disagreeing Agreeably* to respond to a shortsighted idea or say "no" to a request (module eleven).

Epilogue: Weaving the Skills into Your Life

In this curtain call, we'll identify and address four predictable challenges of implementing *Straight Talk* skills: faltering Self-Talk, people you don't like, the "fade-out factor" that plagues any training, and back-home culture obstacles.

Takes One to Know One

I don't claim to have perfected everything in this book. Far from it. Many thought leaders teach, write, and coach skills that they most need to learn themselves. For instance, the Greek orator Demosthenes was initially a stutterer, so he went down to the river every day and put pebbles in his mouth to practice speaking clearly. He became one of the greatest speakers (GOAT) after struggling. This book isn't about public speaking, but the example fits. Using good communication skills and managing my own emotions within my own relationships is sometimes a struggle for me, even though I teach the stuff! It's part of my own journey toward ongoing self-improvement. I like to say if we're not growing, we're withering (or dying).

Once, when I was being defensive and wasn't practicing what I preach during a family conversation, my wife, Cheryl, lovingly ribbed me, "Oh, hello, Mr. Listening Skills!" She broke the tension, so I continued the kidding by quipping, "Oh, you misunderstand, honey. I only use listening skills when I'm being paid!" We laughed, I apologized, and we got back on track. I believe that we all do the best we can. As my old friend Ed Lisbe used to say, "We're all bozos on this bus." We all blow it at times. What matters is whether we commit to doing something about it. Please join me in the courageous vulnerability of admitting that we can always improve our interpersonal skills.

Ready to Rock and Roll?

My intent with this introduction was to orient you to the purpose of this workshop-in-a-book and how to get the most out of reading it. While I can't coach you in person, I trust that my explanations, activities, demos, and drills will result in your:

- *Understanding:* grasping of the rationale and how-to steps.
- *Implementing:* expertise and confidence to use the skills.
- *Coping:* the ability to use the skills even under stress.

Part I

Core Communication Skills

Module One | Communication Chaos

The Need for Straight Talk

> The Chinese use two brushstrokes to write the word *crisis*. One
> brushstroke stands for danger, the other for opportunity. In a
> crisis, be aware of the danger—but recognize the opportunity.
> —JOHN F. KENNEDY

Defining *Straight Talk*

Communication challenges have existed since the birth of language, and monumental new needs have been sparked by the dynamics of our current work world. Healthy interpersonal performance is essential not only to survive, but also to thrive. Our real-world work pressures are eased with these interpersonal influence skills:

> **Straight Talk:** *Assertive Speaking* to express our viewpoint directly
> and respectfully; *Active Listening* in ways that invite open expression
> from others, promote productivity, and cultivate positive working
> relationships; and using proven, step-by-step *Conversation Formats* for
> executing critical day-to-day discussions at work and home.

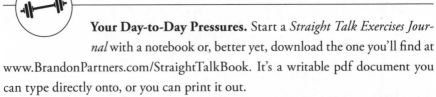

Your Day-to-Day Pressures. Start a *Straight Talk Exercises Journal* with a notebook or, better yet, download the one you'll find at www.BrandonPartners.com/StraightTalkBook. It's a writable pdf document you can type directly onto, or you can print it out.

Now, list all the problems you've had at work in the past few weeks—big or small. Jot down a word or phrase for each problem, as long as you know what it means. I'll wait . . .

OK. Have I cheered up your day yet?

Okay, now examine your list of pain-in-the-butt situations and consider how many are purely Task Problems and how many are Relationship Problems—stressful situations around your communication and interaction with others. For most people, there are at least as many Relationship Problems as Task Problems, and many find far more Relationship versus Task hassles. ∎

What's the Point of the Above Exercise?

We all have both Task Problems and Relationship Problems that drain our time, energy, results, morale, job satisfaction, and health. It's often the Relationship Problems—communication challenges—that keep us awake at night, create stress, erode our morale, and lower our productivity. Our stomachs keep score with ulcers from interactions that drive us crazy.

It's common sense, but not always common practice, to work on our interpersonal skills in order to address Relationship Problems with greater confidence and competence. But the real-world needs for optimal communication extend far beyond your own Relationship Problems and Task Problems sparked by the dynamics of our current work world. Organizations are having a wake-up call about the urgent need—an interpersonal imperative—for world-class communication skills.

Straight Talk Overcomes Today's Hurdles

In mapping out all the below current workplace obstacles that demand optimized people skills, I hope you won't see me as a cynic who can light up a room just by leaving! It's just that in order to address and solve our demanding work life, we first have to recognize and admit that problems exist. Work conditions are tougher than ever before. *Straight Talk* skills form a survival kit for today's arduous workplace conditions. Let's put a magnifying glass on the tough business conditions you face that necessitate the *Straight Talk* skills you'll learn.

Miscommunication Mayhem

Rising performance bars, busy schedules, and constant voicemails, emails, and texts pull us in every direction. The warp speed pace of work leaves everyone too stressed to focus on relationships. Today's complex, matrix-oriented, global companies make effective communication more elusive than ever. The bump in skills demanded is analogous to the leap a high school basketball star must make to even make the team at a college level, much less the professional NBA level.

On top of that, managers under-communicate or miscommunicate due to limited time and resources, ridiculous deadlines, runaway organizational change, and massive responsibility without authority. Senior leaders' communication capabilities are also taxed by being stewards of their companies' resources, reputation, and profits—facing perpetual financial pressures, competition, and customer demands.

Faulty Communication Torches Organizations

Within the maelstrom of challenges plaguing organizations, the cost of faulty communication hits billions each year. Countless time drains are traced to faulty communication. Misunderstanding poisons work relationships. Mistreatment sullies corporate climates and breeds alienation. Teamwork atrophies due to interpersonal shortcomings, and morale withers away into apathy.

First-Line Managers' Quandary

Most new managers are promoted based on their technical expertise—achieving their *own* results. Suddenly they're responsible for getting results with and through other people, which introduces a grab bag full of Relationship Problems. Supervisors inherit an array of headaches, especially if they're managing the same people they used to commiserate with about management (e.g., "I'm happy about my promotion, but it's tough to give my friends feedback or hold them accountable"). This typical dilemma demands stellar communication skills.

Executive Derailment

When an executive is axed due to communication deficiencies, the cost can reach hundreds of thousands per replacement. The Conference Board reports that rehiring costs 150 percent of an exempt professional's salary, 176 percent of an IT professional's salary, and 241 percent of a mid-manager's salary. Intelligence and technical skills are important for mid-level and senior leaders, but these are merely threshold capabilities—entry-level requirements responsible for only 20 percent of an executive's success.

Research reveals that the true success determinant is "Emotional Intelligence" (EI)—a critical group of non-cognitive skills and capabilities: empathy, social skills, self-awareness, self-motivation, and self-regulation of one's emotional responses. The guru of Emotional Intelligence, Daniel Goleman, found that the higher a leader advances, the more critical EI becomes.

Engagement and Retention Shaky Ground

"My boss just doesn't listen to me! . . . The communication around here sucks . . . Raising new ideas isn't safe because they just get shot down . . . I can't get through to her—she commits to following through, but no . . . I know it shouldn't bother me, but I can't get that conversation out of my mind . . . Do I dare tell my boss what I really think of her latest idea?"

Sound familiar? Gallup research reveals that only 30 percent of workers are fully engaged, and the number-one reason given is one's manager. If you ask your family, friends, and work associates to tell you their biggest job complaint, many will likely identify troubling communication patterns and a demoralizing company atmosphere. Employees at every level thirst for positive "dia-logue" because they are weary of managerial "mono-logues" and toxic "duel-logues"! *Straight Talk* skills ameliorate this distress.

Breakneck Rates of Change

Runaway organizational change prompts us to *under*-communicate due to time crunches when, ironically, that's exactly when it's better to *over*-communicate so that requirements don't fall through the cracks. Alvin Toffler's *Future Shock*, a bible for change management, prescribed three coping mechanisms for the exploding rate of change: (1) learning to learn, (2) learning to choose, and (3) learning to relate. *Straight Talk* hits the bull's-eye for the third strategy by enabling effective communication.

Remote Work's Downsides

The need for *Straight Talk* skills is paramount given our migration toward virtual communication and resulting disconnected relationships. Teleworking, remote offices, and virtual communication were escalating before the COVID crisis, more than doubling between 2005 and 2015, according to Global Workplace Analytics (GWA).

The COVID-19 pandemic put this trend into overdrive, doubling it again in 2020 to 50 percent of all workers. Tens of millions of workers around the world were redeployed to basements and home offices with video conferences and other virtual conversations replacing face-to-face interaction. GWA projected that 30 percent of workers would remain remote through 2022. The real impact is even greater.

The Gartner Report research found that by 2022, 53 percent of the U.S. workforce will be a mix of hybrid and fully remote workers. Up to 60 percent of companies will have adopted a hybrid arrangement, many doing so permanently in order to lower brick-and-mortar rent costs, eliminate commute time, and reduce distractions.

Gartner's survey of company leaders reveals that "82 percent of company leaders plan to allow employees to work remotely some of the time" and that 47 percent intend to allow fully remote work. Owl Labs' annual State of Remote Work Report, a study of 2,500 remote workers, predicts that one in two U.S. workers won't return to a job not offering a remote work option. Furthermore, 80 percent of workers expect to work from home at least three days a week after COVID guidelines and restrictions are lifted.

The Human Costs of Remote Work. The balance sheet savings of remote work ignore the price of shrunken in-person contact and corroded work relationships. The collateral damage includes social deprivation, isolation, and loneliness. The *State of Remote Work* study says the sacrifices include difficulty unplugging after work (22 percent), loneliness (19 percent), and lower collaboration (17 percent). Anxiety, depression, drug abuse, and suicide rates have skyrocketed. Virtual work's social isolation is surely a factor.

Noreena Hertz's 2021 book, *The Lonely Century: How to Restore Human Connection in a World That's Pulling Apart,* says one in five adults is suffering from loneliness. Lonely workers are less productive, more likely to quit, and 30 percent more likely to die. Interpersonal contact and the enrichment of relationships through *Straight Talk* skills aren't the cure, but they can certainly ease the pain of separation, isolation, and depersonalization.

Remote Work: A Glass Half-Full or Half-Empty? Please don't get me wrong. Virtual technology brings opportunities for connectivity in our increasingly remote and global world. COVID prompted families to spend more time on video meetings—*seeing* one another rather than only having telephone contact. Virtual technology brings other benefits, like reduced commuting time, increased international interactions, greater ease for disabled workers, and admirable technical savvy in increasingly younger children.

However, let's also be cognizant of the drawbacks of virtual and remote work that are here to stay. Our virtual volcano is erupting into dwindling relationships and a more disconnected and depersonalized status quo. Our voice-to-voice and face-to-face interaction has become massively restricted, as documented in the frightening film *The Social Dilemma.* Our remote world isn't mutually exclusive from human connection, but the term *virtual communication* has increasingly become an oxymoron—like vegetarian meatpacker . . . jumbo shrimp . . . diet ice cream . . . the Village People's greatest hits (oops, sorry, "YMCA" fans!).

The remote work explosion also sends up a red flare warning about technology addiction. Organizational psychologists and human resources officers decry the pipe dream of a high-tech/high-touch balance going up in a puff of smoke. Mental health professionals lament the downsides as stunted personal and interpersonal growth. Has COVID's physical virus not only wreaked havoc on our physical health, but constituted an emotional virus that we also need to cure?

Module Wrap-Up

This module surfaced day-to-day problems requiring top-notch interpersonal prowess, the human and financial pain to individuals and organizations due to flawed interactions, and the unsettling relationship costs of our mushrooming virtual world. I hope the individual, organizational, and societal needs mapped out in this kickoff module whet your appetite for maximizing your *Straight Talk* skills.

The technology of the future—artificial intelligence, online classrooms, and more—will stretch our communication muscles. Interpersonal expertise will be instrumental for productivity and healthy relationships. Failing to optimize the communication aspect of virtual work will squander the tremendous opportunity for staying connected in a disjointed world.

Is optimizing communication in our increasingly high-pressure, remote, and virtual work world a utopian fantasy? NO! This book's messages are hopeful:

1. *Straight Talk* skills give individuals and organizations a fighting chance for surviving and even thriving in today's demanding workplace.
2. *Straight Talk* skills counteract miscommunication caused by work-world pressures.
3. *Straight Talk* skills optimize the in-person contact we still enjoy.
4. *Straight Talk* skills can enrich virtual communication and buffer us from the depersonalization of our virtual, remote lives.

The short story writer Damon Runyon quipped, "The race is not always to the swift nor the battle to the strong. But that's the way to bet." In today's challenging business environment, which individuals and organizations would you bet on? My money is on those that grab the competitive edge offered by stellar interpersonal skills. World-class communication proficiency gives us a fighting chance—maybe even the upper hand—over competitors who are complacent about communication. *Straight Talk* to the rescue!

Module Two | The *Straight Talk Mindset*

Staying Mentally "F.I.T."

> The final weapon is the brain, all else is supplemental.
> —JOHN STEINBECK, *THE ACTS OF KING*
> *ARTHUR AND HIS NOBLE KNIGHTS*

O ur journey's first step is to put a magnifying glass on the heart of the above model—the *Straight Talk Mindset*. We'll learn "Self-Talk" as an *internal* prerequisite skill and enabler for every *external Straight Talk* skill. Self-Talk is integral to the *Straight Talk Mindset*. Next, we'll do some head and heart shaping to ensure that we're mentally and emotionally "F.I.T." as we:

- *Foster the Business Case for Straight Talk* by embracing a bottom-line rationale for positive communication in the workplace.
- *Identify Your Communication Patterns* by knowing where you fall along the *Straight Talk Continuum* of *Passive*, *Aggressive*, or *Assertive* communication.
- *Take the Straight Talk Challenge* by accepting personal accountability for positive communication in spite of its challenges and obstacles.

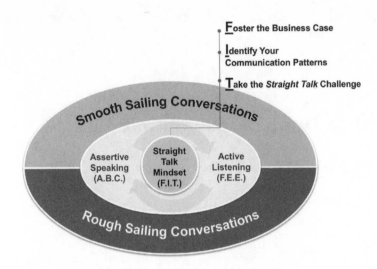

Diagram 2.1 | The *Straight Talk* Model

The Inner Game of Communication: Self-Talk

What Is Self-Talk?

In the classic movie *Cool Hand Luke* (popular shortly after the wheel was invented), an abusive southern prison camp guard drawls to an upstart prisoner (Paul Newman) while torturing him, "Luke, what we have here is a failure to communicate. We gotta get your mind right." I won't torture you in this module, but I do want to "get your mind right" for optimizing *Straight Talk* skills!

Think Back. How many times in the past two weeks have you consciously thought about the words you were going to use to influence somebody? At least a few, right? Now consider how many times in the past two weeks you've consciously thought about the words you were going to use to influence *yourself*. Far fewer times, yes? We don't typically think about how we think. Think about that!

That's what we'll do now—focus on how we think, because influencing *others* with constructive *Straight Talk* demands being in charge of how we influence *ourselves*—how we manage our thoughts while communicating. Every *Straight Talk* skill's comfort and effectiveness requires being in the right frame of mind. Therefore, let's explore Self-Talk as part of the *Straight Talk Mindset* that drives our skill usage. Later, we'll reinforce Self-Talk through "Self-Talk Shifts" sprinkled throughout the book.

What's Self-Talk? Self-Talk is that voice in your head—your self-statements about you, your job, the future, politics, power—everything (including how you think about interpersonal communication and each *Straight Talk* skill). Cognitive psychologist Aaron Beck calls it "automatic mind chatter," and Arnold Lazarus writes: "As long as you're alive, your brain is always active, and a lot of what it does is talk to itself, mainly about you."

You won't optimize your *Straight Talk* skills and may not even try them out if your head isn't in the right place, which involves the "inner game" of *Straight Talk*. Self-Talk can generate negative, demotivating feelings that detract from your communication competence *or* positive, constructive emotions that fortify you for successfully entering the arena of interpersonal influence.

Self-Talk Dynamics: Nonstop Programming

Your Self-Talk goes on all the time whether you're aware of it or not—awake, asleep, daydreaming . . . constantly. Listen to it right now. Hear it whirring away in your head? Yeah! There it is! We all talk to ourselves. Some of us even argue with ourselves. (If you lose those arguments, a therapist may be helpful!) Your Self-Talk programs your brain about everything in your life. As with programming any computer, including the most sophisticated one in the world—the human brain—"garbage in, garbage out."

Self-Talk Dynamics: An Automatic Habit

Please clap your hands (just think about how you feel about this book so far!). Then applaud with the opposite hand on top. Cumbersome, eh? Now cross your arms and notice which hand is on top. Then reverse how you fold your arms. It feels foreign!

You have mental habits—how you talk to yourself—that are just as baked in as your physical habits and just as awkward to alter. We all know people who *habitually* nag themselves (e.g., "I'm such a klutz . . ." or, "I suck at remembering names . . ."), intimidate themselves about business (e.g., "This colleague will never agree to my request . . ."), or disempower themselves socially (e.g., "I shouldn't voice my idea in the meeting because I'm just an assistant . . ."). You may be hurt by counterproductive thinking patterns about your job, your relationships, an upcoming interpersonal challenge, or any of the *Straight Talk* skills. The good news is that negative Self-Talk is a habit you *can* kick.

Self-Talk Dynamics: Sabotage or Support

Henry Ford said, "Whether you think you can or think you can't, you're right." Athletes psych *out* opponents with trash talk designed to get inside each other's head, while supportive coaches psych *up* their players with affirming messages. Your Self-Talk either sabotages or supports your self-concept, feelings, actions, and communication—as well as how well you implement each *Straight Talk* skill and whether you even use a given skill. It's vital to pay attention to your Self-Talk about *Straight Talk*.

Changing Self-Talk: Awareness

The first step in changing Self-Talk is *awareness* of our counterproductive mental programming. Marshall McLuhan is the culture thought leader who coined the phrase "The medium is the message." He also said, "Fish did not discover water . . . because they are completely immersed in it. They live unaware of its existence." Similarly, we're often unaware of what constantly surrounds *us*—our nonstop Self-Talk, especially our negative thinking. We all slip into it, even the experts on Self-Talk (including yours truly).

Confucius Carrie Episode I: From the Mouth of Babes. When my son and daughter were eight and five, respectively, our family was in the Paris airport when my computer and passport were stolen. We had to stay overnight before getting a new passport at the embassy. I was distraught, nearly in tears, until little Carrie reassured me, "Daddy, 'member Self-Talk. You coulda lost *us*." Budding wise philosopher or budding psychologist?

My pal Marty Seldman first taught me about Self-Talk, and he describes how he developed negative mental programming about singing. It stems from a grade school choir teacher saying, "You there in the back row, Martin. Just move your lips, but don't let any sound come out." Ouch. To this day, Marty wrestles with this Self-Talk demon about singing, but his self-awareness helps.

Awareness of Your Trash Talk. In your *Straight Talk Exercises Journal,* jot down your negative Self-Talk about various interpersonal challenges, upsetting situations, and other stressors in your work or personal life.

Negative Self-Talk is any internal statement that triggers negative emotions, especially stronger reactions than you want to have. Identify your thinking patterns that lead to *Fight* feelings (e.g., resentment, anger, etc.) or *Flight* feelings (e.g., anxiety, insecurity, intimidation, etc.). Notice when you "awfulize," predict catastrophe, beat yourself up, worry excessively, over-criticize yourself or others, jump to conclusions, or place demands on yourself with "shoulds" ("should-ing" all over yourself!). Jot down what you say to yourself when you slip into negative Self-Talk. ∎

Easy Does It! When you're finished making notes, notice your Self-Talk *about* your Self-Talk. When you become aware of your own counterproductive Self-Talk, instead of getting self-critical, try to non-judgmentally self-correct with more supportive Self-Talk.

- *Negative Self-Talk:* "Wow, I'm always trash talking myself with put-downs. My Self-Talk sucks. I'm *so* messed up." (How's *that* for lousy Self-Talk? Let's build awareness, not guilt, about our negative Self-Talk.)
- *Positive Self-Talk:* Try on more self-supportive Self-Talk. "Great that I can recognize where I can improve my mindset. We all slip into negative thoughts, but I'm a professional always striving to get better." ∎

Self-Response-Ability. Two fifth graders, Mark and Louise, are in the school lunchroom. Mark has eaten the same thing every day—Monday, Tuesday, Wednesday, and Thursday. He finally explodes on Friday: "Peanut butter, peanut butter, PEANUT BUTTER! I'm sick of peanut butter! It's all I ever have for lunch!" Louise says, "Well, just ask your mom or dad to make something else for you." Mark snaps, "Mom? Dad? They go to work before I even wake up. I make my own lunch!" Do you disempower yourself from having choice and ownership for more "nourishing" Self-Talk? That can stop today if you *believe* you can change.

Changing Self-Talk: Belief in Change

Some people say, "I can't change my Self-Talk. You said it's awkward to change automatic habits." More negative Self-Talk! It's a self-defeating, vicious cycle of self-programming sparking an imprisoning, self-fulfilling prophecy. I didn't say you *can't* change your Self-Talk. I just said it's awkward. If *you* can't change your Self-Talk, who can?

Changing Self-Talk: Choosing Each Moment

To paraphrase Shakespeare's Hamlet: "Nothing is. Thinking makes it so." The *Straight Talk Mindset* tool of Self-Talk assumes that we can choose our mood and attitude about anything. In the *Star Wars* movie franchise, there is a "Dark Side of the Force" (Darth Vader) *and* a "Light Side of the Force" (Obi-Wan Kenobi). Similarly, Self-Talk is a force. You can choose to focus on the "Light Side of the Force" with constructive, positive thinking about any interpersonal situation, unpleasant person, or inner resistance to experimenting with a *Straight Talk* skill.

Positive Self-Talk is not naïve, overly positive thinking that denies reality or real challenges. It's not like walking through the woods saying, "Oh, the sun is shining through the trees and everything's fine, and that snake isn't there at my feet . . . ouch!" It's a more grounded reconditioning of our minds with realistic and *appropriately* optimistic self-statements that calm us down and adjust our perspective.

Switch Channels. Whenever you're tuned into negative thinking about a person or interaction, or when you're being cynical about one of the *Straight Talk* skills, imagine your mind is a television and "switch channels" to a positive, or at least more realistic and less upsetting, program.

- *Negative Self-Talk:* "*Straight Talk* seems like a bunch of 'touchy-feely' soft skills."
- *Positive Self-Talk:* "Interpersonal skills are productivity-driven performance tools that impact my results and work relationships for a competitive advantage."

- *Negative Self-Talk:* "I should have put more time into prepping for this sales presentation. If I screw up, these execs are going to eat me alive. My competition is much more experienced than me. I'm just a rookie."
- *Positive Self-Talk:* "I know my material much better than my audience. They don't know what they don't know, so they won't notice if I do make a mistake. Besides, we're tops in our industry and they're not out to get me, just to see what I offer." ∎

So Many Opportunities! Each skill set in this book is an opportunity to get in touch with your positive or negative thinking. Notice your counterproductive Self-Talk and switch channels to constructive Self-Talk when:

- You have a thought or fear that triggers *Passive* or *Aggressive* behavior.
- You're tempted to cop out from using *Straight Talk* skills.
- You start to shy away from *Assertive Speaking* when expressing your opinion.
- A customer raises objections and it's hard to *Actively Listen* instead of arguing.
- It's hard to start *Recognizing* a direct report because he bugs you.
- A peer proposes an unreasonable policy, so you must *Disagree Agreeably.*
- A person you're *Confronting* gets defensive and hooks you.
- You get discouraged or pessimistic about even trying *Straight Talk* skills.

F = _Foster the Business Case_ for _Straight Talk_

A former colleague once playfully offered a slogan for interpersonal skills training: "Soft Skills for Hard Results." I yelled, "I love it! Let's merchandize it as a bumper sticker!" Some _Straight Talk_ program attendees worry that they've been sent to "Charm School" to learn "touchy-feely skills." They quickly realize that these skills are anything but _soft_, because they achieve _hard_ results. In fact, enhancing positive communication skills is mission-critical for effective companies.

That's why the _F_ of being "F.I.T." means to _Foster the Business Case_ for positive workplace communication. The previous module outlined the challenges facing individuals, companies, agencies, and nonprofits around the world, all of which drive our call to action—an "interpersonal imperative." Now let's detail further reasons that _Straight Talk_ prowess makes good business sense and provides individuals and organizations a competitive advantage.

Interpersonal Influence

An Essential Competency. As this book's subtitle previews, a key business case for _Straight Talk_ skills includes today's necessity for stellar influence skills. In over thirty-five years of teaching around the globe, I've seen inadequate influence skills derail careers. A leader's, manager's, and employee's success rests upon the ability to exert interpersonal influence, especially in our increasingly competitive world where it's hard to differentiate ourselves. Approval for our ideas, recommendations, proposals, and requests is determined more by how we communicate them than by their actual substance.

The Influence Pyramid. Learning leaders and teams often request "influence skills training" without targeting the exact kind of influence needed. I differentiate between the six dimensions on Diagram 2.2's "Influence Pyramid": (1) _Substantive Influence_ (having sound ideas), (2) _Interpersonal Influence_ (core interpersonal skills), (3) _Style-Based Influence_ (personality and communication style considerations), (4) _Presentation-Based Influence_ (small- and large-group presentations), (5) _Strategic Influence_ (factoring politics and power dynamics into the equation through organizational savvy), and (6) *Self-Influence* (managing one's own reactions and motivation). While we teach courses on each dimension, this *Straight Talk* book targets dimensions number two (Core *Interpersonal Influence*) and number six (*Self-Influence*).

Your "Influence Ship." Influencing interpersonally in our challenging business environment is analogous to a ship sailing in stormy weather. Swells of turbulent changes buffet us about. Lightning bolts of new policies and priorities strike down our ideas. We crash into unforeseen icebergs like hidden agendas or frozen, inaccurate perceptions about us or our function, and it takes only one shark-like coworker to kill our ideas.

The *content* of our ideas forms a *powerful engine* that propels our Influence Ship forward. We also need communication that provides essential *steering* so that our ideas reach their destination. *Straight Talk* skills keep our Influence Ship "steady as she goes," like Captain Jim Kirk did at the helm for the Starship *Enterprise* on *Star Trek*.

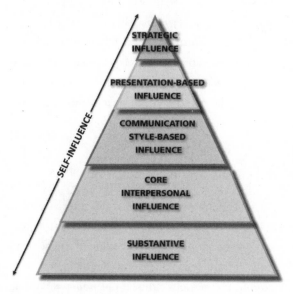

Diagram 2.2 | The Influence Pyramid

Performance Results and Quality

Straight Talk skills give companies a competitive advantage through improved collaboration and commitment. Ineffective "non-leaders" are either bossy, resulting in mere compliance rather than true commitment, or they are unclear, resulting in confusion about expectations. Effective leaders blend *Assertive Speaking* and *Active Listening* skills to gain give-and-take buy-in to goals, roles, quality standards, assignments, projects, responsibilities, and requests for assistance. Peak performance and productivity blossom from positive relationships with direct reports, peers, bosses, cross-organizational business partners, vendors, suppliers, clients, and customers.

Greater Innovation

Another business outcome of world-class interpersonal influence is innovation, which demands an open and honest free flow of ideas, feedback, and suggestions. Companies thwart innovation when employees stifle their opinions for fear of others' abusive reactions. For years, Kodak was the thought leader in their industry, but innovation atrophied when *Passive* people no longer surfaced ideas. A sadder example is NASA's *Challenger* shuttle disaster. Some scientists knew of flawed parts but were unable to convince officials to delay the launch. *Straight Talk* practitioners appreciate people's ideas rather than breeding a nation of sheep. It's said that just one voice at just the right pitch can start an avalanche. It's true for generating innovation, too.

Improved Work Climate and Job Satisfaction

We've stressed the productivity resulting from interpersonal expertise. But there's no shame in wanting satisfying work relationships, too! Warmth and positive regard from interpersonal bonds are some of the goodies we want from work, right? Job satisfaction, engagement, and enjoyment flow from stress-free, smooth, and gratifying interactions. Plus, a harmonious work atmosphere fosters the trust, team spirit, and unity that are precursors to performance quality and quantity.

How are we doing so far? Do you "buy into" the interpersonal performance imperative for leaders and organi-
zations to thrive? If so, you've embraced the *F* of a mentally "F.I.T." *Straight
Talk Mindset, Fostering the Business Case* for positive communication. Any
time you get discouraged about implementing *Straight Talk* skills, use Self-
Talk to remind yourself of positive communication's real-world payoffs. If
someone asks you why you're reading a book about "soft skills," nudge yourself to describe the business results of interpersonal prowess.

I = *Identify Your Communication Patterns*

The *Straight Talk Mindset's I* for staying attitudinally "F.I.T." stands for *Identify
Your Communication Patterns*. We can be *Passive, Aggressive,* or *Assertive*—weak,
harsh, or firm—in our interactions. Or we may slip into less extreme *Borderline
Aggressive* or *Borderline Passive* behavior. Diagram 2.3's *Straight Talk Continuum*
helps us to increase times when we use balanced, *Assertive* communication. Each
position on the *Continuum* involves characteristic ways of interacting.

		Borderline Passive		Borderline Aggressive	
Passive		**Assertive**		**Aggressive**	
• Submissive		• Direct and Honest		• Abusive	
• Weak		• Firm		• Harsh	
• "Nice:" Acquiesces		• "Noble:" Collaborates		• "Nasty:" Bullies	
• Holds Back, Withholds		• Constructive Debate		• Dominates	
• Disengaged		• Shared Leadership		• Command and Control	
• Lose-Win		• Win-Win		• Win-Lose	

Diagram 2.3 | The *Straight Talk Continuum*

Passive Communication

On the *Passive* end of the *Straight Talk Continuum*, people are submissive and weak. They try too hard to meet others' needs at their own expense. *Passive* and *Borderline Passive* communicators avoid tough conversations. They're so concerned about being "nice" and avoiding conflict that they opt out of key discussions. They shy away from speaking directly out of intimidation.

Passive people's low self-worth destroys their credibility. They accept a lose/win, one-down position, apologizing for using up the air they breathe! They bend over backward to accommodate everyone else, to their own demise (e.g., "Krista, did you really think it was okay to drop the axe on my foot? Sorry I got blood on your carpet!").

Some people are *Passive* because they've checked out from the job. They are disengaged, bored, and uninvested in their work. When discouraged and resigned, *Passive* people relinquish their voice and their organizations suffer from decreased engagement, ideas, and results. Some organizations' cultures are so relationship-oriented that they breed "nice" but *Passive* teammates and leaders who are under-influential, marginalized, and dispirited. They exist in a gray zone of watered-down, unmet work needs and a lack of fulfillment.

Aggressive Communication

We also want to avoid bruising others by dominating or being in their faces. People at the *Aggressive* end of the *Straight Talk Continuum* obsess over coming out ahead, adopting a win/lose stance in conflicts and negotiations. In the *Aggressive* or *Borderline Aggressive* mode, people use actions, body language, tone of voice, and words that are abusive, harsh, and intimidating. These bullies are not amenable to input and want to have the last word. Their dominating style makes others hesitant to speak candidly, so valuable input is lost. A command-and-control mentality permeates the company, muffling cooperation and collaboration.

Aggressive people don't realize that true power doesn't require loudness or abuse; tyrants are unaware of their bruising behavior—or they don't care. If you're more into pop culture, think of "baddies" from the movies: Biff Tannen from *Back to the Future,* Regina George from *Mean Girls,* and Joffrey Baratheon from *Game of Thrones.* Got the picture? *Aggressive* behavior yields resentment, demotivation, and tuned-out, disengaged employees. When I asked one *Aggressive* manager how many people work for him, he wryly replied, "About half of them." If you manage people, minimizing *Aggressive* speaking patterns is vital. Otherwise, you'll be like a caretaker at a cemetery—a lot of people beneath you but nobody listening.

Assertive Communication

Our target zone on the *Straight Talk Continuum* is *Assertive* communication that's open, direct, and firm without being harsh. *Assertive* communicators live by the maxim "It hurts when I bite my tongue!" When we are *Assertive*, others recognize, appreciate, and emulate us. *Assertiveness* yields win/win joint solutions and multiple winners. Cooperative problem-solving is the preferred mode, rather than hierarchical dominance (*Aggressive*) or subservient acquiescence (*Passive*).

Assertive people are vibrant and inspiring because they live out loud, encouraging others to communicate as if the words of Mahatma Gandhi are their mantra: "I want freedom for the full expression of my personality." Or, if you're partial to Oprah Winfrey, let's go with, "Every day brings a chance to draw in your breath, kick off your shoes, and dance."

Assertive communication is two-way and collaborative, rather than "ask-only" (*Passive*) or "tell-only" (*Aggressive*). Rather than avoiding or crushing others, *Assertive* communicators blend asking and telling to achieve balanced candor. They are "noble" rather than "nasty" or overly "nice" like *Aggressive* or *Passive* people. *Assertive* managers cultivate commitment rather than mere compliance, because people have a say. *Assertive* interaction is a portal to motivation, engagement, teamwork, and results.

Keep Yourself Honest

When are you *Passive, Aggressive,* or *Assertive*? With what kinds of people do you tend to be too submissive (*Passive*), too harsh (*Aggressive*), or balanced (*Assertive*)? Does it depend on their personality, role, function, gender, age, or other demographic trait? Are you different depending upon the positional power involved? Does the situation dictate your manner, like whether you're in a performance appraisal, negotiation, or car mechanic conversation? What Self-Talk is percolating when you're *Passive* or *Aggressive* versus when you are *Assertive*?

As an example of the kind of self-awareness I hope you'll capture in a moment, here are some of my patterns:

I'm generally a straight shooter—*Assertive* and direct—without bullying or being *Aggressive*. When briefing my trainers about a client, I may talk too long without *Checking Reactions*, which can seem *Borderline Aggressive* by dominating. I have to be careful not to be *Borderline Passive* with clients out of my desire to please. When my kids were teens, I sometimes wasn't tough enough or would crack a joke, like Phil Dunphy wanting to be the cool dad on TV's *Modern Family*! After I give someone touchy feedback, I want to be sure our relationship is OK the next day—that we're cool with each other—so I may use humor about the situation. At times it's fine, but other times it is *Borderline Passive,* diluting my message.

Identify Your Patterns. Now you know my vulnerabilities and triggers. It's your turn! Jot notes in your *Straight Talk Exercises Journal,* or at least make mental notes about your tendencies.

- What situations, types of people, or fears trigger you to be *Passive*?
- What is the Negative Impact of being *Passive*—on you, teams, or results?
- What situations, types of people, or fears trigger you to be *Aggressive*?
- What is the Negative Impact of being *Aggressive*—on you, teams, or results?
- What situations, types of people, and conditions help you to be *Assertive*?
- What is the Positive Impact of being *Assertive*—on you, teams, or results? ∎

Way to go! If you're a bit more self-aware, that's terrific. Awareness is the first step to responsible behavior change.

If you're not proud of your answers above, don't beat yourself up. Instead, try healthier, gentler Self-Talk: "Great that I can look in the mirror and not cop out. A pro always tries to get better. I can congratulate myself for my courage to be imperfect."

Fears Trigger *Passive* and *Aggressive* Behavior

We know the negative costs of *Aggressive* and *Passive* stances, so we surely don't intentionally sabotage ourselves, others, and our organizations. Our hearts are in the right place. We aren't trying to be "Meek Manager" or "Samurai Supervisor." We just sometimes slip into counterproductive habits. If you don't think that you ever gravitate toward *Borderline Passive* or *Borderline Aggressive* actions, then check your pulse to make sure you're alive!

Welcome to the Human Species. If you *have* identified some unhelpful behavior, YOU ARE STILL A GOOD PERSON! What matters is trying to fix it. Sometimes, our fears and insecurities prompt overly weak or overly pushy actions, vocal tones, or words. Let's forgive ourselves, as long as doing so isn't an excuse keeping us from improving. The writer Toni Morrison, noted for novels like *Beloved* and *A Mercy*, counsels us, "Correct what you can; learn from what you can't."

My Cutthroat Friend. Even abusively *Aggressive* people have a story. I once coached an executive VP I'll call "Jonathan," who was widely known to be a ruthless, cutthroat, ladder-climbing, power-addicted, intimidating bully. Other than that, he was a great guy! Seriously, I was dreading coaching him.

I admire the wisdom of Michael Pritchard, the beloved Bay Area comedian renowned for his healing work in curbing bullying in elementary schools. He tells kids, "Hurt people hurt people." So I wasn't proud of my advanced judgment of Jonathan, because I try to bring an open mind and heart to coaching "difficult people" (aka S.O.B.s).

Jonathan greeted me with an amazing admission: "Look, I know I'm an ass. I know that I step on people and act like I don't give a crap about their feelings. I know *you* know I'm cutthroat, acting only for my own naked self-interest. What you *don't* know is that for nine months in my late twenties, I lived out of my car." Jonathan's eyes glazed over as his voice cracked. "For two of those months, my eight-year-old son lived with me in that beaten up old Chevy. I decided that I would never be in that situation again."

Wow. *Hurt people hurt people.* That softened me big-time. Jonathan had taken off his armor and let his inner light out. We had a bonding, rich two days together. People may act *Aggressively* due to being bruised themselves. *Aggressive* and *Passive*

behavior are rooted in vulnerability. Let's be careful of how we judge others. There
may be secrets in their hearts that would make us weep.

Aggressive Fears. In this spirit of compassion and empathy, please admit what
may trigger your subpar communication. When you slip into being *Aggressive* or
Borderline Aggressive, what fear ignites your over-the-top, harsh "Fight" stance? Is
it fear of:

- losing respect if you don't lay down the law in an autocratic way?
- losing control with an unruly group or chaotic situation?
- losing your authority?
- losing essential results?
- appearing weak or caving in, losing face?
- enabling someone to avoid being accountable?
- allowing the other person to hurt you?
- letting someone take advantage of you?

Passive Fears. When you slip into *Passive* or *Borderline Passive* communication,
which of these fears cause you to engage in "Flight" behavior, subjugate your own
needs, or muffle your true voice? Is it fear of:

- being disliked?
- offending someone?
- hurting others' feelings?
- having negative perceptions spread and tarnish your reputation?
- being ostracized?
- experiencing retaliation by the other?
- dealing with retribution by a boss?
- losing something you need or want from the other?

Did you identify any fears? If you didn't detect any of the above fears in yourself,
then you might be living on that river in Egypt—Denial!

Extremes Are Appropriate at Times

We sometimes behave at an extreme end of the *Straight Talk Continuum* because
it's appropriate and necessary to do so. If a crowded theater catches fire, you can

count on me to adopt *Aggressive* behavior, even using colorful French language ordering you to "GET OUT! NOW!" If I'm in in a dark alley and a scruffy ruffian demands my wallet at knifepoint, I will *Passively* surrender. After all, it's a dog-eat-dog world out there, and I'm wearing Milkbone underwear! Seriously, these two situations are *not* examples of dysfunctional communication, because the *Aggressive* and *Passive* postures would be choiceful—strategically adopted for sound reasons. Make sense?

T = *Take the Straight Talk Challenge*

The *T* of the *Straight Talk Mindset*'s "F.I.T."-ness asks us to *Take the Straight Talk Challenge,* to hold ourselves accountable for being part of the communication solution rather than part of the problem. This noble vision and purpose can become our "True North." Focusing steadfastly on our purpose helps us to cope with the interpersonal challenges tackled in this book.

Confucius Carrie Episode II: Performance Purpose. Since age four, helping the world through music has always been my daughter Carrie's expressed sense of purpose. When she was twelve, about to sing the National Anthem solo at a San Francisco 49ers football game, I inexplicably asked, "Carrie, there's going to be seventy thousand people watching you sing. Are you nervous?" Slick move, psychologist dad! Why plant a seed of anxiety? Never fear. My grounded, pint-sized teacher looked at me and patiently instructed, "Dad. There could be seven or seventy thousand people watching. It's *still* about the music." Wow . . . Schooled again.

Straight Talk's Purpose: Two North Star Goals

Ancient mariners kept their bearings when navigating high seas by having the North Star in their sights and aiming their ship toward it. *Taking the Straight Talk Challenge* demands having the North Star Goals of *Straight Talk* in our sights. Keep your "Influence Ship" on course by always sailing toward two simultaneous goals: (1) *Getting the Results You Want* and (2) *Building a Trusting Relationship.*

Getting the Results You Want. *Aggressive* people try to get the results they want by pushing people around abusively and disrespectfully, pointing their finger like a critical parent and sharply barking, "Do it or else!" Ironically, they lose out by only achieving compliance versus true commitment to what they want. Hopefully, you don't lose your cool to that level, but do you ever fall into *Borderline Aggressive* communication that's still off-putting?

Building a Trusting Relationship. *Passive* people are misguided in their attempts to build positive, trusting work relationships at all costs, because their submissive behavior is a turn-off. They think others will like them if they avoid displeasing them, so they're overly nice and accommodating. Ironically, relationships are eroded as they lose others' respect. You may not falter to this degree, but are you sometimes *Borderline Passive*?

The Magic of Blending Both North Star Goals: Assertive Communication. *Aggressive* people don't need a book or workshop to teach them how to get the results they want (or so they think). They just barrel over people, bully, and don't let others get a word in edgewise. *Passive* people don't need a book or workshop to teach them how to build a trusting relationship (or so they think). They just avoid speaking their truth and stifle their own needs for fear of imposing on others. Both approaches backfire.

Most of us *do* need a book or workshop in order to learn how to *both* fulfill our work needs for desired results and behaviors *and* build a trusting, positive relationship. Instead of an *Aggressive* stance where we win and others lose, or a *Passive* posture where we lose and others win, *Assertive* communication aims for win/win outcomes. Reaching both North Star Goals simultaneously is our reward for aspiring to balanced, *Assertive* communication.

Straight Talk Even When It's Hard

It's easier to use *Assertive* communication when all is well in our lives, on good days under favorable conditions. But, hey, s*** happens! Being part of the work climate solution rather than part of the problem means striving for positive communication no matter what. A healthy work atmosphere happens by one person at a time being interpersonally direct and respectful—firm and fair—regardless of excuses. *Taking the Straight Talk Challenge* is a humbling mission that requires honesty with ourselves about our interpersonal behaviors and impact.

As I said in the introduction, "It takes one to know one." I don't know about you, but I sometimes need to use *Straight Talk* with myself to call "foul" on my own justifications for being *Passive* or *Aggressive*. Which of these reasons for non-*Assertive* communication do you wrongly claim at times?

- Time binds
- Work pressures
- Fatigue
- Stress
- How the other has acted
- Power dynamics
- Environment constraints

- Usually I'm so good, so it's OK
- The stakes being too high
- Upset about other life frustrations
- Being angry about injustice
- The effort demanded
- They started it
- That's how you were raised

Guess it's time to drop our "poor me," broken wing victim mindset and adopt greater self-accountability, eh?

Module Wrap-Up

Straight Talk skills begin in your mind, with awareness and intention through constructive Self-Talk and the *Straight Talk Mindset*. We introduced Self-Talk as the heartbeat and driver of the *Straight Talk Mindset*. You can decide your focus and mood at any moment—about people, events, and your skills. The *Straight Talk Mindset* grounds us as we strive to be mentally and emotionally "F.I.T." to apply positive communication:

- We *Foster the Business Case* for positive communication by shifting our Self-Talk about interpersonal skills from being "soft" to yielding bottom-line benefits.
- We're honest with ourselves, without guilt, to *Identify Our Communication Patterns* of where and when we are *Passive, Aggressive,* or *Assertive*.
- We *Take the Straight Talk Challenge* of being vigilant about our interactions in order to get the work results we want while building trusting relationships.

You'll encounter self-doubt, resistance (yours and others'), and challenges on this journey. Gandhi knew something about overcoming obstacles and discouragement through self-control and resilience. His wisdom underscores Self-Talk and the *Straight Talk Mindset*:

> Your beliefs become your thoughts.
> Your thoughts become your words.
> Your words become your actions.
> Your actions become your values.
> Your values become your destiny.

Module Three | *Assertive Speaking*

As Simple as "A.B.C."

> Be who you are and say what you feel, because those who
> mind don't matter and those who matter don't mind.
> —BERNARD BARUCH, AMERICAN FINANCIER,
> STATESMAN, AND ADVISOR TO PRESIDENTS

> You can speak well if your tongue can
> deliver the message of your heart.
> —JOHN FORD

With the *Straight Talk Mindset*, we embraced a business rationale for improving our interpersonal performance and took responsibility for where we are along the *Straight Talk Continuum* in order to avoid counterproductive communication. Let's now ground ourselves in *Straight Talk's* two Core Communication Skills, beginning with *Assertive Speaking*.

> *Assertive Speaking:* Conveying our frame of reference in firm,
> respectful ways so others understand and are more likely to agree.

Effective interpersonal influence demands that our *Speaking* turn is direct yet fair. Enter the "A.B.C."s of *Assertive Speaking*. This acronym doesn't mean that

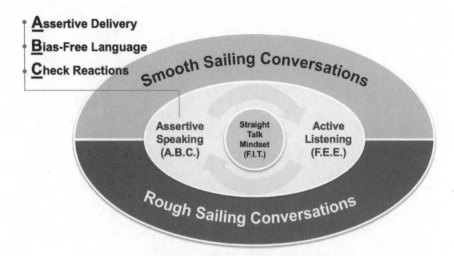

Diagram 3.1 | The *Straight Talk* Model: *Assertive Speaking*

the sub-skills are as "simple as ABC," but rather to indicate that they are essential building blocks. Analogous to the fundamentals of reading and writing, the "A.B.C."s of expressing your opinions, ideas, and needs are:

- *Assertive Delivery* that is firm while being even and considerate.
- *Bias-Free Language* versus opinion-oriented, judgmental, or inflammatory wording that is not factual.
- *Checking Reactions* from the other person before shifting to *Active Listening*.

These *Assertive Speaking* "A.B.C."s are the fundamental requirements for conveying opinions, ideas, feedback, and reactions. Just as a football player must drill the basics to eventually win the Super Bowl, these "A.B.C."s are the basics for communicating well, especially when performance pressure is high.

A = *Assertive Delivery*

Module two's *Straight Talk Mindset* described *Assertive, Passive,* and *Aggressive* communication. Let's now put a magnifying glass on the exact behaviors that comprise these three postures. Any message's delivery is composed of behavioral cues that are visual (what we see in the body language, face, eye contact, and gestures), vocal (what we hear in the voice's volume, pace, pitch, pauses, and filler words like *um*), and verbal (the actual words we are digesting).

Borderline Passive		Borderline Aggressive	

Passive	**Assertive**	**Aggressive**
VISUAL • Body • Eyes • Face • Gestures	VISUAL • Body • Eyes • Face • Gestures	VISUAL • Body • Eyes • Face • Gestures
VOCAL • Volume • Rate • Pauses & fillers	VOCAL • Volume • Rate • Pauses & fillers	VOCAL • Volume • Rate • Pauses & fillers
VERBAL	VERBAL	VERBAL

Diagram 3.2 | *Passive* and *Aggressive* Behaviors

Diagram 3.2 depicts the visual, vocal, and verbal components for expressing yourself. We'll learn the *right* delivery (*Assertive*) by first exaggerating the *wrong* way (*Passive* or *Aggressive*). As we deep-dive into behavioral specifics, imagine how each spot on the *Straight Talk Continuum* looks and sounds.

Visualize yourself in my *Straight Talk* workshop, sitting in small groups at round tables in a lavender-colored carpeted conference room. You've just returned from a scrumptious coffee break featuring a fresh fruit salad and hot oatmeal cookies.

***Passive* Visual Behaviors.** After positioning <u>A</u>ssertive Delivery as the *A* of *Assertive Speaking*, I approach your tablemate, Jorge. I ask the group to imagine that I'm an old Gumby clay figure that they will mold into a *Passive*, wimpy person making a request of Jorge. Then I crack, "Or, if you live in *this* century, pretend I'm a CGI that you're programming into a super-submissive image by naming my weak and self-defeating body language."

"What facial expressions should I make? How about my gestures? Where should my hands go?" The group has fun "molding" me to assume a slumping posture, facing sideways from Jorge at an angle, and backing up as I ask for Jorge's help. Ahmad suggests extending my arms with palms facing Jorge as if apologetically signaling, "It's OK to say 'no' if it's too much trouble." DeShawn suggests wringing my hands with anxiety or shoving them into my pockets as I shuffle pathetically. Cal urges a fearful grimace with pursed lips and a nervous twitch. "What kind of eye contact should I adopt?" You coach me to avoid eye contact and look at the floor. Emile astutely says that my eyes dart around and only intermittently make contact with Jorge. I call that the "Butterfly Flit."

Passive **Vocal Behaviors.** Next, I elicit what qualities describe my voice. "What's my volume? Rate of speech? Tone and pitch? What other vocal habits make me *Passive?*" Jaleeba says my voice is soft and slow, since I'm unsure and insecure. Denise suggests stammering, starting and stopping my sentences while clumsily interjecting "fillers" like "uh . . . so . . . um . . ." You're spot-on in telling me to either speak slowly with uncertainty *or* frantically and quickly with a flood of fitful self-interruptions. Hey, you should teach this class! ∎

Passive **Verbal Behaviors.** Let's leave the workshop behind for a while as we move from *Passive* visual and vocal cues to verbal ones. *Passivity* is also manifest in our actual words. Submissive vocabulary undershoots the mark, lowering respect from others (especially power-oriented people). Weak language opens the door for people to be dismissive and not take seriously our ideas, feedback, suggestions, or requests. Do you see your own shadow in any of the following patterns?

- *Apologetic: Passive* people contritely mutter: "Sorry to bother you . . . I hate to bother you at such a busy time . . . I should have thought through the environmental impact more, so my bad if it's an incomplete report . . ."
- *Self-discounting:* Meek people may gingerly mumble, "Would I be crazy to suggest suspending clinical trials until we gather more data? I guess maybe I'm being a bottleneck by being so nitpicky." They sound like a pimply, awkward fifteen-year-old sheepishly asking for a date: "I know you're probably busy, so you don't want to go to the movies on Friday, do you?"
- *Ambivalent:* Imagine a *Passive* person fretting, "I'm not totally sure if this is the way to go. I've gone back and forth a few times . . . plenty of people might disagree . . ."
- *Tentative:* Submissive influencers dilute their power and conviction with qualifying language: "Uh, I sort of think that maybe one way to, like, go

on this system configuration would be, uh, if it's OK with you . . . to, you know, kind of explore opening the door to . . ."

- *Vague:* Passive speakers may withhold their point, droning, "I have an issue that deserves our attention since these kinds of areas can be problems for lots of companies. At the thirty-thousand-feet level, some factors may bear examination." . . . Oy! Could they *be* any less specific?
- *Checked Out:* Passive people may adopt a "whatever" or "if you say so" stance that timidly follows others. Their apathy and lack of passion extinguishes others' enthusiasm.

Back in the workshop, I joke that I've now morphed into the power-driven maniac "Heisenberg" from TV's *Breaking Bad*, so the group should mold me into an *Aggressive* tyrant. I stomp up to poor Jada and demand ideas from the group that demonstrate my being over-the-top abusive, bullying, and harsh.

Your eager, fun-loving group gets into the spirit of the activity. They tell me to stand squarely in front of Jada, invading her personal space. "How about my face?" The group hesitates, so I adopt an S.O.B. persona and yell, "C'mon, you stupid people!! It's easy!! Shape me!!" Through her laughter, Carmen tells me to wrinkle up my face in disgust and to sneer or scowl. "And my eye contact?" Soon I'm eye-to-eye with Jada, burning a hole into her brain. Your team leader, Imani, offers the option of squinting my eyes in an accusatory, skeptical expression and shaking my head back and forth vigorously in disgust. "My hands and gestures?" I end up pointing at Jada in a scolding, demanding way. Kai yells, "Put your hands on your hips like a critical, angry teacher or parent about to punish her!" The group howls when I slap the inside middle of my right arm and clench my raised right hand into a fist, as if telling Jada to kiss off.

Aggressive Vocal Behaviors. The group prompts me to raise my volume and to speed up my vocal pace. Hiko says, "Use sharp, biting articulation and inflections that sound annoyed." I clarify and demonstrate how an *Aggressive* hard-ass might also use a slow, soft, threatening tone so Jada knows she is in hot water: "Look, Tomkins [Jada's surname], if you can't handle this . . . [I pause, glaring at her] . . . I'll find someone who can. Got it?" . . . Whoa, heavy duty! ■

Aggressive Verbal Behaviors. Phrasing on this end of the *Straight Talk Continuum* goes overboard in disrespectful, alienating, and intimidating ways.

- *Autocratic:* "That's the way it is. My way or the highway." This command-and-control mode says, "I'm the boss!" (Even if you're not.)
- *Abusive:* "Did you stay up all night dreaming up something that stupid?" Being overly critical is bad karma and invites retaliation. People will spread the word about you and purposely drag their feet. The word *sabotage* comes from the French *sabot*, for "shoe." In France's early factory days, folklore has it that workmen resenting oppressive bosses threw their wooden shoes into the machines on purpose to vandalize production.
- *Overly Critical: Aggressive* people may not be "colorful" or foul, but still be off-putting by constantly being a fault finder. You know this kind of boss, parent, coach, or teacher—forever having antennae to detect what's *wrong* with you rather than what's *right*.
- *Threatening:* Pulling rank may work in the military, but you'll rarely achieve esprit de corps anywhere else. "Do it, or else" ultimatums won't get the results you want because people will only do the bare minimum.
- *Exaggerated:* Inaccurate, absolutist language overstates the case: "That meeting was a TOTAL failure [Really?] . . . This report is the WORST I've ever seen [Come on, get real.] . . . You NEVER come on time [How about that time last decade?] . . . You ALWAYS miss the point when you implement my instructions and it's KILLING me" [We wish!]. The receiver gets defensive and mired in disputing the fine points of these hyperboles, dismissing the overall validity.
- *Opinionated:* Don't prematurely pat yourself on the back just because you don't abuse with such harsh tactics. *Aggressiveness* can be less obvious but real. "Dominating Daniel" was an opinionated know-it-all who regularly flaunted his intellectual rightness: "The only true option, like I learned at MIT, is to . . ." Or he'd say, "It would be folly to ignore Six Sigma's efficacy." Whoa. "Folly?" Are we back in Elizabethan England? Daniel's self-proclaimed genius offended his boss, who didn't appreciate his pompously lecturing, "Look, this one's a no-brainer. Here's what we have to do . . ." His manager barked, "No, Einstein, we don't *have* to do anything, and do you remember who the hell you're talking to?" Oops. Daniel wasn't over-the-top abusive, but he was still offensive.

Borderline Passive and *Borderline Aggressive* Behaviors

Fortunately, when most of us stray from the *Assertive* range of the *Straight Talk Continuum,* it's usually with less blatant *Borderline Aggressive* or *Borderline Passive* behavior. These modes aren't as preposterous as the above exaggerated extremes but can still hurt you and others.

It's not full-scale *Aggression* to react to a manager's idea by saying, "That's kind of shortsighted and unrealistic." But try that with an ego-tripper and it will be *you* who was shortsighted (and short-lived!). Letting a peer's cell phone "ping" incessantly during a meeting instead of asking him to silence it isn't the utmost in *Passivity,* but it enables thoughtlessness. In workshops, we point to such milder slipups and ask participants to "fess up" to their less exaggerated communication bloopers at their tables. Which of the following examples sound familiar?

- *Borderline Passive Behaviors:* Staying silent when you disagree . . . stifling your idea during a brainstorm . . . speaking with an upturned voice at the end of sentences so that they sound like questions instead of statements (no offense to our lovable Canadian friends!) . . . saying "Sorry" too often (e.g., when knocking on a colleague's door with a needed update or letting a stranger know that he's accidentally cut in front of you in a checkout line) . . . sacrificing too much in a negotiation and regretting it . . . saying "yes" when you want to say "no" . . . nervously smiling while expressing annoyance . . . letting someone highjack your time in a meeting by switching topics, and so on.
- *Borderline Aggressive Behaviors:* Arriving late and not apologizing . . . interrupting others . . . checking your cell phone too often at a meeting . . . "dissing" someone's idea in a meeting before they even finish it (e.g., "That'll never fly with Legal.") . . . saying you think you speak for the whole team when you *don't* . . . impatiently tapping the table. . . standing when it's more appropriate to sit . . . leaving a meeting during someone's presentation without excusing yourself . . . overstating your point . . . blaming someone for missing a deadline when there were extenuating circumstances . . . clenching your fist and sighing when supposedly listening, and so on.

Assertive Communication

By now you know the drill! What firm but open and receptive *visual, vocal,* and *verbal* behaviors make you *Assertive?* Think of your body, eyes, face, and hands, as well as your volume, rate, and tone. Hey! No fair skipping ahead to the ideas below! Nudge yourself to think of *Assertive* behaviors . . . Keep imagining *Assertive Delivery* . . . OK, now read on!

***Assertive* Visual Behaviors.** Sit level with the person, face them squarely, and use a slight forward lean and an outrush of energy while making your point. Maintain relaxed eye contact without staring intrusively. While inviting the other's views, avoid slumping in your chair, although you might sit with your back against the chair back and make a beckoning gesture.

***Assertive* Vocal Behaviors.** Aim for a balanced volume of 7 or 8 on a 10-point scale, depending on the topic's content and mood. Your vocal speed should also vary according to the topic but never speed-rap or pedantically plod along. Imagine your voice is a ball smoothly and steadily rolling forward. This momentum also conveys belief in what you're saying. After all, the last four letters of the word "Enthus-I.A.S.M." stand for "<u>I</u> <u>A</u>m <u>S</u>old <u>M</u>yself"!

Applied behavioral scientist Ralph Nichols measured typical speaking rates as being 125 to 150 words per minute, three to four times slower than the rate at which most people listen (400–600 words per minute). If you talk too slowly, your receiver's brain races ahead to mentally complete your sentences, filling in the blanks (often inaccurately and with assumptions). That's why I suggest aiming for a vocal pace in the 7 or 8 range, or even faster in a virtual meeting where folks otherwise may tune out.

***Assertive* Verbal Behaviors.** Avoid *Aggressively* pushy wording like Meryl Streep's Miranda Priestly in *The Devil Wears Prada*: "By all means, move at a glacial pace. You know how that thrills me." Also steer clear of the *Passive* wimp's anxious and insecure language like Seymour's in *Little Shop of Horrors*. Banish phrases like "I think . . . maybe we could . . . if it's OK with you . . . I'm not sure, but . . ." Embrace phrases like "We strongly believe that . . . I'm sure you'll find . . . I'm confident that . . ."

You can further nuance your *Assertive* language by calibrating your suggestions and requests with "Conviction Phrasing" or "Invitation Phrasing."

- *Conviction Phrasing* is declarative, making statements that are on the bolder end of being *Assertively* firm, without becoming *Aggressively* harsh. All of these lead-in stems are tell-oriented: "My point of view . . . I recommend . . . I suggest . . . In my opinion . . . If this were my decision, I'd . . . My vote is that we . . . Based on our experience . . . My advice is . . ."

- *Invitation Phrasing* is still firm but makes your opinion known in a more ask-oriented fashion. You're not being *Passively* weak. You're just stating your recommendation more provisionally and deferentially: "What if we were to move forward with . . . Would it be possible to . . . I'd suggest the option of . . . One alternative . . . I'd like your thoughts on an idea . . .We're leaning toward . . . Of course, it's your call, but would you consider . . ."

A = *Appropriate Honesty*

We've said that the *A* of *Assertive Speaking*'s "A.B.C."'s stands for *Assertive Delivery,* but we could alternatively call it *Appropriate Honesty.* People often put honesty on a pedestal, as if it's all that matters. They justify a bruising statement with phrases like, "I'm just saying . . ." or "Just being honest!" Well, yeah, but are they "just saying" it in a way that alienates, insults, or backfires with resistance or retribution? There's a difference between honesty and idiocy! Just because you open your mouth and sound comes out doesn't mean you're practicing *Appropriate Honesty.*

The Right Stuff

The *Right Stuff* movie and book by Tom Wolfe depicts the character traits embodied by America's early astronauts. Accordingly, we call the criteria for *Appropriate Honesty* "The Right Stuff." Please ponder times you've shared feedback, asked for cooperation, or expressed opinions. Did you alienate others by not adhering to the following "Right Stuff" guidelines for *Appropriate Honesty*?

The Right Way. This mainstay of *Appropriate Honesty* entails this module's earlier *Assertive Delivery* standards—being firm rather than weak or harsh. This aspect of *Appropriate Honesty* is so crucial, we've devoted a full section to fleshing out specific *Aggressive, Passive*, and *Assertive* behaviors.

The Right Time. Was the person ready to hear your honesty? Did you ask permission to give feedback? Were you sensitive to timing? What else was going on in the person's life? Was there enough time to discuss the issues? Would you have been more successful at another time?

The Right Place. Did you assert in a private setting to minimize distractions, reduce awkwardness, and avoid humiliation? Or was it in a group where the receiver became more defensive and resistant? Was the setting less than optimal in other ways like being noisy or full of interruptions?

The Right Reasons. Time for some *Straight Talk* with yourself to consider whether your honesty was based on fair and appropriate reasons, to:

- help or develop the other
- make input to inform a decision
- strengthen the organization
- improve the relationship
- maintain your own integrity
- convey a needed image or quality
- forge greater accountability
- set a positive tone or motivate

OR . . . did you speak up for flawed reasons, to:

- power trip
- hurt the other
- prove how smart or right you are
- hear yourself talk
- get even
- gripe and complain

The Right Risk Level. Many people get into trouble by saying the wrong thing to the wrong person. If you're overly trusting of everyone and always say everything on your mind without regard to power and politics, you'll regret it. Consider the ego issues and potential risk level involved. Are you getting yourself into hot water? Is the receiver an overly political player who will exact revenge?

Naïve Nick joined a new team and took his boss's invitation too literally: "Nick, our team norm is the phrase you see on the laminated poster over there,

'Challenge Conventional Wisdom.' Constructive dissent is healthy." Nick took the bait, voiced concerns about a marketing strategy, and wound up in the doghouse. He realized it when he tried to join a social gathering in the conference room, and a coworker closed the door on him with a smile so sweet he couldn't feel the knife go in. He clearly wasn't in the inner circle! However, considering the "right risk" doesn't mean you should kiss up or never speak truth to power. Just be savvy and prudent about what you're saying and to whom. To learn more about political savvy at work, please read my book, *Survival of the Savvy: High-Integrity Political Tactics for Career and Company Success.*

When You Had The "Right Stuff" . . . or Not? Reflect on times you weren't at your best—you weren't using *Appropriate Honesty.* Record these instances in your *Straight Talk Exercises Journal.* How did you falter with the "Right Stuff"? What did you omit: right time, right place, right reasons, or right risk level? ∎

Salvage the Situation. Maintain a sense of humor to hold yourself accountable with this tough exercise.

- *Negative Self-Talk:* "I don't mess up much. This is a ridiculous self-critique. Besides, it's too late to do anything about mess-ups now."
- *Positive Self-Talk:* "There goes my whole repertoire of screwups! (Ha ha!) Hey, it's not too late to repair the relationship damage. At least I can 'own' it and apologize. They'll forgive me." ∎

B = <u>B</u>ias-Free Language

As part of *Assertive Delivery*, we detailed harsh and weak verbal behaviors to avoid and suggested Conviction Phrasing and/or Invitation Phrasing. Another antidote to the interpersonal perils of *Passive* and *Aggressive* verbal behavior is found in the B of *Assertive Speaking*'s "A.B.C."s: *Bias-Free Language.*

Snap yourself back to the workshop, where I'm standing by a modern art painting you'd admired during a break. I preview a quick skit and then yell, "ACTION!" You then witness this: I walk in front of the group with my head down, nod and smile nervously, shuffle up to the flip chart easel, and fumble through the first few sheets looking confused. I frown, roll my eyes, and let out an exasperated sigh as I slap my hand against my thigh and mutter, "Great! Again!" I storm to my materials table and rifle through some papers. I pace back and forth, visibly upset. I stomp to a table with six participants, grab Malika's backpack, glance inside it, and glare at Malika with my hands on my hips and a scowling facial expression. I trudge to the flip charts again, rip off a sheet, crumple it up, and throw it on the floor as I pound my fist against the easel. I call out, "CUT SCENE!"

Debriefing the Skit. I pause and deadpan, "Well, that was fun!" Next, to debrief this over-the-top role-play, I ask the group, "What did you see?" I repeat the question over and over again as I write the group's answers on the left side of a flip chart. What would *you* call out? These answers come flying back: "Unprofessional . . . disorganized . . . inappropriate . . . anger . . . total loser . . ."

I keep pushing for more answers, repeating the same question louder and louder as I furiously scribble to capture the input onto the left side of the flip chart. "What did you see?" ["Immature . . . a jerk . . . exasperation . . . confusion . . ."] "What did you SEE?" ["No respect . . . frustration . . . complete incompetence . . . a future unemployed freeloader!"] The group bursts out laughing as I speed up my voice and get louder each time: "What did you SEE? . . . WHAT DID YOU *SEE*?!???!"

Steph finally gets the point: "You slammed the easel with your fist!" I scrawl "slams easel" quickly, placing that observation on the right-hand side of the flip chart. People see that their initial responses are on the left side, but I've jotted Steph's input on the right side. More right-side ideas bubble up: "You threw down your pen . . . you stomped up to Malika's table . . . you crumpled up the paper . . ." Suddenly, I mix it up: "What did you see and *hear*?" More right-side behaviors are cited: "You cursed . . . you sighed . . ."

I ask, "How am I sorting your ideas?" Skylar answers, "The right-side items are what we actually saw and heard—facts. The left-side words and phrases are our interpretations and conclusions about what we saw and heard—opinions." I give a thumbs-up, noting that the right-side items are *factual*, objective observations and the left-side items are subjective *opinions* about what we observed. I promise Skylar a copy of my book and will even sign it, driving up the dollar value exponentially. She can put it on eBay and retire! ■

Guidelines for <u>B</u>ias-Free Language

It's challenging enough to give feedback or seek commitment from others without creating obstacles with our sloppy wording. The purpose of this *B* sub-skill of *Assertive Speaking* is to screen our language for *subjective*, opinion-oriented words and phrases and to replace them with *objective*, factual descriptions. Which language below is more likely to lead to understanding and less likely to trigger defensiveness or other emotional reactions?

Objective Versus Subjective. Watch out for giving feedback like, "You're unprofessional and sloppy . . . be more of a team player . . . you don't make the grade . . . that presentation was a loser . . ." This wording shares your subjective interpretation rather than objective truth. Such opinions merely broadcast your annoyance without specifically describing the disagreeable performance or action that you're evaluating as the Supreme Judge. *Bias-Free Language*'s measurable and provable phraseology fosters greater understanding. It points to the actions and results you want when assigning a task or correcting someone.

There are no absolutes in this book. There *is* a time and place for evaluation and judgment, like in performance appraisals, when ratings are required. But performance evaluations are ideally based on objective specifics, examples, and metrics as opposed to making personal judgments with subjective, loaded labels.

Fair and Even Versus Inflammatory and Loaded. Emotional put-downs and volatile accusations provoke defensive reactions (e.g., "jerk . . . immature . . . really pissed off at you . . . like a selfish, bratty kid . . ."). Replacing polluted anger with clean anger (see module ten's *Confronting* skills) will help the other be more open to your message. "I was angry when you . . ." still sobers a person plenty. Take your language down a notch to build bridges rather than walls.

Realistic and Accurate Versus Absolutist and Exaggerated. Inferential language isn't believable. Hyperbole leads receivers to say, "C'mon, man. Get real." Extremist claims like "You're always late" launch the person into an expedition to find the times they weren't tardy. Absolutist claims (e.g., "you never . . .") invite quibbling about your wording, which misses the point.

Facilitating and Exploring Versus Playing Amateur Psychologist. Suppositions like "Your anger is clouding your thinking . . . you're being paranoid . . . positions of power intimidate you . . ." are presumptuous. Labeling or analyzing someone's emotions, motivations, and attitudes is intrusive. Are you the authority on someone else's inner workings? No. They are.

Imperialism means to "expand the rule and authority of one country over another country and territory, often by military force." I call playing amateur psychologist "psychological imperialism." The territory you're usurping is a person's internal world. It may trigger, "What are you, a mind reader?" or "Back off, Dr. Freud!"

Concrete and Specific Versus Vague and General. We addressed this under *Passive* verbal behaviors earlier. "It's just a sense I get that something's off . . ." makes you seem confusing and afraid to tell it like it is. Out-of-the-blue generalities without evidence or examples (e.g., "You need to be a better meeting leader . . .") leave a colleague guessing or feeling attacked because they can't fully grasp your point. Instead, *Bias-Free Language* is concrete and specific (e.g., "You didn't check whether the group had any questions. . ."). It paints a vivid picture of your meaning. The recipient might not *like* what you're saying, but they won't fault you for lack of clarity or beating around the bush.

The <u>Bias-Free Language</u> "Just the Facts" Test

A litmus test for whether your language is objective or erroneously subjective is the "Just the Facts" Test. My grandfather (!) used to watch an old TV police show called *Dragnet*, in which Sgt. Joe Friday would always say to crime scene witnesses, "Just the facts, ma'am." In a court of law, would "angry" be allowed as a fact or be considered an inadmissible opinion?

Imagine that Ali is presenting and his team leader, Robby, interrupts and barks, "Sit down. That ridiculous proposal will never fly!" We might later tell Robby he was "abusive" to Ali, but this will trigger defensiveness. The "Just the Facts" test would never allow "abusive" to be said as an opinion in court—only factual, objective language about Robby's behavior (i.e., interrupting, telling Ali to sit, and sharply rejecting the proposal) and its impact (e.g., Ali shuffled to his chair, rolled his eyes, and didn't utter a word for the rest of the meeting). Even though anyone would agree that *abusive* is a fair descriptor of Robby, we're better off just describing the behavioral, objective facts and the results.

I'm not saying to never use an adjective to label someone's actions when delegating a new project role, giving feedback, or confronting. But you'll get further by *also* giving objective descriptions and examples of what happened or what you'd prefer, so that there's no ambiguity and less defensiveness.

<u>Bias-Free Language</u> Pop Quiz. Let's see if you can differentiate objective, descriptive, and concrete wording (i.e., *Bias-Free Language*) from subjective, judgmental, or inflammatory vocabulary (i.e., inferences). Mentally code each phrase below as *F* for Factual wording or *O* for Opinion-oriented wording, or write your answers on the "fillable pdf" version in your downloadable *Exercises Journal*. For any item you code as *O*, what alternative wording or examples would make the phrase more Factual, observable, and objective? Answers are after the exercise, so no fair looking ahead!

_____ 1. "Tom, I really need you to be more of a team player."

_____ 2. "During weekly team meetings, I'd like you to share written file notes you have about customers we are transferring to our new sales reps, and to make a time to coach each one about each customer's style and buying habits."

_____ 3. "You wore blue jeans to the client meeting today."

_____ 4. "You were unprofessional in the meeting."

_____ 5. "We sure need a lot of people to facilitate meetings better."

_____ 6. "We need shift supervisors to end each meeting with a summary of decisions and action items with who's responsible."

_____ 7. "You've obviously been really disengaged since vacation."

_____ 8. "I've noticed since you got back this week, you've been late to each meeting and haven't spoken up except when I call on you. This isn't like you. What's up?"

_____ 9. "Jordan really has to do things on a timely basis."

_____ 10. "Elki threw two pink elephants off the Empire State Building." (Sorry, just had to make sure you were still with me!)

_____ 11. "I'd appreciate Sydney's Friday finance reports being submitted by 11 AM so that I can integrate everyone's numbers by 5 PM."

_____ 12. "Damnit, Kareem! All of your technology status reports to the ABC account totally miss the mark and show me that you don't give a crap about ever being client focused! Who do you think you are pretending to be committed to our company values of customer focus when you clearly *aren't* on board?!"

Please do not check out the next page until you have thought through your answers!

Exercise Answers. Let's assess your learning here:

1. **O**—Too general. What specific actions does "team player" mean to you? Tom may say, "Huh? I'm early to each team meeting, unlike most others."

2. **F**—Now Tom knows what comprises "team player" in your mind. Besides, you avoid labels and describe the exact behavior change you seek, which gets the results you want *and* builds positive, trusting work relationships, the dual goals of *Straight Talk*.

3. **F**—This is a tricky one because you might not like it if I gave you this feedback, and it omits skillfully saying the Negative Impact. But the wording is behavioral. Saying "you had jeans on" reports "just the facts."

4. **O**—What the heck was "unprofessional"?

5. **O**—Who are we talking about in this potential cast of thousands, and what is the exact desired behavior?

6. **F**—This clearly and specifically conveys the needed behaviors factually and objectively.

7. **O**—This plays psychologist, labeling someone's inner world without them expressing it. If you do say "disengaged," at least add, "You seem less engaged than I usually experience you as being." That's less likely to trigger defensiveness. Also, what actions led you to have a hunch about the other's inner experience?

8. **F**—Bingo. On the money.

9. Part **F**, Part **O**—This item is closer to the mark than some of the others. It's not as precisely descriptive of the exact lack of timeliness, but at least the receiver knows the problem is missed deadlines. It would benefit from an example.

10. **F**—Here, the *B* is for "boring" (and also "behavioral").

11. **F**—Now the specific target and expectation is clear and goodwill is captured in the "I'd appreciate . . ." phrasing.

12. **O**—This dump is exaggerated ("*all* reports"? . . . "*totally* miss the mark"? . . . "*never* committing"?). Also, presumptuous claims to know Kareem's inner motivation are risky ("You don't give a crap . . . never being committed . . ."). He may feel invaded and resent you playing shrink about his intentions. This example is unspecific (e.g., how do the reports "miss the mark"?), not to mention *Aggressive* with the four-letter kickoff and accusatory tone (e.g., "Who do you think you are . . ."). Other than these problems, it's a *perfect* feedback message! Ha! ■

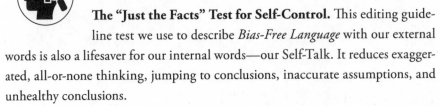

The "Just the Facts" Test for Self-Control. This editing guideline test we use to describe *Bias-Free Language* with our external words is also a lifesaver for our internal words—our Self-Talk. It reduces exaggerated, all-or-none thinking, jumping to conclusions, inaccurate assumptions, and unhealthy conclusions.

A client yawns during your sales presentation. What do you think to yourself?

- *Negative Self-Talk:* "Oh no! This guy is totally bored and hates my pitch."
- *Positive Self-Talk*: "Hold on. I'm upsetting myself by thinking 'totally' and 'hates,' and I'm making a mountain out of a molehill even if he *is* bored. Besides, *is* he bored? Is *bored* what a video camera factually records? No, it just shows him yawning. Maybe he was up all night with his newborn baby, and he's actually intrigued by my talk."

But this "Just the Facts" Test Self-Talk tool is *not* about being in denial about actual problems. If everyone in the meeting yawns, then be honest with yourself. ■

C = *Checking Reactions*

Andrew Grove, the former CEO of Intel Corporation, wrote, "How well we communicate is not determined by how well we say things, but by how well we are understood." We may be legends in our own minds for how brilliantly we've conveyed a point, but until we take the pulse of others' understanding, we may be deluding ourselves.

The *C* in *Assertive Speaking*'s "A.B.C."s stands for *Checking Reactions*. A key ingredient in the art of communication is knowing when to *stop* speaking and to *start* listening—to invite the other to share their understanding and reactions. It's their turn with *Assertive Speaking* to express their own frame of reference.

The "Stop" and "Go" of Communicating

The Core Communication Skills of *Assertive Speaking* and *Active Listening* require a traffic signal to ensure the smoothest flow of communication. No traffic signal is constantly on green, or there'd be an eventual crash. Notice when your speaking turn's traffic light has turned to red for STOP and the listening light has flashed green to GO. Otherwise, you'll cause the communication version of road rage.

The transition between *Assertive Speaking* and *Active Listening* is the sub-skill of *Checking Reactions*, a simple yet spectacular step. It creates trust and safety for others to voice reactions, share an opinion, or speak truth to power. It gauges how well your receiver understands you and how supportive or committed they feel. No true influence can occur without *Checking Reactions*.

Be Your *Own* "Flapper"

The epic Jonathan Swift novel, *Gulliver's Travels*, is best known for the hero's voyages to the lands of Lilliput, where inhabitants are six centimeters tall; Brobdingnad, where seventy-two-foot giants live; and a nameless place, where a race of talking horses lives. His most relevant odyssey for us is to Laputa, an island high above the clouds where the most revered public servants are "flappers" who wave palm branches to signal people who are talking too much.

We all need flappers! Humans can only digest limited amounts of information without a chance to process what's been said. Break longer *Speaking* turns into bite-sized pieces and *Check Reactions* before shifting to your next point. Periodically taking tabs on how your message is coming across ensures comprehension. Enlist the aid of a friendly "flapper" to message you in a virtual meeting or visually signal you (subtly!) in an in-person meeting if your words start to wash over people. Better yet, *Checking Reactions* places the onus of "flapping" on *you* rather than others.

Three Ways to *Check Reactions*

My family and I marveled at the genius of Lin-Manuel Miranda's *Hamilton*. We walked around for days singing, "Talk less, smile more." This book's adapted lyrics are: "Talk less, *Check* more. Don't let them think that you're a hopeless, rambling bore! Talk less, *Check* more." Here are three *Checking Reactions* categories:

1. *Check Understanding:* "Does that make sense? . . . How's my clarity? . . . What is your understanding so far?"
2. *Check Reactions:* "Does this sound good? . . . What's your reaction? . . . What do you think?"
3. *Check Agreement:* "Can I get your support on this? . . . Where do you agree or disagree? . . . How comfortable are you with this?"

More Than Meets the Eye

The above three ways to take the pulse of your receiver are more sophisticated than they may seem. Each type of *Checking Question* elicits a different kind of reaction. It's one thing to ensure *understanding*, another to take the temperature of positive or negative *reactions*, and yet a different goal to gauge the level of *agreement*—whether there is buy-in to your idea, recommendation, or request.

Open or Closed *Checking Questions*. Notice how the first question in each category of *Checking Questions* is closed-ended while the others are open-ended. Each first item prompts a limited "yes" or "no." The other queries invite more expansive responses about someone's understanding, comfort, or commitment. Closed-ended questions force-fit and control answers. You risk seeming like the cross-examining lawyer Elle Woods in the film climax of *Legally Blonde* as she goes for the jugular with rapid-fire, driving, closed-ended questions. Sure, Elle is a likable heroine, but the scene does *not* depict a relaxed dialogue.

When to *Check Reactions*: Look for the Clues, Sherlock!

If you don't have the services of a "flapper," how do you know when to put a sock in it, catch a breath, and *Check Reactions* to see how your *Speaking* turn is landing? There are clues within yourself and from the other.

Internal Clues. How long have you been talking nonstop? How much of what you've been blabbing can the receiver digest? If what you're saying were in written form, how many paragraphs would be safe to share before *Checking Reactions*? Two? Three? Ten?

External Clues. Have your antennae up to pick up clues from your receiver. Are they pursing their lips to get a word in edgewise as you race onward? Are they leaning forward and inhaling to share a reaction or clearing their throat to talk? Shuffling of the feet and looking down dejectedly signals an emotional reaction worth exploring. A raised pointer finger shows a desire to interject. A raised middle finger may come next if you don't *Check Reactions*. No offense, but what were your first forty clues? Is the person screaming with their mouth shut, nonverbally begging you to ask about their understanding, reaction, or agreement? As NIKE purports, Just Do It!

Virtual Variations: *Assertive Speaking*

Face-to-face or at least phone-based conversations are ideal, but these days, it's not always practical. The challenge of feeling connected in our virtual and remote work environment necessitates optimizing whatever in-person interactions we do enjoy. Quality interpersonal skills are all the more important. We can also adapt the "A.B.C."s of *Straight Talk* skills to the virtual communication channels of phone, email, text threads, and virtual meetings.

<u>A</u>ssertive Delivery Virtually

Telephone Conversations and Conference Calls.
- Use *Assertive* body language, eyes, gestures, and facial expressions along with energetic vocal pace, volume, and tone.
- Stand at times and speak clearly to emit an *Assertive* aura.
- Announce your name upon entry (group calls).
- Avoid being steamrolled if you have an "airwave pirate" monopolizing the call, by tactfully thanking them for their enthusiasm and saying that you'd also like to hear from others (group calls).

Voicemails.
- Counter the tendency to talk fast to squeeze it all in (it's frantic and flighty).
- Rehearse and time yourself, and listen to your recording before leaving it.
- Invite the receiver to discuss the content voice-to-voice.

Video Meetings (as a Participant).
- Avoid *Passive* behaviors: talking too softly or slowly; lack of participation; forgetting to unmute yourself so that you seem "asleep at the wheel."
- Avoid *Aggressive* behaviors: interrupting others; speed-rapping or talking too loudly; monologuing without *Checking Reactions*.
- Use bold while respectful and caring *Assertive* behaviors: making proactive contributions like asking for self-introductions (if appropriate); stating

your name when speaking so you're remembered; previewing if you must depart early and chat your thanks upon leaving.

- Appear empowered rather than submissively victimized by your technology: testing your computer to avoid glitches or fumbling; raising your computer screen so your gaze isn't always downward; looking into the camera to simulate confident, involving eye contact; if sharing your screen, be aware of what else is on your desktop and move anything private.

Video Meetings (as the Leader).

- Greet others as they join (at least with the chat function if not verbally).
- Ask whether your voice is too loud, soft, fast, or slow; limit fillers ("um . . . uh . . .").
- To maximize engagement without being heavy-handed, preview that you'll call on people.
- Paraphrase questions or comments to show understanding before responding.
- Use a forward rolling pace in your voice and vary voice inflection; turn off the "Assign Privileges" feature if someone is texting onto a slide.
- Review ground rules up front so you sound less parental if you need to correct the group; try to do so without naming a rule-breaker (e.g., "Folks, let's all remember our agreed-upon ground rule to not side-bar in Chat").
- Slow your pace for international attendees; vary meeting times to accommodate their time zones.
- Close with a recap, group comments, or chat reactions; end on time or renegotiate the ending time to show respect.

Emails, Texting, or Messaging.

- Avoid *Passive* behaviors: emailing requests or assignments in tentative or apologetic ways; asking too many questions in replies; coming across as insecure.
- Avoid *Aggressive* behaviors: seeming harsher than intended due to lack of visual or vocal cues; using all CAPS or too many exclamation points that convey UPSET; being so short in a reply that you seem curt and uncaring; forgetting to scroll through an email thread and accidentally including

someone you didn't intend to see your message; excessively repeating your point in verbose ways that dominate; not replying to emails (implying that the sender isn't important).

Social Media Posts. If someone ignores your Facebook "Friend Request" or LinkedIn invitation to connect, how does it feel? Do you similarly ignore others who might become an enemy? Think before you act. In the movie *Chef,* the lead character loses his job at a trendy Los Angeles restaurant after impulsively posting an over-the-top rant against a food critic and it goes viral.

Bias-Free Language Virtually

Especially when body language is absent, monitor your verbal behavior to stay in the *Assertive* rather than *Passive* or *Aggressive* zone on the *Straight Talk Continuum.* Vigilantly self-correct any judgmental, absolutist and exaggerated, nonspecific, or overly emotional phrasing. If you're upset, try to phone or video-meet the person so that your tone of voice and body language aren't misread. If you must email, count to ten before hitting "Send," reread the message, and edit dangerous wording.

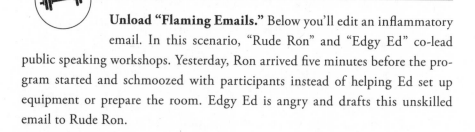

Unload "Flaming Emails." Below you'll edit an inflammatory email. In this scenario, "Rude Ron" and "Edgy Ed" co-lead public speaking workshops. Yesterday, Ron arrived five minutes before the program started and schmoozed with participants instead of helping Ed set up equipment or prepare the room. Edgy Ed is angry and drafts this unskilled email to Rude Ron.

From: Edgy Ed
To: Rude Ron
Subject: Thanks for NOTHING!
WELL, "FRIEND," YOU REALLY DID IT THIS TIME!!!

I can't believe how unprofessional you are! This is the last time I'll count on you to co-lead a workshop for top management. You made me look pitiful with your total lack of consideration, and now my course evaluation numbers will show it.

First, you didn't even show up on time an hour before class to help set up the room. When you did grace us with your esteemed presence, you figured that mingling to get in good with the executives as they filtered in was more important than helping me troubleshoot the video cameras. So the equipment was crap! Maybe if you'd shown a little bit of teamwork, we wouldn't have had to apologize for not being able to videotape their presentation drills like we promised in the prework.

I thought we were supposed to be equal partners, but nooo. You're NOT my boss, so where do you get off acting like you're above the grunt work? Feel free to reply here, not that I expect you to even bother. Anyway, "sorry" doesn't do much good now!

Ed

Fortunately, Ed shows the email to you, and you predict a disastrous outcome if he doesn't rewrite it to be less inferential and loaded. Ed knows that difficult conversations are best conducted in person or by telephone. However, Rude Ron is known for insisting upon an email to preview any meeting so that he can digest the issues and prepare.

In your *Straight Talk Exercises Journal* or on a blank sheet of paper, help Ed identify problematic language and rewrite it with *Bias-Free Language*. This doesn't mean Ed can't say that he has a real issue with yesterday, but how can he express it cleanly, crisply, and fairly with objective descriptions of the activating event? ■

Amping Up Voicemails. Make sure you apply the above *Aggressiveness* self-monitoring with voicemails, too. We've all regretted leaving a volatile voicemail that drained our time and energy as we de-escalated and salvaged the blowup. Laurence Peter counsels in *The Peter Principle*, "Speak when you are angry, and you'll give the best speech you'll ever regret."

Other times, we are *Borderline Passive* or outright submissive. Again, it's best to work issues voice-to-voice, but if you do leave a quick voicemail with your reason for wanting to meet, be sure you're not self-discounting. Let's help "Meek Maurice" to amplify this undershooting voicemail:

> Um, uh . . . hi, Joe. Maurice here . . . Maurice from the task force? Anyway, I was just wondering if maybe it'd be OK to grab a few minutes sometime to chat about something that, you know, I was a little surprised happened. I mean, it can wait if you're too busy, I guess. But it's about the monthly meeting? I sort of wish it'd gone in a little bit different direction, you know? No offense, 'cause your input was right on and everyone said so. I just wondered if maybe you took a little too much time? I felt a little rushed and now I'm not sure how to meet my deadline of briefing everyone before the off-site. So maybe you'd be willing to coach me on ways to make up the lost time? I mean, if it's OK, I'd really appreciate it.

Could Maurice *be* any less *Assertive*? Let's fix his message by writing a new voicemail for Maurice to leave. Jot it down in your *Straight Talk Exercises Journal*. ■

Checking Reactions Virtually

Phone *Checking*. On the phone, you can't see body language signals indicating the other person wants to jump in, so proactively check in rather than waiting till the end of your long diatribe. Your listener may not fully hear your last five points if they're stuck back on your first two.

Video Meeting *Checking*. There's a silver lining in the storm of the COVID crisis, because online conversations have become more of a norm than only texting or telephoning. At least in video meetings we can see visual clues and reactions as we do in face-to-face meetings. It's tougher with a group larger than five since people's faces are only thumbnails. Look for nonverbal and verbal signals that it's time to ask a *Checking Question*.

Email *Checking*. Who ever said sending an email must always be a one-exchange process? For critical or sensitive messages, consider asking recipients to email a reply summarizing their understanding and reactions. Then you can paraphrase and address their reactions.

Module Wrap-Up

One of the two core *Straight Talk* communication skills is *Assertive Speaking* to directly and firmly express our needs and opinions while maintaining a respectful tone. Avoiding *Passive* or *Aggressive* extremes requires three fundamental "A.B.C." building blocks:

- *Assertive Delivery* through our body language and vocal qualities.
- *Bias-Free Language* that isn't exaggerated, judgmental, inflammatory, or unclear.
- *Checking Reactions* to prevent the other person from losing track of what we are communicating, and to gauge how our message has been received.

Action Planning Journal. Cap off our work on *Assertive Speaking* by making notes in your *Straight Talk Exercises Journal*. Please jot down your most salient *Assertive Speaking* key insights along with possible changes you might benefit from making. Later, you can convert these into action plans with behavior change goals and action steps.

OK, OK, I get it. Taking time right now in your *Journal* is a pain because your reading is so engaging that you can't wait for the next module, right? Try to contain yourself! Seriously, I do urge taking a few moments upon completing every module to capture possible topics for action planning later. This is how you can make the training stick—by making a few self-commitments. ∎

Module Four | *Active Listening*

The "F.E.E." We Pay

> Courage is what it takes to stand up and speak; courage
> is also what it means to sit down and listen.
> —WINSTON CHURCHILL

> No man ever listened himself out of a job.
> —CALVIN COOLIDGE

P ay attention" is a fitting phrase because we truly do *pay* a fee when we listen. There are costs to listening, including our agenda, time, energy, patience, and concentration. It's hard work! Of course, there are massive payoffs of listening as a way to convey understanding of and empathy for others. As with the "F.I.T." and "A.B.C." acronyms for the *Straight Talk Mindset* and *Assertive Speaking*, we have a mnemonic device for *Active Listening* skills. The "F.E.E." skills we "pay" to reap listening's business and personal rewards are:

- *Focusing* our environment, mind, and body on the other's perspective.
- *Exploring* with acknowledgments, open-ended questions, and encouragement.
- *Empathizing* by validating and paraphrasing others' thoughts and feelings.

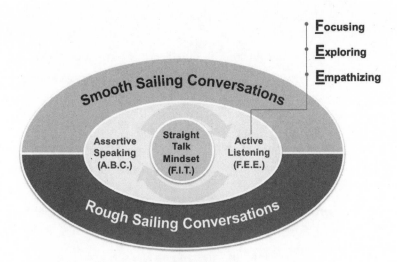

Diagram 4.1 | *Active Listening* "F.E.E." Skills

Wake Up! The Traffic Light Just Changed!

Active Listening is the *Straight Talk* linchpin—used when we need to shift from focusing on our own frame of reference to the other person's. As we *Check Reactions* to what we're communicating, our interpersonal traffic signal metaphor turns to RED for our speaking turn and to GREEN for our listening turn as the other person takes their speaking turn. Our own GREEN light for speaking will return when we respond to the other's reactions, questions, or concerns.

A Rigorous Definition

The following *Straight Talk* definition of listening is far more demanding than garden-variety listening skills.

> *Active Listening*: A mindset and set of nonverbal and verbal behaviors that convey vigorous interest and openness to another person's point of view, and show that you understand (not necessarily agree with) what's being said from other person's perspective, not yours.

Let's unpack this unique and specific definition.

"A mindset and set of nonverbal and verbal behaviors . . ." We call this skill set "active" listening because it demands that we invest all of our being—including mental, physical, and verbal behaviors. No wonder real listening demands such concentration and energy!

". . . that convey vigorous interest and openness to another person's point of view . . ." The *Focusing* and *Exploring* skills we'll hone show a willingness and desire to hear others. Demonstrating *openness* is a necessary, but not sufficient, criterion in our precise listening definition. Many people equate merely hearing someone with true listening, but we must offer more than polite silence until it's our turn to speak.

". . . and *show that you understand* (not necessarily agree with) . . ." It's easy to fake receptivity by looking at a person, nodding, and saying, "I hear you," as we take a mental vacation (e.g., "I wonder who will be at the party tonight."). But we can't fake *understanding*, which is the true test of *Active Listening*. We're forced to be mentally and physically alert in order to fully understand. Our lofty listening definition says it's not even enough to think we understand. We must *prove* it to the other person to their satisfaction through the *Empathizing* skill of paraphrasing. We'll make sure we accurately and deeply "get" what the other person has said.

". . . what's being said from the other person's perspective, not yours." We often listen from our own frame of reference, conflating our listening with another speaking turn. We may only listen long enough to interrupt, or we distort what someone's saying through the filter of our own viewpoint. We often disagree internally—mentally reacting instead of first absorbing. We may half-listen while rehearsing our push-back response. That's not *Active Listening*.

These Are Survival Skills

You may think of listening as "fluff" skills applicable only in your personal life, having nothing to do with results, performance, or productivity. Nothing could be further from the truth!

Listening Improves the Bottom Line. Today's organizations demand quality listening to avoid costly errors, prevent wasting time, surface new ideas, gather information for solving problems, and defuse upset during conflict. To achieve stellar business outcomes, we must harness the cooperation and contribution of all employees. This demands an open environment where people feel free to express their ideas without concern about hierarchy, functional affiliation, or internal politics. Enter *Active Listening* skills as integral to our success.

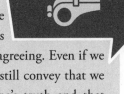

Please don't confuse empathic listening's *understanding* with agreeing. Even if we don't agree, we can still convey that we comprehend someone's truth and that we accept their right to voice it. Then, if we don't agree, we can take our *Assertive Speaking* turn to say so.

When to Use *Active Listening*. "Paying the listening 'F.E.E.'" is a worthwhile investment of your time and energy in order to:

- Understand instructions before executing a task or responsibility.
- Gather needed data to analyze a problem or provide advice and recommendations.
- Empathize with a person's problem when counseling or coaching them.
- Show receptivity to reactions to your feedback, recommendations, or instructions.
- Summarize decisions and action steps so that nothing falls between the cracks.
- Stay calm before arguing, so that you don't say something you'll regret.
- Create readiness to hear your input when someone brings you a problem.
- Tactfully disagree or challenge an idea without turning off others.
- De-escalate volatile emotions during a conflict.
- Mediate a dispute.

F = *Focusing* Skills

The *F* of *Active Listening*'s "F.E.E." stands for *Focusing* skills. We begin with these three elementary sub-skills, not to insult you, but because we often *know* much more than we actually *do*. Also, without the following *Focusing* behaviors, the higher order *Active Listening* skills fall flat or come across as phony:

- *Focus* your environment.
- *Focus* your mind.
- *Focus* your body.

Focus Your Environment

Ensure that the physical environment is conducive to effective listening and conveys openness and receptivity. Set aside and silence your phone, close folders, turn away from your computer, stop clicking your pen, and ask your assistant (yeah, sure, like *that's* in the budget!) to hold calls. Send a strong message that you intend to be present—that the other person matters. If your office is large enough, place chairs facing each other away from the barrier of your desk. One participant had a poster in his office that read, "LISTENING ZONE."

The Scourge of Multitasking. Multitasking happens in face-to-face conversation, and it runs amok in virtual meetings. It's commonplace for families at mealtime. Many families pretend to eat together but are actually eating alone in a group while mesmerized by their open cell phones on the table. This mock together time is a missed opportunity for bonding in a world where we're often disconnected, and it's sad.

Listening is NOT Walking and Chewing Gum! You can't do two things at once if one of them is *Active Listening*. Non-listening environments, preoccupation, and multitasking have become contagious. They are antithetical and destructive to meaningful communication. Let's retake the reins to slow the runaway horse of ineffective listening, especially if someone is expressing emotion or providing key input, reactions, or ideas. Do you create an external setting (*Focus* your environment) conducive to listening?

Focus Your Mind

Let's also create an *internal* environment that's conducive to listening. *Focusing* your mind is a conscious decision—an act of will—to concentrate 100 percent of your energies and mind on understanding the other's frame of reference, free from distracting thoughts about your own agenda, what you're going to say next, or your next appointment. If you're explaining a new role or responsibility to someone and a push-back response flares up, it takes self-discipline to listen instead of arguing away the concern. In this moment, how can you *Focus* your mind solely on the task of listening, trusting that you'll get your speaking turn again?

Don't misinterpret this sub-skill as improving your concentration in general, like getting enough sleep, grabbing a cup of coffee, or clearing your mind by meditating. Tactics for alertness are terrific, but here the point of *Focusing* your mind is different. It's mentally nudging yourself to lean into *Active Listening*.

It's midmorning, and our group is discussing ways to *Focus* your mind. The thirtysomething IT guy sitting next to you suggests, "I'll see the word *LISTEN* in capital letters." The artistic woman from marketing shares, "I'm a visual person, so I'll imagine the traffic signal of *Assertive Speaking* turning to red and the *Active Listening* light turning to green." The expressive sales guy says he normally thinks "Overcome" when faced with a client objection, and now he'll think, "Come Over." He says he'll mentally go over to the client's side of the table to understand the concern before responding. How will *you Focus* your mind on *Active Listening*? ■

Stay Present. I don't want to go all Zen on you, but to *Focus* your mind on listening means to stay fully present, which takes discipline and self-control. We excel when we're totally in the present moment, as musicians do during an improvisational jam or when athletes are "in the zone." My favorite adage about this is, "The past is history. The future is a mystery. This moment is a gift; that is why it's called 'the present.'"

Present Focusing Techniques. There are many ways to practice staying present. Focusing your awareness on your breath instantly brings you into the present moment. Mindfulness and meditation books, podcasts, and apps abound. Find your own pathways to "the power of now." Use an internal word ("NOW"), phrase ("Be here"), or visual image (hitting a calculator's "Clear" button). But don't get down on yourself when you're NOT "in the zone."

- *Negative Self-Talk:* "Crap! There I go again letting my mind wander and thinking about my next meeting. Why can't I just listen for once??!"
- *Positive Self-Talk:* "It's OK. This thought is a bird flying through a window to enter the room of my mind. I can just let it fly out of an open window on the other side and return to my present-focused listening." ∎

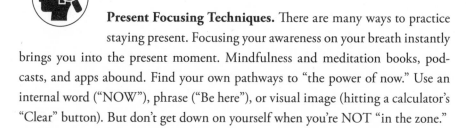

***Sesame Street* Sage.** As we work on staying present, let's also keep perspective by not taking all this stuff and ourselves so seriously that we can't have fun with it, relax, and enjoy life. In the words of the Cookie Monster from *Sesame Street*, "Today me will live in the moment, unless it's unpleasant, in which case me will eat a cookie."

Focus Your Body

With apologies to Olivia Newton-John, "let's get physical" and lock in the all-important body language of *Active Listening*.

Close your eyes and see yourself back in the workshop's brightly lit training room with me. Oh, wait a sec. If you close your eyes, you can't read this. KEEP YOUR EYES OPEN!

I'm standing next to the modern art painting you admired during break time, but your attention shifts to my incredibly gripping teaching (!): "You probably already know how to *Focus* your body, but ignoring this sub-skill now is malpractice in any interpersonal skills training. The body language of attentive listening shows that you're receiving the other person's viewpoint, as if they're the baseball pitcher and you're the catcher."

I continue, "Please shift into non-focusing, non-listening behaviors, whatever that means to you—the opposite of good listening. Reposition your body, chair, head, arms, hands, legs, face, and eyes to show me you're not focused on what I'm saying. Also, show me lousy listening with props like your workbook, belongings, or other items."

As you and the group adopt exaggerated non-listening, *un*-focused actions, I yell, "FREEZE!" I crack, "Well, *that* sure came easily to you." We debrief the Negative Behaviors: slouching, facing away, poor eye contact, flipping through the workbook, stretching, yawning, crossed arms, clicking pen, tapping the table with a pencil, whispering to a neighbor, and other tidbits.

I next explain, "OK, now imagine that what I'm saying will win you the lottery, so you will pay rapt attention. You're vitally interested, and you want me to feel heard. Please shift into positive listening body language." As the group adopts constructive *Focusing* behaviors, I again yell, "FREEZE!" I look around, pause, and with mock sincerity utter, "OK, that's better. Stay in this position for the rest of the workshop."

Above the snickers I ask, "What do you see?" People teach themselves, citing how they are facing me, moving chairs closer, leaning forward, and using relaxed but steady eye contact. Joanne says she tilted her head with one ear toward me, and Kenny mentions interested facial expressions, raised eyebrows, and receptive smiles. I give one more instruction (please do this as you read): "Extend your arm out in front of you. Stretch it straight up toward the ceiling. Reach around behind you. Pat yourself on the back! You already know how to *Focus* your body!" ■

The Body Language of Listening. Let's review attentive behaviors that show others we are listening.

- *Face the Other Squarely:* If the chair arrangement makes this hard, you can still turn your body or head.
- *Sit Up and Lean Forward:* Leaning back says we aren't taking seriously what someone's saying. No big deal while watching TV and casually chatting,

but it matters if someone's disclosing something important. Leaning forward transmits, "I'm intently taking in what you're saying." Occasionally sit back to convey, "OK, it's your airtime now."

- *Assume an Open Position:* Avoid crossed arms that exude a judgmental "prove it to me" attitude. Plant your feet on the floor. If you're sitting cross-legged, don't also lean back in your chair or you'll appear too casual. The same caution applies to sitting with one leg cocked at the knee with the ankle resting on the other leg's knee. This might look too relaxed in an intense discussion, but you can adjust any guideline if everything else you do broadcasts that you're really listening.

- *Maintain Focused Eye Contact:* Some people are less comfortable with eye contact, so don't scorch their brain with laser vision! One maxim says, "The eyes are the windows to the soul," so keep a steady but not unwavering gaze to project receptive, relaxed alertness. Oh, yeah. It's OK to blink!

A Chip Off the Old Block. One day, my wife, Cheryl, and I discovered our son, Eric, was picking up attentive listening skills from Daddy. He was four years old playing with his bestie, Pomme, who was sitting in our foot-pedaled plastic car engrossed in planning his route. Eric was describing the latest episode of *Sesame Street* and growing annoyed with Pomme, who wasn't paying attention. Eric suddenly put his hand on the hood of the play car to stop it, leaned down, planted his face squarely three inches in front of his buddy's face, and sternly scolded, "Pomme! Yook at my eyes. Just yook at my eyes!" My wife and I rolled with laughter. The apple does not fall far from the tree.

- *Make Appropriate Facial Reactions and Gestures:* The word *appropriate* applies to each *Focusing* behavior. Match the mood of the sender's emotions and the topic. If a person is venting about her car being smashed, we may grimace, clench a fist, and roll our eyes. A pleasant smile might prompt them to smash *you.*

- *Nod Your Head:* This shows that you're tracking and encouraging further disclosure, but don't perpetually bob your head up and down like one of those toy doggy bobbleheads on a car's dashboard mantle! That gets distracting and might rush the speaker.

Different Strokes for Different Folks. "Appropriate" *Focusing* takes into account cultural differences, so adapt nonverbal listening behaviors according to region. In some Arab countries, eye contact by women to men is considered flirting, and some Native American tribes view eye contact as rude, so they show respect by averting their gaze. Physical distance norms vary across countries. This isn't a book on cross-cultural differences, so do research interpersonal norms for other countries. When you're abroad, take your cues from the other person because they may have adapted to the parent company's norms even though they're overseas.

Beware of Incongruent Communication. Imagine that Rami pops his head into your cubical asking, "Got a couple of minutes? I need to bounce something off you." If you're embroiled in some complex work, honestly say that you'll be better able to give him the time he deserves in an hour. If you're mentally preoccupied, you're not doing Rami any favors by pretending to listen. Saying, "Uh, sure, grab a seat . . ." without consciously deciding to listen will likely result in poor, nonattentive body language that Rami will notice in a heartbeat.

A mismatch between words and body language is called "incongruent communication." A disconnect between words ("I'm listening") and negative body language ("I'm NOT listening") will sabotage any exchange. What do you think people will believe—your *words* or your body language?

Words or Body Language? Second-grader Johnny waves his hand frantically. "Ms. Taylor, Ms. Taylor!" His stoic, world-weary teacher, on the verge of retiring, sighs with exasperation, "Yes, Johnny, what is it?" Johnny asks, "Ms. Taylor, do you enjoy teaching?" She's taken aback and snaps, "Why, of course I do." Her wise and observant pupil retorts, "Then why don't you tell your face?"

The Mind-Body and Body-Mind Connection. Poor listening often stems from being bored or preoccupied, so we drift off and lapse into inattentive nonverbals. But if we consciously will ourselves to adopt the external body language of listening, we can internally become more interested. Some customer contact centers place mirrors at service representatives' desks to show them their own external listening behavior. Seeing themselves prompts reps to *Focus* their body language, in turn increasing their alertness.

Simple Yet Spectacular. Have I told you that I used to perform mind-reading shows at corporate events? I haven't? Oh. That's probably because I never did that. But I *can* read your mind right now . . . You're thinking that this *Focusing* your body stuff is too elementary. I'm always apprehensive about teaching these obvious skills, but I do it because common sense isn't always common practice. If these fundamentals are absent, rapport with others dwindles, and work associates may extricate themselves from conversation.

E = <u>E</u>xploring Skills

The first *E* of the "F.E.E." skills we invest to "pay attention" stands for *Exploring* skills. These simple skills are also easy, so we'll just touch on them briefly: acknowledgments, encouragements, and open-ended questions.

Acknowledgments

These words, brief phrases, or barely audible sounds signal that you're tracking a person's train of thought. These simple "I hear you" statements, especially when blended with *Focusing*'s head nods, convey that you are following someone's point.

Single Words. Even one-word responses prompt further sharing: "Wow . . . Oh . . . Okay . . . Right . . . Gotcha . . . Awesome . . . No! . . . Sure . . . Oy . . . Unreal . . . Yikes . . . Amen . . . Ouch . . . Ooh." The emotional flavor of the word you say has to match what's being expressed. "Yay!" is a tad off if a person is worried.

Phrases. "I hear you . . . I see . . . Is that right? . . . I follow you . . . OK, I'm tracking . . . I see where you're coming from . . . I understand . . . You bet . . . No way! . . . Too much . . . No kidding!" Such interjections reassure a speaker that they're making sense and that you're paying attention. Be brief to avoid interrupting the flow or distracting. Mix in a variety of these "spices in the communication stew" so that you don't seem technique-like or mechanical.

Barely Audible Sounds. "Uh-huh . . . Hmmm . . . Tsk-tsk." These "grunts and groans of communication" are less sophisticated and almost involuntary, but they lubricate conversation. Acknowledgments are even more important on the phone when people can't see whether you're *Focusing* your body or really checking emails.

Don't Overdo It! I'm thinking of a kind-hearted acquaintance, Dee, who means well but overdoes acknowledgment skills. I ran into her at the supermarket and was answering her question about my vacation. Dee kept interrupting me every three or four words to interject, "Wow," "No kidding," or "Uh-huh . . . uh-huh . . . uh-huh" to the point where it was hard to maintain my train of thought. I was getting exhausted listening to *her* listen to *me*! I thought, "Stop trying so hard to listen to me! It's Chill Pill time." But since Dee's overzealousness was due to her social nervousness, I just let it go.

Encouragements

Like acknowledgments, encouragements are short and convey that you're hearing the person. But they also prompt further disclosure. Urge hesitant speakers to continue sharing opinions, facts, and feelings with phrases like "Go on . . . tell me more . . . please say more . . . it's OK to be straight with me . . . and then?" These verbal invitations nudge others on, especially if they're worried they've spoken too much.

Acknowledgments and encouragements convey interest and maintain involvement without agreeing, disagreeing, or stealing the focus. Be careful, though, because acknowledgments and encouragements are so easy that we sometimes slip into going through the motions of paying attention while actually being on a mental vacation.

Don't Get Busted Faking It! I was in a college band, Swamp Buggy, that opened for Cheech & Chong. (Did I  just earn your respect or erode it?) One time at rehearsal, our guitarist-song-writer, Alan, was explaining his vision for a new song arrangement. I had just pulled an all-nighter cramming for a midterm exam, so I was running on fumes. As Alan mapped out the tune's ending, he knew I was faking my listening while being "out to lunch" in a fog.

As I kept nodding my head and flatly uttering "sure" and "gotcha" with a glaze over my eyes, sly and fun-loving Alan explained: "So, guys, let's build the third verse into a crescendo . . . [Rick with glazed eyes: "Yeah, sounds good."] . . . and right as we kick into the chorus, the horns and guitars drop out so it's just a cappella three-part harmony on top of bass and drums . . . [Rick drearily nods and mumbles, "I gotcha . . . un-huh."] . . . and then for the finale we drive a Chevy through the speakers." [Rick in a daze: "OK, I get it . . . cool."]. Alan stopped, silence ensued, and he calmly and slowly repeated, "We drive a Chevy through the speakers," and the whole band burst out laughing. Only then did I sheepishly catch on that I had been caught red-handed at faking my listening.

Open-Ended Questions

Open-ended questions personify the *Exploring* skill by fostering deeper responses. Invitations like "What happened next? . . . What else should I know? . . . How'd that feel?" tell a person that you're willing to invest time and energy to listen longer and more fully without rushing. What a gift!

Open-ended questions can kick off a conversation (e.g., "What's on your dance card for today?" . . . "How did the big off-site turn out?") or segue into deeper exploration (e.g., "What do you think were the contributing factors?" . . . "So, what are Tim's best career development steps?"). Open-ended questions assume that it would be productive to explore someone's thoughts and feelings further. When it's your own agenda driving a discussion and you're *Checking Reactions,* asking open-ended questions will invite broader responses that enrich the interaction and foster trust.

Limit Closed-Ended Questions

As we noted with *Checking Reactions*, closed-ended questions narrow the scope of possible answers. "Yes," "No," and other one-word answers are elicited by "Did you? . . . When? . . . Which? . . . Where? . . . Do you? . . . How many?" These are helpful when data gathering and fact finding, or when time is short. However, if used excessively, their directive nature makes you sound like a Grand Inquisitor or drill sergeant, squelching openness and shutting down conversation. It pains me to watch unskilled TV talk show hosts interviewing a child who isn't very forthcoming. The interviewer wishes the kid would give fuller, more interesting answers when it's actually the host's exclusive use of "yes" and "no" questions that's creating the awkward situation.

Pay attention to personal and casual work conversations—lunches, getting acquainted, dates, family holiday gatherings, networking events. You'll be fascinated by how often people seem unaware of hogging the spotlight and "airtime." Some folks talk exclusively about themselves and forget to ask about you, your day, your job, your life—your world. Besides building rapport and connection through sharing about yourself, also focus on others with open-ended questions. Otherwise, you'll be like the stereotypical self-absorbed actor who rambles on and on about his latest project and finally pauses to ask, "But enough about me. Let's talk about you. What do *you* think of my latest movie?"

E = *Empathizing* Skills

Relying on the *Focusing* and *Exploring* skills alone can seem empty. Just saying "I understand" may leave the other thinking, "No you don't," or "Prove it." The *F* and first *E* skills of *Active Listening*'s "F.E.E." skills only show that you *hear* the other, not necessarily that you *understand*.

The second *E* of the "F.E.E." acronym stands for *Empathizing* skills, what puts the "Active" in *Active Listening*. Let's augment our *Focusing* and *Exploring* skills with the two pillars of *Empathizing*: validating and paraphrasing.

Validating

This first *Empathizing* skill is one you do all the time while listening.

> ***Validating*:** Making brief statements that convey alignment and agreement.

Most interpersonal skills programs don't categorize validating as a listening skill, adhering to a stricter definition of listening as focusing only on the *other* person's frame of reference. Making "I" statements about your agreement or acceptance technically does come from *your* frame of reference, but I'm OK with validating, as long as you're *quickly* affirming what someone is saying in order to convey empathy.

Briefly commenting that you share their opinion or can genuinely relate conveys that you've been there: "Way out of line! . . . That's a ridiculous request she's made . . . So weird, huh? . . . Yeah, that makes no sense at all . . . I'd feel left out, too, if I were in your shoes." Here are some cautions about validations.

- *Who's the Speaker?* Validations are short reassurances that you are in harmony with what someone is saying. Validations backfire if you start expanding on why you agree or detail your own experience to the extent that you commandeer the conversation. Now your momentary interjection becomes a runaway train (e.g., "I'm totally with you on that. Man, you think *you've* had a bad day. Lemme tell you about *mine*, blah, blah, blah . . .").
- *What If You* Don't *Agree?* We use validations when we agree or at least can really relate to how a person is feeling. Don't feign alignment or say "I've been there" if you haven't! Not to worry. You don't have to agree with someone to cultivate rapport and connection. You can still show empathy for the person's feelings and beliefs, even if you disagree—by paraphrasing.

Paraphrasing

> **Paraphrasing:** Summarizing in your own words your understanding
> of a speaker's thoughts and feelings in order to ensure understanding
> and to convey acceptance.

This bedrock of *Active Listening* prompts many participants to exclaim, "Wow. I thought I was a good listener. I didn't have a clue about what real listening is." In the classic novel *To Kill a Mockingbird*, wise Atticus Finch counsels his daughter, "If you can learn a simple trick, Scout, you'll get along a lot better with all kinds of folks. You never really understand a person until you consider things from his point of view, until you climb into his skin and walk around in it."

Remember our *Active Listening* definition: "A mindset and set of nonverbal and verbal behaviors that convey vigorous interest and openness to another person's viewpoint, and show that you understand (not necessarily agree with) what is being said from the other person's perspective, not yours." *Focusing* and *Exploring* skills demonstrate our *openness* to another person's viewpoint. Paraphrasing skills prove that we *understand* what's being communicated (at least to check whether we have). Program attendees have aha! moments when they realize that they're good at *hearing* others, but not necessarily proficient at showing that they truly *understand*.

Paraphrasing is deceptively hard to master, as you'll see when you practice in the next module's Listening Lab. You'll also be stretched to paraphrase when *G.A.I.N.-ing Commitment* and encountering resistance (module seven), when you're hit with volatile reactions while *Confronting* (module ten), and when *Disagreeing or Saying "No"* and your boss pushes back (module eleven). In such situations, paraphrasing will save you.

How to Paraphrase

Feeding back someone's thoughts and feelings in your own words double-checks to ensure understanding. As you dissect someone's message, picture two bins—one for the speaker's thoughts and ideas, and the other for the feelings you detect. Next, boil down and rephrase the content and feelings following these guidelines.

Be Succinct. Share your understanding of the message's core rather than hitting every point a person says. Focus on the essence of the speaker's point— the kernel—rather than listing everything that was said. You're *not* a court stenographer!

Be Comprehensive. Don't be so intent on being concise that you omit key pieces, which may cause the speaker to not feel fully heard. Leaving out key dimensions of someone's message makes your paraphrase seem empty. Listen for what is being said and for what is *not* being said but is implied. Help the person get out what's on their mind. You might need to read between the lines, searching for deeper meanings not literally expressed. Just be careful not to assume or analyze motivations or feelings that aren't present.

Use Your Own Words. Paraphrasing is *not* merely parroting what's said verbatim. You don't need a human being for that. Just turn on a tape recorder. The person may say, "I just said that. What's the purpose of just spitting it back?" Agreed! "Polly want a cracker?" Aping someone at least focuses on the speaker, but it falls short of paraphrasing's greater understanding. Paraphrasing a speaker's thoughts and feelings takes more concentration. This extra effort shows the speaker that you care.

Focus on the Other's Perspective. Rephrase the speaker's viewpoint without leaking out your own perspective. Instead of tainting your paraphrase with your biases, keep it neutral and free from agreement or disagreement. You'll communicate that when it's *your* speaking turn. Keep the focus on the other with these "Paraphrase Lead-Ins":

- *Paraphrasing Thoughts:* "Your opinion is . . . In other words, you think . . . So, the way you see it is . . ."
- *Paraphrasing Feelings:* "You seem . . . You sound like you're feeling . . . That made you (insert an emotion) . . ."
- *Paraphrasing Thoughts and Feelings:* "Sounds like you're [*insert an emotion*] about . . ."
- *Paraphrasing Questions:* "You're wondering . . . You'd like to know . . . So, you'd like clarity about . . ."

When you were a tadpole learning to ride a bicycle, your parents attached training wheels to keep you from falling. Similarly, the above paraphrasing lead-ins are "listening training wheels" that keep you from "falling" into another speaking turn. These "lead-in" phrases all have in common the word *you* or *your* to keep the focus on the other. If your lead-in phrases are instead "*I* think . . . *My* . . . Well, *our* take on this is . . . ," that's called "speaking"! Remember the traffic light has turned. You'll get your turn to react and respond next.

Some participants worry that the paraphrasing lead-ins sound phony and people will feel "technique-ed." Others get concerned that these "training wheels" make it obvious they're learning a new skill: "Won't others feel like my guinea pigs?" We'll soon teach you ways to sound more natural with these paraphrase starters. Besides, they save you from spouting your own views when others prefer that you listen. Premature speaking is far more annoying to others than sounding a little stilted, especially when they see you making a good-faith effort to understand them.

Convey Empathy for the Emotions Expressed. When a speaker shares directions, data, or other content, paraphrase their thoughts. But when feelings are involved, acknowledge them or your listening will come up short. Even if someone doesn't say a "feeling word" (e.g., "angry," "confused," etc.), you can still read body language and vocal tone while asking yourself, "What would I be feeling if I looked and sounded this way while talking about that?" Part of the paraphrasing feelings equation is to use accurate emotion words (more on that in the next module's *Listening Lab*), and the other part is showing empathy with your body language and voice. Paraphrasing, "You sound upset . . ." with a monotone voice and face devoid of expression will fall flat.

Use Empathic Questioning. Some listening skills programs insist that paraphrases must only be in the form of statements (e.g., "So that really baffled you because you never committed to the job."). They warn that paraphrasing with an upturned voice rather than a downturned one gives it a questioning tone that seems uncertain and tentative. They also caution that you may be misinterpreted as skeptically challenging the speaker (e.g., "So, you think he was out of line?").

This workshop is less rigid. It's fine to have an upturned voice occasionally since every paraphrase implicitly does ask the question "Am I hearing you correctly?" As long as you don't use an upturned voice exclusively, you won't sound wishy-washy, and as long as the speaker senses you're seeking to understand versus judge, you won't come across as challenging.

In fact, feel free to repackage your paraphrasing *statement* of empathy into an "empathic *question*":

- "That baffled you, didn't it?"
- "Where does he get off lecturing you when you're his manager, eh?"
- "Are you distrusting what he was saying, sort of skeptical given his track record?"
- "Hard to believe that he'd throw you under the bus like that, huh?"

Sounding and Feeling Natural. We've said that the paraphrasing lead-in phrases ("Sounds like . . . So, you're saying . . .") ensure that we're truly *Listening*, but that they can sound gimmicky or phony. They announce the presence of a new skill ("Been reading a book on listening skills?"). Here's how to nuance paraphrasing to sound more natural and less obvious:

- *Mix Up Lead-Ins:* It's obvious that you're a novice paraphraser if you use the same starter over and over. I once cringed watching a participant become annoyed at her learning partner's fifth consecutive "Sounds like you're saying . . ." lead-in. Just as the listener began his sixth paraphrase with the same lead-in, his frustrated practice partner preempted it by mocking, "So please, please tell me. What does it *sound* like I'm saying?!" Ouch. Use different lead-ins. Variety is the spice of life.
- *One Lead-In at a Time:* It's uncomfortable, even bizarre, when an overeager listener packs every conceivable starter into one paraphrase: "In other words, if I'm hearing you correctly, it sounds like you're saying that from your perspective, you feel . . ." Whoa, easy does it!
- *Don't Sound Too Syrupy:* Some lead-ins come across like a new-age psychotherapist by using an overly gentle, soothing voice: "What I hear you saying is . . . I get the sense that you're feeling . . ." Yuck! Be yourself!

- *Break the "I" Guideline:* Paraphrasing "training wheels" contain the words *you*, *your*, and *yours* versus *I*, *my*, or *our*. But it's OK to include *I* if it's in the context of an empathic response (e.g., "*I* can't help thinking that *you* were really put out by Randy's demand . . ." or "Wow. *I* can tell *you're* still simmering . . .").

- *Drop the Lead-Ins:* Once you were comfortable riding a bike, your mom or dad removed the training wheels. You'd look weird using them today. When you're comfortable paraphrasing, occasionally drop the paraphrasing "training wheels" altogether and simply say whatever you normally would say after a lead-in: "She threw you a real curve that caught you off-guard . . . That had to be disappointing . . . They really floored you . . . It seemed way out of line to you . . ." No need to start the above examples with "Sounds like . . ."

- *Pretend to Be the Speaker:* A higher order paraphrasing technique is to speak as if you *are* the other person: "So you're thinking, 'Who the hell do you think you are anyway? You're not my mother! Back off!'" You might use this technique without a lead-in ("So you're thinking . . .") if it's clear what you're doing. Let's say Kelly voices skepticism about how one of her sales reps submits annual projections: "I *know* Lou withholds deals that are almost ready to sign and then sets low targets that he knows he'll easily reach." You could figuratively step into Kelly's shoes and paraphrase with an exasperated sigh, "Hey, Lou, I'm not an idiot. I know you're sandbagging accounts."

Paraphrasing's Payoffs

I have a blast as front man singer and trumpeter in my R&B band, The New Hip Replacements, so I must pay homage to Ray Charles's epic song "What'd I Say." A speaker may not pause to ask, "tell me what'd I say," but you can still do so before reacting with your own viewpoint in order to gain the following benefits.

Payoff #1: Corrects Misunderstanding. We *ass*-ume that we understand what someone is saying (which makes a "you know what" out of U and ME). This workshop-in-a-book says to assume that you *don't* understand. Here's why:

- *Speaking Is Flawed:* Our message may be fuzzy in our minds, we may not formulate our thoughts accurately, our wording may be imprecise, or emotions may cloud our clarity. Other times, we may intentionally obscure what we want to say until we're sure we can trust the other person to really listen.

- *The Environment Is Flawed:* Communication is also constrained by telephone or computer limitations, noise, language differences, and time delays while trying to remember what a client said at yesterday's meeting.
- *Listening Is Flawed:* Our own frame of reference filters block us from accurately hearing and understanding. The lens through which we see the world colors what others say to us. It's as if we wear multiple pairs of "Subjectivity Sunglass" that tint and blur what others are saying. The various tints that distort our listening are the many ways that we differ: age, gender, race, nationality, culture, education, industry, job function, training, socioeconomic factors, religion, values, upbringing, and life experiences. It's preposterous to assume that we can accurately understand each other's world and feelings at a deep level through our Subjectivity Sunglasses.

Even Twins Can Misread Each Other. I have an identical twin, Bob. Many of our tints are similar, but some are not. Our talents, personalities, and fears constitute our different lens colors

When Bob was in law school, he was worried that he'd become duller and less charismatic than when he was a rock and roll musician. When people asked how classes were going, he sometimes droned on about torts and contracts, so his "village" started good-naturedly reminding him, "TMI, Bob. Put a sock in it."

Bob and I were once at a party and an acquaintance asked, "What's it like being twins?" I gushed, "It's fantastic. We go way back. We were 'womb mates' taking bets on who would come out first. This great-looking guy has been my best friend since before he was even BORN!" Instantly, Bob tossed his drink in my face! Perplexed, I asked, "Uhhhh . . . Thanks for sharing your scotch, but what do you think I just said?" A little tipsy, Bob retorted, "You said you've known me since before I was BORING!" I had said "born," but Bob heard "boring" through his filter of self-consciousness about becoming less engaging. Wow. The tinted lenses strike again!

Paraphrasing is a fail-safe mechanism that lightens the shade of our distorting sunglasses' tint by double-checking whether we've accurately tracked someone's thoughts and feelings. We wisely remove our Subjectivity Sunglasses by paraphrasing to check understanding—especially if we disagree or don't like what is being said.

Payoff #2: Checks the Accuracy of Your Understanding. Feeding back what you hear is how you double-check the accuracy of your understanding. It's especially important to verify that you've grasped the speaker's message if it is complex.

Years ago, I was lost in Rockland County, New York, trying to get back home to Manhattan. A good Samaritan gave me complicated directions. I was rushed and didn't paraphrase. You guessed it. I wound up in New Jersey. Especially with complex messages, paraphrasing is like a communication sifter when a speaker includes lots of superfluous detail and offshoots that muddy their core message. Just as a sifter separates fine particles from coarse ones, paraphrasing separates out "detail debris" to achieve accurate understanding of the speaker's intent.

Payoff #3: Conveys Acceptance and Positive Regard. Nondefensively summarizing someone's thoughts and emotions says, "I may not agree with you or like what you're saying, but I accept your right to feel that way. I care about you and have goodwill, so I owe you that respect." A Cuban proverb instructs, "Listening looks easy, but it is not simple. Every head is a world." What a service we offer others by investing our time, energy, and heart into truly understanding their world.

Payoff #4: Saves Time and Money. Faulty listening costs us. Just think of the last time you were in a meeting or conversation and someone said, "Oh, I thought we said the client needed the project plan *next* Friday, not *this* Friday." Add to such mishaps the myriad times listening mistakes cost time as we redo a misunderstood task. Multiply the wasted days by people's salaries, and it's clear that even minor listening errors add up to big bucks.

Payoff #5: Creates Readiness to Solve Problems. You may think, "If I understand someone's problem and know the solution, why waste time paraphrasing? I'm a manager, not a therapist!" Well, *you* may be ready to resolve the issue, but is the person who is still venting and working through their emotions?

I call paraphrasing the "interpersonal Drano of communication." When a plumbing pipe is plugged up, we need to unclog it, or nothing will flow smoothly.

When someone is sorting through a problem, their thinking pipes are clogged with emotions, so they can't yet effectively engage in rational problem-solving. Your brilliant idea for solving their dilemma may not get through the muck of their still unexpressed feelings.

Payoff #6: Defuses Tension During Conflict. Paraphrasing the emotions and perspective of an upset person lowers volatility, defensiveness, and resistance. Ignoring heavy emotions doesn't make them disappear. Feelings may even escalate if neglected or stifled. Shoved-aside feelings can smolder and erupt later. If you paraphrase a person's fiery feelings, you *won't* open up a Pandora's box of emotionality. In fact, empathizing helps venters come to their senses and gradually douses the flames. Telling someone to "Calm down" may result in, "CALM DOWN???!!! Up yours! ##**!!!"

Payoff #7: Improves Concentration. Paraphrasing reduces mental vacations and preoccupation. You're less likely to half-listen, tune out, or plan dinner if you know that when the other pauses, you'll paraphrase. Decoding a speaker's message is hard work that keeps us alert, so paraphrasing is an antidote to boredom.

Payoff #8: Sparks Innovation. Creative thinking is stifled when people don't feel safe to voice an idea for fear of being prematurely judged. The thought is barely out of your mouth before someone pipes up with, "Nah, we've tried that before . . ."

Payoff #9: Helps You Retain Content. Gently breaking in to paraphrase during a speaker's complex explanation helps you to grasp and remember key points. Test this out when attending a presentation, watching a documentary, or listening to a podcast (e.g., "He sounds skeptical about the impact of reorganizing by market segments because . . .").

Payoff #10: Cultivates Intergroup Trust and Cooperation. Teams, departments, divisions, and regions often have competing goals, barriers, and tensions. Paraphrasing promotes intergroup teambuilding through understanding of grievances, challenges, and frustrations of working together. The superhero Black Panther admonishes, "In times of crisis the wise build bridges, while the foolish build barriers. We must find a way to look after one another as if we were one tribe."

Payoff #11: Improves Selling. Paraphrasing is an invaluable tool of master salespeople—to build rapport, explore needs, and defuse objections. You might get away without paraphrasing if you're in transactional retail selling, but you may as well throw in the towel if you're in more relationship-based, consultative selling.

Payoff #12: Enriches Group Process. Paraphrasing in groups draws out viewpoints and urges others to share their reactions and opinions. It clarifies ideas, distills points of agreement or differences, summarizes the status of decisions, and captures agreed-upon next steps.

- *Paraphrase Individuals:* "Theresa, you're excited about launching the nonprofit but are worried that the legal work is massive, so you want to hire outside counsel."
- *Paraphrase Subgroups:* "You three at headquarters seem to like the idea, but you four in remote sites worry that monthly town halls are impractical due to travel constraints."
- *Paraphrase the Entire Group:* "The team is confused about why this policy has floated down, so you want me to seek clarity about the business rationale. Am I tracking?"

Payoff #13: Saves a Q&A Session. Paraphrasing questions in groups prevents answering the wrong question. It's not fun to respond to a question and pause to admire your brilliant answer, only to hear, "That's not what I'm asking." I'm often frustrated watching TV press conferences where sports stars or politicians answer questions from non-microphoned reporters without first paraphrasing. What a fun guessing game . . . NOT! Paraphrasing also buys you time to ponder what the heck to say in response to a question that's from left field.

Payoff #14: Helps in Time Crunches. When you're in a hurry, paraphrasing in certain ways can help a long-winded rambler to wind down:

- Convey that you're in a hurry with staccato, more frequent acknowledgments (e.g., "Yep . . . Got it . . . I'm tracking.").
- Keep paraphrases shorter, crisper, and faster paced.
- Use "wrap-up" lead-in phrases that convey you need to wind down (e.g., "The bottom line seems to be . . . The upshot is you want me to . . .").

- Use closed-ended questions instead of open-ended ones that invite elaboration.
- Often, speakers blab on incessantly because they're unsure whether you've understood or agree. Curb droning by blending paraphrasing and validating (e.g., "Got it, Fiona. You want buy-in from the supply chain. I don't blame you for wanting to check with each region."). Fiona will feel less need to keep convincing you.

Module Wrap-Up

We listen countless times a day unless we're hermits, but we take this core skill set for granted. This module put a magnifying glass on *Active Listening*'s bottom-line payoffs and taught the basics of this all-important *Straight Talk* skill. We committed to *absorbing* what others say before *reacting* with a knee-jerk response.

To stretch your *Active Listening* muscles, notice the lack of *Focusing* or *Empathizing* skills at social gatherings. Notice how many TV talk show hosts, especially comedians, interrupt to steal the spotlight. Mentally think how you'd paraphrase a guest's answers if you were the host. Imagine paraphrasing as you watch TV sitcoms, hear song lyrics, or attend lectures.

Of course, the best practice is with your significant other, family, and friends. Better yet, put your toe in the water using the skills at work. To help you feel more confident and competent before you do so, the next module will provide valuable *Active Listening* practices.

Module Five | Listening Lab

Experimenting with Paraphrasing

> As practice makes perfect, I cannot but make progress; each
> drawing one makes, each study one paints, is a step forward.
> —Vincent van Gogh

> Practice does not make perfect. Only
> perfect practice makes perfect.
> —Vince Lombardi

Active Listening Tips and Drills

Comprehending a skill is much easier than executing it, so this module includes
a series of scenarios in which you'll experiment with paraphrasing, and each practice will incorporate a different teaching point. If you haven't downloaded the
Straight Talk Exercises Journal, you'll find it especially helpful for the upcoming
drills (www.BrandonPartners.com/StraightTalkBook).

For now, tie your questioning arm behind your back, and also set aside validating ("I don't blame you for being ticked off . . .") because you already know
those skills. If you visited Tokyo, you wouldn't go to McDonald's, would you?

You'd check out the sushi! Push yourself to fully digest this interpersonal gourmet dish—paraphrasing to keep the focus on the speaker. Also resist the urge to jump in with your own reaction, solution, or suggestion. Instead, first take a *Listening* turn to *absorb* the other's perspective.

> Don't worry about missing a piece of the speaker's message or being inaccurate. Your speaker will correct any misunderstanding or add any piece you omit. The goal of paraphrasing isn't to be a perfect listener. It's to communicate your understanding so that the speaker can verify or adjust it. Even the experts are off 20 to 30 percent of the time, but that means the process of correcting any misunderstanding is working!

Listening Tip #1: Paraphrase Emotionality or Complexity

When should we use *Active Listening*? Not every time a person speaks, since we'd burn out! Life is too short to always consciously use a skill. Any skill overused turns a good thing into something tedious. I love ice cream, but too much of it packs on the pounds. We don't paraphrase while hanging out casually, because it isn't needed. We use it when someone expresses strong emotion (i.e., there's energy or "juice"), or when the person's message is complicated or multifaceted enough that we need to check the accuracy of our understanding.

Take Paraphrasing with a Grain of Salt! At a meal, if Grandpa says, "Please pass the salt," don't pull your chair over, face him, lean forward, and compassionately say, "What I hear you saying is that you're craving some seasoning." NO! Just pass the freaking salt!

Drill: Paraphrase Emotionality or Complexity. You're in a meeting to plan an off-site function and Juan rushes in venting about his boss. Sure, you could say, "Sorry, Juan. We need to plan the off-site," but you decide to take a quick detour to hear Juan out so he can then refocus. Besides, you care about Juan and can see he's hurting. As you listen to Juan below, absorb his thoughts and emotions. Sort his content into a "thoughts bin" and his feelings into an "emotions bin." Then, in your *Straight Talk Exercises Journal*, funnel these bins into a succinct yet comprehensive, accurate, and empathic paraphrase of Juan's outpouring.

> "Hey, guys, sorry I'm late. I have to get something off my chest. I'm *so* peeved!" [Juan sighs with exasperation and shakes his head back and forth.] "I feel undermined as a manager. Nguyen just dropped in unannounced to my customer contact team like a bull in a china shop. He started [Juan gestures air quotes] 'coaching' my reps on procedures. He *totally* contradicted the new complaint logging procedures I taught the team in last week's training that he skipped." [Juan mutters an expletive.] "He threw my guys way off track and now I have to unravel his mayhem! To make matters worse, he didn't even tell me that he was coming, much less ask permission! He's incredibly inconsiderate!"

Pull the content and emotions bins together to write a paraphrase of Juan's message. ∎

Check Your Practice Response. OK, how did you do? Did your paraphrase merely pass the "Accuracy and Empathy Test" or did you earn an A+ so that Juan would say, "Exactly!" Rinse your paraphrase through the rigorous standards below. The goal isn't perfection; it's learning and improvement.

- Is it a listening response with a *you* focus or actually a speaking turn from your own frame of reference?
- Is it reasonably *succinct* or too wordy?

- Is it *comprehensive* enough so that Juan won't need to say more to be sure you absorb his full message?
- Is it *accurate* at a content level? (Only Juan can really say.)
- Does it *convey empathy* and resonate with Juan's emotions with a lead-in like, "You feel . . ." or "You were . . ." or "You sound . . ."?
- Does it use your *own words* or too many of Juan's? Does it even capture Juan's emotions using different words? If he says, "That *irked me big-time* when he barged in . . ." you might paraphrase, "You're *ticked off* that he waltzed into your unit."
- Does it sound natural or too "technique-y"?

Sample Paraphrases. There's no one right way to capture Juan's upset, and he's not here to affirm our accuracy or empathy, so who knows! Some of these may seem too wordy, others too concise. But they all focus on Juan, avoid parroting him, and include both thoughts and feelings. Juan would likely appreciate any of these:

- "Wow, Juan, you're really angry that Nguyen blindsided you by not checking in before giving your unit flawed feedback that ignored the new service protocols."
- "Sounds like you resent the extra work Nguyen's created and are worried about your reputation with your team now that they've gotten mixed messages."
- "What an unnecessary hassle your boss dumped on your lap! You're furious that he went around you, blew it with his input, and eroded people's confidence in you."
- "What a mess! You're ticked off that he may have hurt your credibility by barging in. And you're stuck cleaning up the turmoil from his off-message and uninvited input."
- "You're mad as hell about Nguyen's out-of-the-blue and misguided micromanagement. From your perspective, he's undercut your managerial role and burdened you with a huge mix-up. You resent his intrusion—like, 'thanks for nothing!'"

Listening Tip #2: Paraphrasing Feelings Enrichment

The hallmark of empathic listening is the craft of paraphrasing feelings. An artisan level of this craft demands pinpointing the exact intensity of the feelings being expressed. Strive to expand your repertoire of emotion words. Any category of emotion (e.g., anger, happiness, sadness, etc.) has different degrees—like hot, medium, or mild taco sauce. Some adults have an extremely narrow range in their feeling words vocabulary: happy, sad, glad, mad, good, bad. That's it! This limits their ability to hit the mark and pass the "Accuracy and Empathy Test" with flying colors. Emotional fluency involves the ability to accurately convey understanding of the exact level of an emotion that a speaker is experiencing and conveying in their message. For instance, if someone seems ANGRY, are they "irritated" and "irked" (Mild), "mad" and "angry" (Medium), or "furious" and "livid" (Hot)? If their emotion is FEAR, are the right feeling words "nervous" and "worried" (Mild), "afraid" and "scared" (Medium), or "terrified" and "petrified" (Hot)? SADNESS can be paraphrased as "down" and "blue" (Mild), "unhappy" and "sad" (Medium), or "depressed" and "despondent" (Hot).

You'll increase your emotional fluency and ability to pinpoint the right feeling word when paraphrasing others if you can expand your feeling words vocabulary when you're expressing your own emotions. Do you "like" someone (Mild), "love" someone (Medium), or "adore" the person (Hot)? For ANXIETY, are you "uneasy" (Mild), "nervous" (Medium), or "distressed" (Hot)? How HAPPY are you? Are you "pleased" and "content" (Mild), "happy" and "glad" (Medium), or "joyful" and "thrilled" (Hot)? If you pair a bull's-eye feeling word with congruent body language, vocal pace, volume, and tone, your paraphrase will resonate so much that the speaker may say, "Wow, you really get me. Thank you."

Don't Overshoot. Let's say someone expresses mild annoyance: "It kind of bugged me when Raj was late yesterday . . ." and you respond, "Wow, you're *livid*—just *furious* about his inconsideration!" Whoa, back off, Dr. Freud! Don't use "hot sauce" if "mild sauce" will do (e.g., irked, ticked, etc.). Such overly dramatic, emotive paraphrasing is not empathic. It's laughable.

Don't Undershoot. Now imagine a colleague is seething and lays into you, yelling, "I'M INCREDIBLY PISSED THAT YOU PURPOSELY HUMILIATED ME AT THE MEETING! I CAN'T WORK WITH YOU ANYMORE!!" If I were you, I wouldn't paraphrase, "You seem a bit perturbed." You'd miss the mark with "mild sauce." A more empathic response might be, "Wow, you're obviously furious that I asked my budget question at the meeting, and you think I threw you under the bus. You feel like throwing in the towel on the project if you have to deal with me."

Be Careful with "You Feel That . . ." This common lead-in phrase doesn't really paraphrase feelings, because it's always followed by an opinion, thought, or belief—not an emotion. Saying, "You feel that it was a mistake to hire Keyshawn given his lack of experience with our products . . ." accurately paraphrases *thoughts*, and if said with empathic body language and voice is just fine. But if your goal is to paraphrase *feelings*, replace the word *that* with an actual feeling word or feeling-laden phrase: "You feel *skeptical* about hiring Keyshawn given his lack of experience with our product."

Unpack "Concerned." Many paraphrasers habitually use the lead-in "You're concerned about . . ." which isn't specific enough to hit the bull's-eye. What *kind* of concern is expressed? Is the speaker concerned-anxious, concerned-skeptical, or concerned-worried? Figure it out and name it.

Use Feeling-Laden Phrases. You don't have to literally name an emotion (e.g., angry, unsure, excited, confident, etc.) in order to paraphrase feelings. Mix in feeling-*laden* phrases like: "You're between a rock and a hard place . . . You feel hung out to dry . . . You're at the end of your rope." If a workmate is wrestling with a tough decision between two job candidates, each with strengths and weaknesses, you might paraphrase, "You're feeling *damned if you do and damned if you don't* with either choice since neither choice is ideal." Or, "So, you're *up against the wall* and worried about each candidate. If only human hybrids were possible, huh?"

Drill: Paraphrasing Feelings Enrichment. Let's experiment with feeling-laden phrases and avoid overshooting or undershooting the emotions. Remember Juan, who is upset about Nguyen intruding into his customer service unit with out-of-date coaching input? Your paraphrase before prompted Juan to continue:

"Yeah, you're on target that I'm upset with Nguyen for sabotaging my credibility and for wasting my time by triggering confusion." [Juan slumps, looks at the floor, and murmurs.] "You know, I'm also discouraged. I don't understand why he doesn't trust me to coach my own people. Maybe he has a problem with me as a newer manager." [Juan sighs as he slows down.] "He's probably skeptical that I can get the job done on my own. I guess I feel a little insecure myself with this new role, so no wonder he doubts me. Maybe I'm letting him down."

Write your second *paraphrase* of Juan's thoughts and feelings in your *Straight Talk Exercises Journal.*

Sample Paraphrases. There are 1,534,000 terrific ways to paraphrase Juan (that's how many readers I figure have purchased this book), so the following are just examples to compare to yours:

- "The more you're digesting this bummer, the less angry you feel. You're still upset with how off base he was with his input, but now you're wondering if his intrusion stemmed from him being worried about your role."
- "As you think about Nguyen's botched intervention, you suspect that he's anxious about whether you're adjusting to being a supervisor and that he's overcompensating by micromanaging. You're realizing that you have your own misgivings about the new position, that perhaps you're a bit out over your skis."
- "Sounds like you're uncomfortable as a first-time manager. You seem worried that maybe your self-doubt is getting picked up by Nguyen and triggering his distrust."
- "On one hand, you're upset that Nguyen disrupted your team, and you're perplexed about why he went behind your back. On the other hand, you're acknowledging your own part since you feel a little out of your league with being a team leader."

How does your paraphrase stack up with the above examples? ■

Listening Tip #3: Peeling Away the Artichoke Leaves

We've cited two metaphors for paraphrasing: (1) a *sifter* to clear away the clumps of a jumbled communication message, and (2) "*interpersonal Drano*" to unblock emotion-clogged pipes to allow a person to settle down enough to engage in rational problem-solving.

A third listening metaphor is that of *peeling the leaves of an artichoke* to help a speaker get to the "heart" of the matter. Deeper layers of thoughts and feelings can exist with multifaceted or emotional issues. Paraphrasing facilitates moving through the outer surface–level issues to the inner, deeper issues. This dynamic operates when a speaker is:

- only dimly aware of deeper issues and needs a "sounding board" to uncover them.
- fuzzy about complex issues.
- unclear about their feelings.
- embarrassed.
- unsure whether they trust you enough to reveal the real problem.

Patiently paraphrasing prevents misreading the initial issue as being the only one. We often jump in too soon with reactions, suggestions, or solutions. "But, Rick, we're *paid* to solve problems!" Sure, but if you prematurely mistake the first level of a problem as being pay dirt, you risk never getting to the deeper, real issues. Solving the wrong problem wastes time and the person won't trust you enough next time to divulge their deeper, true issue.

I'm *not* suggesting that anyone approaching you with a problem or reacting to something you're requesting is always unintentionally or purposely withholding deeper issues you need to uncover. Sometimes the initially presented issue or problem *is* the only issue and doesn't have deeper layers. I still recommend paraphrasing to *absorb* before you *react*, so the speaker can finish venting before hearing your advice or other input.

Drill: Peel the Artichoke Leaves. The following scenario is scripted to move from an initial surface issue to a deeper, true issue. You'll paraphrase to uncover deeper layers of the problem. Notice what kind of solution you'd normally be tempted to give (too soon), since we'll examine your tendencies in the next module. Below, Donna is your direct report needing to unload.

"I'm so fed up with so many useless meetings. Why do we need six people and two hours to make mundane decisions? We often don't even make decisions. It's a lot of talking and discussing, going round and round." [Donna pauses to see if you understand.]

Think of how you'd paraphrase Donna. Preferably, write it in your *Straight Talk Journal.*

[Donna validates your paraphrase and continues:] "Right. I'm in constant meetings with our team, sales, marketing, supply chain, and external vendors. Something's got to give! I often don't start my regular work until 2 PM, and don't finish until 7 PM, if I'm lucky. Why spend time planning the work if there's no time left to work the plan?" [Donna hopes you'll check your understanding, so you do.]

Paraphrase Donna's thoughts and feelings in your *Straight Talk Journal.*

[Donna feels heard and unfolds more:] "It's affecting my health. I think I'm getting an ulcer from all these meetings. And it's hurting my home life, never seeing my kids. Last night I got home, and my husband sarcastically said, 'Hi. We haven't met. My name is Mario.'" [You and Donna are in rhythm. She pauses for your paraphrase.]

Paraphrase Donna's thoughts and feelings in your *Straight Talk Journal.*

[Donna seems calmer and trusts you enough to "get real."] "Look, it's not *all* the meetings. I'm overstating things because I'm stressed. Actually, some meetings are helpful. It's mainly *your* staff meetings that have been driving me crazy lately." [WAIT! It's tempting, but don't react or even ask the obvious question, "What's wrong with my meetings?" First just paraphrase.]

Paraphrase Donna in your *Straight Talk Journal* or at least think of how you'd do so.

> [Donna reveals the real issue.] "Let me clarify. Staff meetings that *you* conduct are super. You facilitate well and we get things done. But our new client means you travel two weeks a month, so George runs our meetings. He doesn't send out the agenda like you and he totally dominates. Everyone's discouraged because he doesn't call on anyone. Maybe we could rotate who, facilitates or get him some coaching." [AHA! This is the real problem. Still, resist the urge to jump in with solutions. I know I'm pushing my luck, but paraphrase one last time. Then, of course, you'll thank Donna and problem-solve.]

Write a bottom-line paraphrase or practice one mentally.

Examine your responses for how well you're adhering to the criteria for effective paraphrasing (e.g., succinct yet comprehensive, your own words, includes thoughts and feelings, sounds natural, etc.). ■

Listening Tip #4: Paraphrase Reactions to Your Agenda

So far, each practice situation has started with a request or concern that someone brings to you. But also use *Active Listening* when it's *not* the other person's agenda kicking off the conversation. It's *yours*. You're forging an agreement, giving feedback, announcing a change, outlining procedures, or voicing an opinion at a meeting. You *Check Reactions* to what you've said. Your receivers are now the speakers with opinions, concerns, or questions that you need to paraphrase before you respond. You'll paraphrase the person's reactions so that the conversation doesn't devolve into a series of back-and-forth speaking turns. Remember, what they say initially may or may not be their real, underlying issue, so peel the artichoke leaves here, too.

Drill: Paraphrase Reactions to Your Agenda. In this vignette, you and Grant give monthly product briefings together to top management. You do the formal stand-up presenting, and Grant answers technical questions from his seat. This formal to informal format works well. However, you must suddenly fly to a plant in China, so you ask Grant to present solo at this month's briefing. You are surprised by his resistance, but you wisely paraphrase to explore it.

> "I'm really sorry, but I just can't squeeze in taking over the full presenting responsibilities. I'd love to help while you travel, but my schedule won't allow for all the extra prep." [You resist pushing back and instead paraphrase.]

Paraphrase Grant's message in your *Straight Talk Journal* or on a sheet of paper.

> [Grant confirms your paraphrase and elaborates:] "Right. I'm fine with fielding questions as the technical expert after you present, but taking on both roles with the meeting five days away doesn't give me enough planning time. But Ahmad from engineering can handle it." [OK, he feels put out so you paraphrase.]

Paraphrase Grant's unfolding thoughts and feelings in writing or mentally.

> [Good job. You've opened the door to hearing Grant's fuller picture:] "Look, I'm a little embarrassed to bring this up, but stand-up presenting isn't my strong suit. I get flustered and nervous. I just think Ahmad or anyone else would make a better impression and have more prep time." [Grant looks to you for your answer, but instead you paraphrase one more time in case there's a deeper layer (and there will be).]

Paraphrase Grant's next layer of thoughts and feelings in your *Straight Talk Journal*.

> [Grant feels safe and reveals the real issue:] "OK, this is incredibly confidential, but . . . the truth is, I have a serious presentation phobia. In my last job, I was presenting to the executive committee and had a full-blown anxiety attack. Sweating, heart palpitations, stammering, brain freeze— the whole nine yards. It trashed my reputation. I had to leave the company. Ever since, I've avoided taking that risk. That's why I prefer sitting and facilitating more informally." [Ah! Now it makes sense! No wonder. Good thing you listened instead of reacting. You use one last summary paraphrase to wrap things up before problem-solving.]

Write your paraphrase of Grant's "real problem" in your *Straight Talk Journal*.

Now that you've reached the true issue, you might brainstorm solutions (e.g., agree to Ahmad's subbing, reschedule, you present the data and Grant conduct Q&A like always, practice with Grant, suggest a presentations coach, explore anxiety management counseling, etc.). It's a very different conversation once you paraphrase to uncover the real block to Grant saying "yes." ■

Listening Tip #5: Don't Get Hooked!

Perhaps the toughest time to paraphrase is when a speaker criticizes or attacks you. It's easy to get hooked and push back from your own frame of reference. It's hard not to take what's coming at you personally—because it *is* personal.

But you're better served by *Active Listening* before you stick up for yourself or apologize. It takes self-control and the Self-Talk from module two to avoid saying something you'll regret, especially with a boss. Remember to *absorb* before you *react.* There may be a deeper issue, or the person may backpedal from their initial angry claims if you demonstrate a non-defensive desire to understand.

Stay Cool in the Heat. Whenever you're attacked, resist the urge to punch back. Try to curb your anger both in the moment and after the interaction. Simmering with anger is like drinking poison and hoping it'll kill the other person!

- *Negative Self-Talk:* "This guy is a pompous, incompetent ass! I'm not going to sell out by kissing up and accommodating his verbal attacks just to get ahead and advance."
- *Positive Self-Talk:* "Okay. This executive has an ego. I protect my own best interests by using self-control and verbal discipline. When they go low, I go high, choosing my words carefully. It might help to paraphrase his upset when he's throwing his weight around." ■

Drill: Don't Get Hooked! Your manager, Lina, is conducting your performance appraisal. You're confident, since your region's sales production numbers have increased for the third consecutive quarter. Lina begins in a flat, matter-of-fact tone (uh-oh):

> "Well, I think it's clear that as far as the numbers go, you hit the ball out of the park again, with strong sales results and metrics for your team. As far as productivity goes, I have no issue." [Lina's tone of voice and body language hint that there is a *but*. You decide to paraphrase the good news as well as the possible negatives she's telegraphing with her nonverbals.]

Paraphrase Lina's positive feedback *and* her reservations in your *Straight Talk Journal*.

> [You're *Focusing* your body skills and empathizing, so Lina continues.] "Yeah, no kidding there's a downside. The problem is *how* you get your numbers. Your communication habits baffle me. I can't fathom how or why you just don't get it about our core values of *respect* and *team focus*. You need to treat your reports and colleagues more like you relate to your customers." [Lina pauses to see whether you are taking in this feedback.]

Paraphrase Lina's disappointment and the "why" behind it in your *Journal*.

> [Great job of showing non-defensive listening! It's tough work as Lina unloads more:] "Your interpersonal behavior abuses people. You alienate your team, berate them in public, and delegate new tasks without listening to reactions. And the way you set sales goals is way too autocratic and unilateral. You're forcing compliance but not fostering enthusiastic commitment." [Here's your chance to at least prove that you *do* know how to listen.]

Paraphrase why Lina's upset in your *Exercises Journal*.

> [You reach Lina's bottom line:] "Look. I've already coached you on this. I may return you to just selling instead of supervising unless you can speak in less inflammatory ways and listen to your subordinates." [Prove to Lina that you fully understand and are willing to hear the whole truth and nothing but the truth, which will earn her respect.]

Paraphrase Lina's bottom-line concern in your *Straight Talk Journal*. ∎

Taking Your *Active Listening* "Progress Pulse"

Great job! I hope these paraphrasing exercises give you confidence! Just as we do in courses, let's debrief your *Active Listening* practice. Please assess yourself as Low, Medium, or High for each of the four categories below:

Rate Your COMPREHENSION. How well do you cognitively grasp *Active Listening*'s "F.E.E." skills—especially *Empathizing*'s paraphrasing skill? Can you teach someone the paraphrasing guidelines (own words, feelings and thoughts focus, etc.)? Can you cite reasons to paraphrase? Is your rating at least Medium for understanding effective paraphrasing? If not, you've been reading in bed and dozed off! Re-read this module since most people rate themselves as Medium or High.

Rate Your COMPETENCE. Based on the above drills, rate your skill level. You aren't assessing your comfort level, only your capability with *Active Listening* skills. Your *Competence* is probably lower than your above *Comprehension* rating.

Rate Your COMFORT. Finally, how natural do you feel with *Active Listening*? How second-nature is paraphrasing? If you graded yourself as Medium, you're integrating paraphrasing fairly easily. If you gauged your ease as High, you must be in human resources! (Ha!) If paraphrasing feels really awkward and foreign, a Low rating, relax. Almost everyone rates themselves lower on this question since paraphrasing isn't a usual reflexive response when others speak.

The Price of the Dream of Learning Any Skill

You're not alone if this all feels unnatural. We are more used to *reacting* than to *absorbing*. Paraphrasing goes against the grain—especially for managers. We're paid to solve problems—quickly. That lures us into telling and advising, when we should be listening in order to fully comprehend what the heck we're trying to fix or solve!

Some people don't like stumbling with new skills. That's OK. Others resist behaviors that are out of their comfort zone. That's OK. Lots of people wrestle with how "fake" or "phony" paraphrasing feels. That's OK. You may worry that you're having a personality transplant. That's OK, too. These sentiments are all typical and understandable. Here are some thoughts to help you through the discomfort of learning.

Any New Skill Is Awkward. When you first learned to walk, it felt cumbersome and strange. Discomfort is part of the learning process. In fact, if you're *not* experiencing uneasiness, you're probably not trying to up your game.

You're *Not* Being a Phony. You're not trying to be someone you're not, no more than you are being a "fake" if you're practicing a new tennis backhand method that feels unnatural. You're not pretending to be Rafael Nadal or Serena Williams. You're still *you,* just working on an unfamiliar stroke.

You're in Charge! Don't feel pressure to use these skills when it doesn't feel right. They are simply tools, but *you* are the carpenter deciding if, when, and how to use each *Active Listening* tool (or not). We all sometimes think, "No thanks. I've had enough personal growth for the century." If you don't want to make any behavior changes right now, I get it—as long as you're making the decision with awareness of your options.

Don't Resist Changing. Then again, I do take issue with people rigidly rejecting all self-improvement while they are bruising others. Their stance is, "If you don't like who I am, then sue me!" They suffer from the "Popeye Disorder," named after the cartoon sailor and his catchphrase, "I yam what I yam and dat's all dat I yam!" Lady Gaga's "Born This Way" song urges accepting and being your authentic self, but Gaga surely *isn't* advocating stubborn refusal to change lousy communication habits or treatment of others.

Feeling Mechanical Is Part of Learning. Any training at first involves repetitively adhering to rigid techniques. That's true with ballet positions, musical scales, golf's driving range, and basic training in a military boot camp. It's normal to dislike paraphrasing's reliance on strict rules, criteria, and "training wheels." Initially, you'll feel robotic and mechanical. Soon, you'll feel more natural and integrated. You *can* retain the uniqueness and beauty of your own style and personality.

Retain Your Uniqueness. One day when my son, Eric, was three, he had napped until dinnertime. I gently tapped his arm, kissed his forehead, and whispered, "Time to wake up for supper, buddy." Eric grouchily barked, "No, Daddy, I'm sleeping!" I gave him a few minutes before trying a second time, when he rolled over to doze off again. I picked him up and carried him to the kitchen, playfully reminding him, "Mr. Sack of Potatoes, you know we always eat together, so we need you to wake up, honey." Eric, knowing exactly how to disarm psychologist Daddy, cried through his tears, "No, Daddy! I don't want to wake up! Why can't you just let me be the person I AM?!?!" The moral of the anecdote? Filter the *Active Listening* techniques through your own fantastic style. BE THE PERSON YOU ARE!

Virtual Variations: *Active Listening*

Let's adapt modules four and five's *Active Listening* skills to our increasingly remote work environment and virtual communication modes.

On the Telephone

Others can't see your body language, but still use attentive *Focusing* skills. They will sense your forward lean, interested facial expressions, and other body language. This keeps you alert, since the body and mind are connected. Emphasize vocal and verbal components of listening (voice tone, rate, pace, etc.). Use more acknowledgments (e.g., "I see . . .", etc.) and encouragements (e.g., "Please go on . . .") to show that you're tracking. Paraphrase more than normal to prove you care and that you understand what someone is saying (e.g., "Let me see if I'm following you so far, since I want to understand what proposal changes you want . . ."). If you gently break in to show empathy and acceptance rather than reacting, others will appreciate your paraphrasing as a service to the conversation.

In Emails or Threaded Texts

You can't see a writer's body language or hear vocal tone, but consider how they might be feeling given their content and emotion words. In your written reply, paraphrase your understanding of the message as a bridge to your response, reaction, or answer (e.g., "Joe, your email made it clear that you're upset about not being kept in the loop about today's meeting. Please let me explain how that happened . . ."). An option is to make sure you're tracking in a first email before responding in a second one. You can write a paraphrase and ask for confirmation that you've understood before following up with your next emailed or texted speaking turn. Such quick back-and-forth exchanges in writing are feasible and simulate a conversation.

Leading Video Conferencing Meetings

Change Your *Listening* Sub-skill Emphasis. On some virtual platforms with camera functions, audible *Exploring* interrupts the speaker, since the camera and audio shifts any time a voice is picked up. Therefore, reverse the above telephone tips by eliminating *verbal* acknowledgments ("I see . . . uh-huh . . .") and encouragements ("Go on . . .") and instead relying more on *physical Focusing* so others can *see* you listening (e.g., looking into the camera's eye, large and slow nods, facial empathy, thumbs up, etc.). Paraphrasing is still your best friend to show that you were truly tracking and understanding.

Paraphrase Liberally. Besides paraphrasing individuals, periodically summarize group agreements, disagreements, conclusions, decision status, and agreed-upon next steps. Send private chat room paraphrases if you think a person doesn't feel heard when the group moves on (e.g., "Hey, Colin. It seems like Carlita didn't really get why you feel so strongly, and you seemed offended. Want to talk later?").

Curb Multitasking. Increase involvement by inviting someone to paraphrase what *you're* saying. So that people don't think this is a "Gotcha," preview that you'll be doing so to maximize focus and energy: "I know it's tough to limit multitasking with emails pinging us and texts popping up. I'd appreciate all of us turning off phone notifications and I'll be calling on people to give reactions or to paraphrase me or others. It's not to catch you off guard—just to keep us all focused. OK?"

Module Wrap-Up

We exercised your paraphrasing muscles to build your *Active Listening* strength and comfort. Then we explored the challenges of learning any new skill set and discussed virtual applications of this module's concepts.

You may have felt it was stilted to isolate and work on these skills outside of a fuller conversation. The rest of this workshop-in-a-book blends your *Assertive Speaking* (module three) and *Active Listening* (modules four and five) skills with procedures for implementing various day-to-day Conversations.

See you after a quick break for module six. I'm serious. The last two modules were long ones, so walk around outside before reading the next module. Please do not take this advice if you're reading this book on an airplane.

Part II

Smooth Sailing
Conversations

Module Six | *Advising and Guiding*

"Lean on Me"

> Service to others is the rent you pay
> for your room here on earth.
> —MUHAMMAD ALI

> The purpose of human life is to serve, and to show
> compassion and the will to help others.
> —ALBERT SCHWEITZER

Applying the Core Communication Skills

You're now grounded in the *Straight Talk Mindset, Assertive Speaking*, and *Active Listening*. For the rest of this workshop-in-a-book, we'll apply these core skills within a range of workplace interactions, with preparation Message Templates and step-by-step Conversation Formats. You'll conduct these discussions with bosses, direct reports, peers, internal or external clients or customers, and people in your personal life. Some conversations are easier ("Smooth Sailing"), while others may involve emotionality or defensive reactions ("Rough Sailing"):

SMOOTH SAILING (Part II)	ROUGH SAILING (Part III)
Advising and Guiding (this module)	*Reminding* (module nine)
G.A.I.N.-ing Commitment (module seven)	*Confronting* (module ten)
	Disagreeing Agreeably (module eleven)
Recognizing (module eight)	

What's *Advising and Guiding* All About?

As a leader, manager, or individual contributor, you're approached by others struggling with concerns, problems, or dilemmas. They ask for advice and suggestions, elicit guidance and input, request coaching, or need your emotional support as they cope with a troubling work or home situation. They need a caring sounding board as well as your experience and expertise.

The goals of the *Advising and Guiding* application are to:
- help others explore and resolve their problems and decisions, and
- provide emotional support when there is no real solution to a dilemma.

COMMUNICATION PROCESS

QUESTION   LISTEN
POSITION/ASK   (F.E.E.)

Questioning Cycle

CHECK

SPEAK   LISTEN
(A.B.C.)   (F.E.E.)

CHECK

Dialogue Cycle

FORMAT STAGE AND STEPS

UNDERSTANDING

OPEN

USE ACTIVE LISTENING AND QUESTIONING AGENDA
- Landscape
- Problem
- Goal
- Action

SUMMARIZE

USE READINESS DOUBLE CHECK

SOLVING (or SUPPORT)
- SPEAK
- CHECK REACTION
- PARAPHRASE REACTION

Diagram 6.1 | The *Advising and Guiding* Conversation Format

This Conversation Format is similar to ones used in consulting, needs-based selling, counseling, and other problem-solving professions. The two stages of *Advising and Guiding* are *Understanding* and *Solving* (or *Supporting*). As we cover each stage in the model shown in diagram 6.1, we'll follow a hypothetical situation involving Janie and her direct report Will, who approaches her for help with an employee.

Let's clarify a few things. The problem someone wants to discuss is NOT you! In this module, they're seeking your help. Next, I don't have your *content*- or *task*-level expertise. I'd never play know-it-all about what actual input you should make. That's what you're paid for and are trusted to do. But I *will* share best practices for facilitating helper-mode discussions that address problems, develop employees, and keep ownership of problems on the other rather than putting the "monkey on your back." Finally, sometimes a person needs to talk through an unsolvable dilemma—a heavy life condition that has no real resolution. They still need your empathic understanding so that they're not alone in their struggle. You can offer emotional support and "en-cour-agement" (from the French word for "heart," *coeur*, so you are literally giving heart to the person in pain).

Remember the overarching purposes and North Star Goals of *Straight Talk*: (1) to get the results you want and (2) to build a trusting, working relationship. The *Advising and Guiding* model directly satisfies the second objective, since helping others in times of need cultivates rapport, trust, and appreciation. This module even impacts the first goal by increasing people's desire to meet your work needs and by removing distractions that may be preventing them from maximizing their performance. You'll improve work results, save time, and develop employees—major payoffs when managing, collaborating, selling, consulting, or parenting.

The *Understanding* Stage

Metaphors for the *Understanding* Stage

The *Understanding* stage of *Advising and Guiding* relies on your *Active Listening* skills plus skillful questioning. This stage has three purposes, each of which relates to one of the three *Active Listening* metaphors introduced in the book:

1. *To fully explore and crystalize an issue:* A person struggling with a problem may be unclear. Listening is a *sifter* that separates out the "detail debris" in their message to accurately understand the essential core of their message.
2. *To avoid prematurely solving a surface or wrong problem:* Initially expressed concerns may cover up the deeper heart of a problem. Listening *unpeels the artichoke* to identify the bottom-line problem.
3. *To create emotional readiness for problem-solving:* Speakers often start right off talking about the real issue but still need airtime to get it off their chest before moving to *Solving* it. The *Understanding* step's listening and questioning blend serves as "Interpersonal Drano" to unclog the person's pipes.

Timing Is Everything! I often ask for a volunteer. I say, "Okay, your task is to ask me the secret of good workshop humor." As the participant begins asking the question, just when the third word is uttered ("Rick, what's the . . .") I rudely interrupt to sharply yell, "TIMING!" Great punch line but awful timing. A splendid, elegant answer delivered before the proper time not only ruins a good joke, it also turns *Advising and Guiding* input into a bad joke!

Timing is everything. The *Understanding* stage allows us to fully comprehend issues before addressing them in the *Solving* stage. Rarely do we explore problems well enough or long enough to even *arrive* at the real issue, much less gather the information needed to adequately address it or clear out the emotions enough to problem-solve.

The Audacity of Premature Problem-Solving

We're paid to have answers to problems or decisions people bring to us, but we often prematurely give input and advice. Who says we must solve problems instantly? Perhaps we've been conditioned by seeing too many TV doctors who miraculously diagnose complex problems and diseases—and they do it in thirty minutes! Fewer, with commercials!

A person has wrestled with a problem or dilemma for two hours, two days, two weeks, two months, or two years—and we jump in with our brilliant solution after two minutes. Isn't that presumptuous, even insulting? Also, we risk solving the wrong problem or getting egg on our face when the person says, "Yeah, I already tried that, and it didn't work." Finally, even if we *do* have the right problem, even if we *do* have the data to solve it, and even if our solution idea *is* sound . . . is the other person ready to work on a solution? Have they sorted through their feelings enough to hear our ideas?

Skills in the *Understanding* Stage

The Questioning Agenda: L.P.G.A. It's acronym time again! Any golfer knows that the LPGA stands for the Ladies Professional Golf Association, but in the *Straight Talk* model it is a sequence of questions to ask when exploring a speaker's problem in the *Understanding* Stage. Training programs often teach salespeople to ask specific questions when exploring client needs to uncover data that will help them propose a solution that will fit the situation. Bankers and insurance agents use their company's questioning protocol to gather information about their clients' financial situation and needs, so they can recommend the best loan structure, investment product, or insurance package.

Unlike questions asked during a sales interview, when *Advising and Guiding*, you'll ask L.P.G.A. Questions to help you understand the person's problem or work challenge that prompted them to seek out your support, advice, and guidance. You've already learned the *Questioning Cycle* of asking a question and paraphrasing the answer. Now, here is a *Questioning Agenda* that is a road map for the information you need to uncover in the *Understanding* Stage.

Landscape Questions. Survey the field by asking questions about the problem's background, situation, and facts. Try to keep your questions open-ended, give the reason you're asking if needed, and usually paraphrase the answers. Often speakers get on such a roll venting about their problem that very few questions are needed and mostly paraphrasing will suffice.

Problem Questions. Ask questions about the problem, challenge, or struggle troubling the person. Your speaker's mood is likely be discouraged or even distressed. Therefore, when you paraphrase, show empathy through your facial expressions, body language, and vocal tone (slow and somber).

Goal Questions. Next, shift from the distressing status quo to ask questions about and paraphrase the person's Goals. Explore (with Questions and Paraphrases) what the person hopes to achieve by resolving the problem. Unlike your tone of voice and body language when you explore and paraphrase the Problem, when you paraphrase the Goal, shift to a quicker, more upbeat energy and forward momentum. This contrast in tone between the first two *Questioning Agenda* steps prevents your speaker from staying immobilized by the Problem, or, worse, sinking in quicksand. It will help you wind up the *Understanding* Stage with a hopeful mood and propel you both into the *Solving* Stage with a motivating, forward-moving momentum.

During the Problem step of the L.P.G.A. *Questioning Agenda*, if the speaker is expressing anger versus melancholy about their Problem, then you will paraphrase with body language, volume, and vocal tone that conveys empathy with their agitated, animated irritation. Then during the Goal step of the Questioning Agenda, you'll use softer, more relaxed, and calmer vocal and visual cues as you paraphrase. You're again modeling an emotional shift that you hope your speaker will adopt for the *Solving* stage.

Sometimes, you'll ask about and paraphrase only the Problem *or* the Goal, but not both. It depends on the content and complexity involved in the *Advising and Guiding Conversation.* Either way, when the speaker confirms that your paraphrasing was on target and you've covered the necessary content in the "P" and "G" steps of the L.P.G.A. Questioning Agenda, move to the "A" step.

Action Questions. Next, inquire about any actions taken by the speaker so far to address and resolve the problem, as well as any new ideas now for resolving the issue. This carries these benefits:

- *Avoids Embarrassment:* You won't waste time or trigger awkwardness by suggesting ideas that didn't work.
- *Tells You About the Speaker:* The speaker's answer sheds light on their critical thinking, task maturity, and motivation to take ownership for their own problem. This data informs the kind of input you'll provide in the Solving stage—how detailed and directive you need to be. If the speaker says, "I haven't thought of anything to fix the problem . . ." then they need more detailed, exacting, and instructional guidance. If the speaker reports several thoughtful actions, then super-detailed advice might be overly directive and insulting.
- *Keeps the "Monkey" Off Your Back:* The famous *Harvard Business Review* article "Who's Got the Monkey?" bemoaned how many managers are overwhelmed with too much work and burdened with too many problems—too many "monkeys on their back." Still, they often shoot themselves in the foot by bailing out a subordinate too quickly (e.g., "Let me think about this issue . . . I'll take care of it . . . I'll get back to you . . ."). So don't *you* unwittingly take on problems, allowing the "monkeys" to leap from the subordinate's back onto your own. Instead, ask what's been tried or considered in order to develop the person's critical thinking and send the message that you expect people to proactively attack their own problems before running to Mommy or Daddy. What a time-saver for you!

Be Flexible with the Questioning Agenda. Life isn't a diagram! Feel free to allow the *Understanding* stage's steps and Agenda to flow organically and not always sequentially (P.L.G.A. or G.P.G.A.). Some narrowly focused, unidimensional problems don't even require exploring both the Problem and the Goal. Imagine that you're exploring a friend's self-remorse about their post-injury rehabilitation.

You paraphrase, "Sounds like the Problem is that you're disappointed in yourself for not shedding the extra thirty-five pounds since the accident." It would be trite to then ask about and paraphrase their Goal as, "So your goal is to lose the extra thirty-five pounds." This is obvious and redundant. You might therefore only cover the Problem or the Goal, but not both. Or instead, you may help the person expand and flesh out how they express and you paraphrase the Goal: ". . . sounds like your goal is to find motivation, self-discipline, and some tactics for tackling your weight-loss hopes, so that you're healthier and back to your marathon training." It's okay to open up the landscape like this if you don't send specific solutions now. That will happen in the *Solving* stage.

The Readiness Double Check. After completing the *Questioning Agenda*, put a ribbon on your exploration of the speaker's issue. You can do this by at times summarizing the Problem, Goal, and Actions already taken or considered, and using a Readiness Double Check to make sure that the speaker is primed to hear your advice, suggestions, encouragement, or support in the *Solving* Stage:

- "Seems like we've fully explored the issues, right?"
- "Sounds like you're ready to address the problem."
- "I do have a few reactions and suggestions if you're ready to hear them."
- "Want to hear some ideas I have?"

A twist on this last *Understanding* stage tactic is, "How can I be most helpful to you right now?" This lets the speaker tell you what exact kind of input is best: advice, training, coaching, brainstorming solutions, referring to a manual or other resource, role-playing the situation, providing encouragement, and so on.

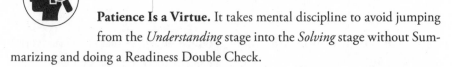

Patience Is a Virtue. It takes mental discipline to avoid jumping from the *Understanding* stage into the *Solving* stage without Summarizing and doing a Readiness Double Check.

- *Negative Self-Talk*: "Come on! It's obvious what the problem is, and I have some good advice that will help this person. I can't spend my entire day helping her!"

- *Positive Self-Talk:* "I may think I know her issue, but I need to fully understand it and find out what she's tried already so I don't waste time with my suggestions. Investing time now will save us time later." ■

Demonstration: The *Understanding* Stage

Let's see the *Questioning Cycle* and L.P.G.A. *Questioning Agenda* in action as Janie explores her direct report

Will's problem with a troublesome salesperson. ACTION!

Janie: [*Invites conversation*] Will, you said on the phone you had a performance issue that's bugging you. I have a few minutes right now. Does that work for you?

Will: That'd be great, Janie. I'm at my wits' end with how to confront Renan, one of the new salespeople from our recently acquired company. He keeps ignoring simple sales protocol requirements. It takes forever to get him to implement easy processes and systems. I'm so aggravated, I'm ready to take disciplinary steps.

Janie: [*Paraphrases*] Sounds like you're really frustrated and mad at how labor intensive it is to get compliance from Renan on straightforward procedures . . . [*Will nods.*] . . . and you're feeling so burdened, you may confront him with an official warning.

Will: Exactly. I've had it.

Janie: [*Positions her L.P.G.A. questions*] Well, to be sure any input I make isn't based on faulty assumptions, may I ask you a few questions? [*Will approves: "Sure!"*]

Janie: [*Positions a _Problem question from the L.P.G.A. Questioning Agenda*] Different performance management tactics fit for different problems. It'll help me advise you if I understand the exact items Renan isn't implementing and the frequency of the pattern. What are some examples?

Will: For one, he regularly ignores basic proposal procedures, like leaving off email attachments. I have to call him, request them, and wait till the next day until he responds.

Janie: [*Paraphrases*] So, an easy proposal process turns into unnecessary hassle and delay. That alone is annoying.

Will: Yeah, and he also "forgets" [*Will gestures air quotes*] to use our uniform template, so I have to cut and paste his content into the correct format. It's not the end of the world, but these mistakes add up time-wise.

Janie: [*Paraphrases*] Sure. It's annoying when he drains time by not following protocol.

Will: Yep. Also, before our joint appointment with RKT Corporation, I'd explained that we always need to start follow-up sales meetings by summarizing client needs before giving our recommendations. Renan blew it. He launched into presenting without building rapport or reviewing needs to align with the client. The client, Ali, is very particular and was visibly turned off. Way too pushy!

Janie: [*Paraphrases*] You're afraid he comes across like a high-pressure hawker of wares instead of modeling the relationship-based selling we pride ourselves in delivering. [*Will nods vigorously. "You're spot on."*]

Janie: [*Asks an empathic question*] It's like being in a marathon. Tiny pebbles in the shoe that slow you down are small, but they're irritating, huh?

Will: Bingo. To say the least!

Janie: [*Positions a second Problem question from the L.P.G.A. Questioning Agenda*] You know, sometimes performance issues have a personal component—a hidden hostility, political agenda, or other dynamic. Since Renan's from a newly acquired company, what about other variables, like resentment or disgruntlement about his job?

Will: Hmmm . . . Great question. We're the top dog company, but I don't sense any hidden agendas or beefs about being managed by me. He's never defensive. He's a good guy. He just doesn't act on my feedback.

Janie: [*Paraphrases briefly*] He means well. He's just a space cadet.

Will: Yeah, you're tracking.

Janie: [*Positions a second Goal question from the L.P.G.A. Questioning Agenda*] Will, you've laid out the problem clearly. You want to turn around his performance. Are there other things you want to accomplish by fixing it?

Will: I think he's starting to feel like I'm piling on and that I'm down on him. I don't want him to quit. He brings real technical expertise to the team and it'd be a loss. He's a good guy and he's not out to make my life a pain, so I actually want to improve our relationship and his morale.

Janie: [*Paraphrases*] You don't sense deeper issues and you're less angry since it isn't intentional. You're worried his demotivation is snowballing, and you're at a loss.

Will: Spot on. I'm less mad than I am clueless. I guess it's a development issue more than a discipline issue. I'm willing to give him the benefit of the doubt if you have some coaching tips.

Janie: [*Summarizes the Problem*] OK, just to be sure I've got it all, it seems like your problem is you're mystified about Renan's continued mistakes with the information he emails you, his product deliverables, like proposals, and his face-to-face selling, like with Ali's sales call. He seems absent-minded or lackadaisical about easy procedures even after you've explained and corrected them. You don't want to discourage him so much that you lose him, but you're exasperated, especially since you now think a warning is overkill. Am I summarizing accurately? [*Will confirms, "Yep, that's it in a nutshell."*]

Janie: [*Summarizes the Goal with an upturned, faster, momentum-filled voice while leaning forward with an out-rush of positive energy*] Sounds like your goal is to find a way of coaching Renan so that he does what's asked the first time, or at least implements your corrective feedback the next time. You want to optimize your time and energy, and you don't want him to be more demoralized than he already is.

Will: Yes! That's music to my ears!

Janie: Janie: [*Positions an Action question from the L.P.G.A. Questioning Agenda*] Well, you've already had sit-downs to lay out expectations in a clear way and provided feedback. Is there anything else you've tried or considered?

Will: I thought of talking to human resources about transferring him to a more experienced sales manager, but like I said, I'd hate to lose the technical knowledge Renan brings, since other salespeople do learn from him. Also, if I can bring him around, it'll up my game as a manager.

Janie: [*Paraphrases*] So, other than reexplaining things, you're stumped and apprehensive about addressing the situation.

Will: That's about it.

Janie: [*Uses a Readiness Double Check*] Well, I have some ideas that fall under the umbrella of coaching more than confronting. Is there any other way I can be most helpful right now?

Will: No, for sure I want your coaching tips. Maybe later we can role-play your ideas.

Janie: Sure! Let's dive in . . .

CUT!

When to Leave the *Understanding* Stage

Often, we don't stay in the *Understanding* stage long enough to even get to the real issues, much less explore them enough to resolve them. Other times we don't segue to *Solving* soon enough, the speaker becomes impatient, and we waste time. How can we know we've achieved mutual *Understanding* of the real problem and that the speaker has expressed emotions enough to rationally address the issue? Hey, this isn't rocket science! The other may say, "So that's basically the issue . . . What do you think? . . . Any suggestions?" Some other signals follow.

Content Clues. It just seems logical that you've reached the *Understanding* stage's conclusion. The spaghetti strands of the problem are less convoluted. The fragmented puzzle pieces have fallen into place. You may not know what input, recommendation, or solution to offer, but it makes sense to enter the *Solving* stage.

Changes in Nonverbal Behaviors. The person's body language and energy shifts:

- *The Speaker Becomes More Animated:* The person starts off talking slowly and softly with low energy, a sinking posture, and a downcast demeanor. They haltingly fumble through what's troubling them. Gradually, as questioning and listening bring clarity, they jerk upward in their chair, open their eyes wide, speed up, and exclaim, "Yes! That's it! That's what's been bothering me!"
- *The Speaker Becomes Calmer:* After initially being frantically agitated, their body language now softens, and they sigh. Their voice softens to a whisper: "I guess I was afraid to admit this to you." They've moved from unrest to relief that the whole problem is finally on the table.

You're on a Merry-Go-Round. You know you're ready to move on when there are no new layers of content or emotion. The person is saying the same thing over and over. Your paraphrases are repetitive. Don't overstay your welcome in the *Understanding* stage. Move to *Solving*.

Is All This Work Worth It? You may feel skeptical about spending so much time and effort in the *Understanding* stage before going to the *Solving* stage, but I guarantee you that your speaker will never resent the interest and focus you devote to exploring their problem. Besides, resolving an issue so that it stays resolved demands this much up-front sweat. Albert Einstein was asked, "If you had one hour to save the world, how would you spend that hour?" He quipped, "I would spend fifty-five minutes defining the problem and then five minutes solving it."

The *Solving* Stage

While much *Advising and Guiding* occurs in the *Understanding* stage, there's essential work to be done in the *Solving* stage with these best practices:

1. Consider a separate *Solving* stage meeting.
2. Use the Dialogue Cycle.
3. Decide how directive to be.

1. Consider a Separate *Solving* Stage Meeting

For straightforward problems, both stages of the *Advising and Guiding* conversation (*Understanding* and *Solving*) can be accomplished in one sitting. However, when issues are complex, you can schedule a second conversation for the *Solving* stage. If so, end the first meeting by bringing closure with a comprehensive paraphrase that captures the person's full scope of the problem and goals. Then check readiness and schedule a second meeting when you'll provide input and recommendations.

You'll use the time between the two discussions to research the problem, consult others, and prepare possible solutions. Begin the second meeting by reviewing the problem and/or goals you surfaced during the first meeting. Salespeople and consultants do this all the time—explore a client's needs in an initial meeting and conduct a follow-up meeting to summarize the situation and propose solutions.

2. Use the Dialogue Cycle

The *Understanding* stage used an exploring cycle (Question-Paraphrase-Question) as the speaker described their problem. In the *Solving* stage, the speaker role shifts to *you* as you use this Dialogue Cycle to interactively give input without monologuing:

- Speak (your first piece of input).
- *Check Reactions.*
- Paraphrase Reactions.
- Recycle the Speak–*Check Reactions*–Paraphrase process with your next input.

Receivers can only digest so much information at one time, so the Dialogue Cycle's interactive process allows the hurting person to consider and react to your first idea before hearing your next one.

3. Decide How Directive to Be

The following enrichment of your Advising and Guiding adapts and builds on leadership guru Ken Blanchard's Situational Leadership model. Some of us are habitually locked into providing only one kind of input for every kind of speaker and every kind of problem. Instead, mix up the range of your responses by adapting your level of detail and directiveness, depending on the speaker's familiarity with this kind of problem, motivation, and task maturity.

Here's the Idea. Overly specific and "tell-oriented" input is micromanaging and insulting with a task-mature, experienced, and motivated employee or team leader. However, speakers who are less motivated or newer to the exact problem being grappled with may feel insecure, uncertain, or abandoned if your input is too sparse, general, and "ask-oriented." More experienced people often want more leeway and ownership to collaborate on a solution, whereas a rookie may need more handholding with directive, precise, step-by-step instructions.

Another variable to consider is how time-sensitive and imperative a specific course of action is. A mission-critical issue might compel you to be more prescriptive and controlling with your input. If you have skin and teeth in the game—because the problem affects you and the whole organization—you'll likely be more directive and tell-oriented. With a less urgent and sensitive decision or dilemma, you may be comfortable giving the other person freedom to come up with their own solution in a less directive fashion.

Expand Your Repertoire. Stretch your versatility in the *Solving* stage by modulating your input among these three levels of directiveness:

- *Least Directive:* With the most experienced and most motivated receivers, and the least critical problems, you may: express faith by asking what they want to do, use facilitative questions to guide the person to their own solutions, or ask the person what they'd advise a friend to do.
- *Moderately Directive:* For medium levels of experience, motivation, and self-accountability, with medium-level problem urgency, options are to: brainstorm ideas and options and let the other decide; provide information that points the person in the right direction so they can take the ball and run with it; share criteria to consider with their next steps without giving a solution; refer the person to manuals, resources, or people; or check for fit as you share your similar experiences and what you did.
- *Most Directive:* With the least experienced, least motivated, and least task-mature receiver, especially if you're heavily invested in the exact nature of the solution, consider these most detailed, tell-oriented methods: make a suggestion, give advice, teach how to handle the situation with detailed instructions, demonstrate how to execute particular steps, take responsibility to handle the problem yourself (yes, now *you've* got the monkey!).

Assess Your *Solving* Habits. Reflect upon your typical ways of giving input to employees, peers, bosses, clients or customers (internal or external), friends, kids, and others.

- Which level of directiveness (Least, Moderate, Most) do you most often adopt?
- Which input options within each cluster do you most utilize?
- Do you vary your level of input based on the speaker's experience and commitment, as well as the problem's gravity, or do you approach most situations the same way?
- How can you develop greater range and versatility with your input? ∎

Demonstration: The *Solving* Stage

This last *Advising and Guiding* demo scene finds Janie moving from the *Understanding* stage into the *Solving/Supporting* stage. ACTION!

Janie: [*First idea's Assertive Speaking turn*] I do have a few coaching tips. First, since Renan has trouble "getting it," how about sending him an email review of whatever expectations or feedback you've talked about? Some folks are more visual than auditory in how they process information. [*Checks Reactions*] Know what I mean?

Will: Yeah, that's true. I thought it was best to meet in person, so he'd see how serious I was, but that means my instructions were only verbal. I can do both.

Janie: [*Paraphrases, speaks, and Checks Reactions*] So, you're up for more documenting. That will help later if you eventually need to confront or give Renan an official warning, right? [*Will nods as he jots notes.*]

Janie: [*Second idea's Assertive Speaking turn*] Next, when you do give corrective feedback, a coaching best practice is to do more than only telling Renan what he did wrong or suggesting alternative actions. Paint a vivid picture of the negative impact of his faulty behavior. An example is how client relations and our sales brand suffer when he jumps into presenting without summarizing needs. When he uses the wrong template, your time and energy are drained. [*Checks Reactions.*] Is this making sense, or do you think you already do this?

Will: No, I just tell him what to do differently, which may come off as bossing him around. This will help lock in the "why."

Janie: [*Paraphrases*] Exactly. Then you think this tweak might be helpful? [*Janie pauses.*]

Will: For sure. What else is in your magical coaching tool kit?

Janie: [*Third idea's Speaking turn*] Yeah, I'm a real Management Merlin, huh? [*They both laugh.*] Seriously, I also want to encourage you to recognize and reinforce the things Renan does right. After a sales call, ask him what he thinks he did well and tell him what strengths you saw, even simple stuff like wearing his underwear on the inside of his pants instead of the outside. [*Will almost spits out his coffee laughing.*] Really, though, catch him doing things right when you correct an action and he does follow through. Your positive feedback and appreciation may gradually build his self-esteem and his thirst for more. [*Checks Reactions.*] How's this idea sound?

Will: Makes sense, Janie. He's gotta feel beaten down at this point.

Janie: [*Paraphrases*] Great. You seem game to experiment with using positive motivation to see if it impacts his performance.

Will: For sure. Next week we have a ride-along day. I'm psyched to try these three ideas.

Janie: Cool. Not to belabor things, but how about a recap of your game plan?

Will: Sure. I'm going to (1) send emails summarizing my directions and corrections, (2) explicitly describe the tangible negative impact of his problem behaviors, and (3) focus more on recognizing his positive actions.

Janie: [*Speaks to preview next steps*] Voila! You nailed all three strategies. I bet you'll see some improvement. You said you'd like to role-play, so let's do that before your trip next week, say Thursday at three o'clock?

Will: I'd really appreciate that, as well as your ideas today. Thanks, Janie. See you Thursday!

CUT!

Short-Circuit Responses

Reacting Versus Absorbing

Janie was successful in *Advising and Guiding* Will partly because she avoided typical habits that cut off exploring and understanding someone's problems, and that derail conversation.

> ***Short-Circuit Responses:*** All-too-common habits that prematurely shift the focus from listening and *absorbing* another's frame of reference to instead *reacting* from our own frame of reference.

The *Understanding* stage of *Advising and Guiding* is ideally a flow of thoughts and feelings that's analogous to an electrical current's flow to turn on the light bulb. Here, the light bulb represents a sound idea for solving a speaker's problem. We may short-circuit the communication flow to lasting resolution by too hastily giving *Solving* stage input instead of first fully absorbing. (Have we beaten this dead horse enough? I mean, Secretariat and Seabiscuit are twitching!)

Short-Circuit Responses aren't always problematic—only when someone is struggling with a difficulty and needs to work through the issues and emotions. These responses are dysfunctional if they cut off the sharing of issues, distance you from a troubled speaker, trigger resentment, foster over-dependency, or chip away at a speaker's self-esteem.

Eight Short-Circuit Reactions

Typical non-listening mistakes cut across four categories:

Power Trip Reactions. These Short-Circuits involve put-downs or pulling rank:

- *Blaming:* Finger-pointing and labeling is unhelpful (e.g., "Well, you're the one that brought this on by . . ." or "That was a little rigid and naïve, don't you think?").
- *Bossing:* Autocratic orders or threats to control the speaker can be out-right *Aggressive* (e.g., "You'd better step up to the plate for once to deliver, or I'll find someone else who will . . ."), or they may be *Border-line Aggressive* (e.g., "You have to fix this yourself. Go tell the customer we won't fulfill his request . . ." or "Listen, this kind of mistake can scar your career.").

Superiority Reactions. These responses make us the "top dog" and convey disrespect:

- *Diagnosing:* Analyzing and playing amateur psychologist is alienating (e.g., "This fits your under-assertive pattern and stems from deeper self-worth issues.").
- *Moralizing:* "Should-ing" all over a person (!) with guilt trips and appeals to higher values is off-putting (e.g., "You should consider the impact on company-wide morale. You should be a team player and bite the bullet for the greater good.").

Misguided "Help" Reactions. These mistimed responses have an honorable intent to help but are brash if the speaker isn't finished with their thoughts, feelings, and ideas.

- *Advising:* Telling someone your solution too soon is presumptuous and minimizes the complexity of the person's problem (e.g., "If I were you . . ." or "Look, this one is a no-brainer. All you have to do is . . . ," leading to, "Well, do you want my help or NOT?!"). Sometimes, all the person wants is listening, understanding, and support. Hitting them with a barrage of advice can be insulting and abrasive.
- *Inappropriate Questioning:* Under the guise of gathering data, we send veiled solutions. It's jarring or even challenging to use too many "Why" questions, especially if we rapidly fire them without paraphrasing the

answers (e.g., "Well, have you talked to Luis about getting more resources? When exactly did you receive the orders? Why aren't other supervisors reporting this problem, too?").

Bail-Out Reactions. These responses avoid hearing a speaker's emotions due to our discomfort with feelings.

- *Diverting:* Instead of following the leader (the speaker), we hijack their train of thought (e.g., "Speaking of red tape hassles, you won't believe the bureaucracy in my department . . ."). Or, we retreat from emotions with logic (e.g., "You're overreacting, so let's calm down and rationally examine the core issues . . .").
- *Minimizing:* Reassuring too soon discounts emotions (e.g., "C'mon, this isn't like you. You're an optimistic, strong survivor."). Other times, we're naïve (e.g., "Don't worry, these things work themselves out. We all go through an initial job adjustment."). Even if you're not being condescending or insincere, beware.

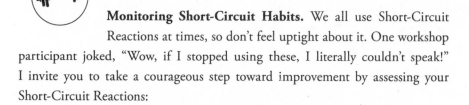

Monitoring Short-Circuit Habits. We all use Short-Circuit Reactions at times, so don't feel uptight about it. One workshop participant joked, "Wow, if I stopped using these, I literally couldn't speak!" I invite you to take a courageous step toward improvement by assessing your Short-Circuit Reactions:

- Which Short-Circuit Reactions do you use too often?
- Which ones are almost always harmful?
- Which ones might be helpful if you first fully listen?

Power Trip Reactions
1. *Blaming:* Finger-pointing and labeling (aka, name-calling).
2. *Bossing:* Autocratic orders and threats.

Superiority Reactions
3. *Diagnosing:* Analyzing and playing amateur psychologist.
4. *Moralizing:* Shoulds, oughts, and guilt trips.

Misguided "Help" Reactions

5. *Advising:* Premature solutions that cut off exploration.

6. *Inappropriate Questioning:* Excessive probing or rushed, veiled solutions.

Bail-Out Reactions

7. *Diverting:* Changing the subject, distracting, or stealing the focus.

8. *Minimizing:* Reassurances that ignore a problem or discount emotions. ■

Fire Your Critical Parent. This Self-Talk tool comes in handy when you're criticizing or labeling yourself in overly negative ways. Did you do this as you discovered ways that you use Short-Circuit Responses?

Transactional Analysis theory says we have four "ego states" that are helpful to monitor: an internal child, rational adult, loving parent, and critical parent. Our critical parent involves negative Self-Talk—beating ourselves, others, or the world up from a judgmental, abusive posture. It's discouraging and demotivating to berate yourself (e.g., "I'm a crappy listener."). Before a meeting, it's self-defeating trash talking to threaten yourself (e.g., "You'd better not screw this up!"). Instead of scolding yourself with put-downs, "shoulds," "musts," or "could haves" after making a mistake, "Fire Your Critical Parent."

- *Negative Self-Talk:* How do you talk to a real child when they're discouraged? Not how you talk to yourself, I bet! You wouldn't critique your kid's soccer play like this: "You stupid idiot. How could you do that? You always screw up games! I told you *not* to come out of the goalie box, but noooo, not you. You cost the team this entire tournament. You never get it!"
- *Positive Self-Talk:* You'd more likely say, "It's OK, buddy. Sure, you let three goals in when you left the goalie box, but what matters is learning from our mistakes. And you still blocked eight shots against the number-one offense in the league! Don't be so hard on yourself, honey. We're still in the top bracket."

We talk to ourselves in ways we would *never* speak to our kids or friends. This Self-Talk tool is about finding your kinder and gentler inner parent, coach, or friend . . . *you*. Compassionate Self-Talk also helps you be less upset with and

Aggressive toward other people, too. I've taught you the Fire Your Critical Parent Self-Talk tool in the hopes that you will not be tough on yourself for any Short Circuit tendencies you discovered in the above Exercise. Forgive yourself and move on to improvement! ■

Virtual Variations: *Advising and Guiding*

Advising and Guiding remotely only takes hopping on the phone and using the exact same process as you would in person. As face-to-face is increasingly replaced by Facebook, it's even more important to be there for others who are grappling with a challenge—including virtually. Sure, when offering support to associates, friends, and family, it's best to be able to put our hand on a shoulder, but we still can "reach out and touch" others across the airwaves of cyberspace by empathically and skillfully *Understanding* and *Solving* problems.

Whenever possible, urge *Advising and Guiding* voice-to-voice, but if you do it in writing, you can send an email reply to paraphrase a writer's (speaker's) "problem data dump" and ask exploratory questions. When the person sends their answers, summarize their problem and goal, and ask what's been thought of or tried (with positioning, especially via email). When the person replies, send a *Solving* stage email to share your input and check the person's reactions before summarizing for closure.

Module Wrap-Up

Advising and Guiding is about *absorbing* during the *Understanding* stage before *reacting* in the *Solving* stage. *Understanding* uses open-ended questions (sometimes with positioning statements for context) and paraphrasing to surface and explore a speaker's issues and feelings. During this first stage, we ask questions about the person's problem, goals, and attempts so far to resolve the work challenge that's troubling them. Four clusters of Short-Circuit Reactions derail understanding before a speaker is ready for input: (1) Power Trip Reactions, (2) Superiority Reactions, (3) Misguided "Help" Reactions, and (4) Bail-Out Reactions.

The *Solving* stage begins by checking readiness to address and solve the problem and then uses a Dialogue Cycle that blends *Assertive Speaking* to share your ideas with *Checking Reactions* and *Active Listening* to know how the other is receiving your input. Adapting the *Solving* stage's level of directiveness for different

receivers helps to break out of one-dimensional input and avoids either micromanaging experienced people or undershooting instruction for novices.

A Touching True Story

Once, I was moved by this testament to the healing power of listening versus
derailing. A half hour before the workshop's Day Two began, I was preparing
the room. Buck, a burly, bearded ex-military warehouse supervisor, strode up and
startled me. "Rick! I need to talk to you." I braced myself, since Buck had been
pretty resistant to *Active Listening* on Day One, saying that it would make his dock
workers view him as a pushover.

Buck's face softened and his eyes glistened with a trace of tears. "I want you to
know that I'm sold. I tried this listening stuff with my high school daughter, and
she talked to me—I mean, *really* talked to me. Usually when I ask about her day,
I get grunts or 'talk to the hand' sullen looks. Last night I could see she was upset,
so I figured what the hell. I paraphrased how she looked kind of sad, and I spent
the next hour paraphrasing her worry about not fitting in with the cool crowd. She
opened up, cried, and felt better afterwards. Katie kissed me good night and said,
'Thanks, Pops. We should do this more.' Thank you, Rick."

THIS is why I teach.

Module Seven | *G.A.I.N. Commitment*

From Bailing or Bullying, to Buy-In

> Unless a commitment is made, there are only
> promises and hopes, but no plans.
> —PETER F. DRUCKER, MANAGEMENT AND LEADERSHIP GURU

Mission Possible: To *G.A.I.N. Commitment*

Last module's *Advising and Guiding* Conversation Format was about giving to others when they are wrestling with a problem, dilemma, or decision. But we can't give from an empty bucket. We need to have our own work needs met, too, in order to be best equipped to help others. This module is about how to be self-ful (not selfish) by getting the results *we* need from our work relationships. Otherwise, we can't really be fully there for others who need something from us.

We've said that *Straight Talk* (1) gets the results you want and (2) builds trusting relationships, as opposed to resorting to *Aggressive* bullying that alienates or to *Passive* bailing that loses respect. This module's Smooth Sailing Conversation Format seeks buy-in in order to:

- gain commitment and alignment about strategies, goals, results, behaviors, new ideas, or changes, and
- achieve buy-in to your suggestions or recommendations.

We'll now use *Assertive Speaking* and *Active Listening* to influence others in order to obtain clear, accountability-oriented commitments from bosses, peers, direct reports, customers, and vendors—anyone whose results and behaviors are critical for our performance success, quality, stress management, and job satisfaction.

Can You Count on Accountability?

Accountability has become a hot buzz word in business:

Accountability: The willingness to accept responsibility for one's actions.

We want others to take ownership for their actions (*and* for their *non*action!). If you're like most people, you're frustrated by people who *aren't* doing what you want, people who *are* doing something you *don't* want them to do, and people who aren't doing something in the *way* you want.

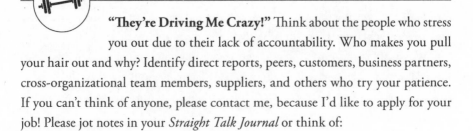

"They're Driving Me Crazy!" Think about the people who stress you out due to their lack of accountability. Who makes you pull your hair out and why? Identify direct reports, peers, customers, business partners, cross-organizational team members, suppliers, and others who try your patience. If you can't think of anyone, please contact me, because I'd like to apply for your job! Please jot notes in your *Straight Talk Journal* or think of:

- people who *aren't doing things* you need done.
- people who are doing things you need them to *stop doing*.
- people who are doing something you need *done differently*.

Please save this list; we'll return to it later. ■

Three Flawed Commitment Expectations

Gaining commitments is supposed to make others accountable, raise productivity, save time, and lower our stress. Then why do so many commitments fall short? Why do so many people drive us nuts, increase team tension, and hinder results? It turns out that *we're* often part of the problem. People have three Flawed Commitment Expectations:

1. Expecting Others to Be Mind Readers
2. Expecting Ineffective Conversations to Produce Effective Results
3. Expecting Without Inspecting

The Flawed Commitment Expectations in Action. Juliana and Jared finish a spaghetti dinner with Cory and Cody, their twin eight-year-olds. They need to finalize their tax returns before tomorrow, so they push their chairs from the table and head to the den. As they leave, Jared glances back and says, "Boys, Mom and I have to work in the den, so clean up dinner. Thanks!"

Two hours later, the bleary-eyed couple finishes the IRS grind and come into the kitchen for a glass of celebratory wine. What's your bet on how well Cory and Cody did with the cleanup? Jared took a stab at talking to the kids, but he missed the boat on all three Flawed Commitment Expectations:

- *Flawed Expectation #1: Expecting Others to Be Mind Readers:* Dad knows his need, but his parting words didn't constitute a clear, commitment-oriented conversation. It was a one-way *expectation* rather than a two-way agreement; he failed to be sure his sons knew exactly what he expected, and he didn't secure buy-in. It was a pipe dream! Jared mistakenly figured the boys would know to handle things because they all had before as a group.

- *Flawed Commitment Expectation #2: Expecting Ineffective Conversations to Produce Effective Results:* Poor discussions consist of a Faulty Communication Process and/or Faulty Content. Jared's communication was subpar. He didn't really *Check Reactions* (e.g., "Any concerns or questions, boys?"). His *Active Listening* body language was flawed (e.g., no eye contact as he talked over his shoulder), and he never paraphrased. He might as well have just left a note on the kitchen table! Pop wasn't *Passive* or *Aggressive*, but he also wasn't proficiently *Assertive*. He won't get the results he wants and the relationship won't be helped when Mommy and Daddy get annoyed and the boys feel blamed for Jared's haziness.

Regarding Faulty Content, Dad's request was, "Boys, Mom and I have to work in the den, so clean up. Thanks!" Plenty of content is missing . . . What does "clean up" mean? Will the table be wiped off or smeared with sauce? Will dishes be off the table but piled in the sink with caked-on food? Will dishes be rinsed off but on the counter? If they're in the dishwasher, will it be turned on? With detergent?! We've said the *B* of *Assertive Delivery*'s "A.B.C."s stands for *Bias-Free Language*. What *specific behaviors and results* define "cleaning up"?

There also weren't clear *roles* assigned. Will the boys fight about who does what? There wasn't *motivation* for them to fulfill Dad's request—no mention of *why* their help was needed (the tax deadline), no rewards for helping (screen time or a percentage of the tax refund?), and no consequences for not helping (the orphanage? Oops, sorry!). What *century* will the dishes be done? Will Cody whine, "We put dishes in the sink and were gonna finish after tossing the football around 'cause it gets dark early now"? Finally, Dad didn't ask whether there were *obstacles or concerns* (like homework), so no removal of barriers could be discussed.

- *Flawed Commitment Expectation #3: Expecting Without Inspecting:* Dad didn't ask the boys to summarize the agreement, set up a time to check their progress, and/or arrange for follow-up. Things were left up in the air, and that's where they stayed.

A Preview of the *G.A.I.N. Commitment* Conversation's "Cures." *Straight Talk*'s steps and skills are antidotes for each of Jared's Flawed Commitment Expectation boo-boos. We'll correct the first error, "Expecting Others to Be Mind Readers," by making two kinds of needed agreements. We'll reduce the second problem, "Expecting an Ineffective Conversation to Produce Effective Results," with the Dialogue Cycle of *Assertive Speaking* and *Active Listening*. We'll fix Faulty Content by funneling the Dialogue Cycle into a proven *G.A.I.N. Commitment* Conversation Format. Finally, we'll handle the third Flawed Expectation, "Expecting Without Inspecting," by how we end the conversation, by *Recognizing* positive results (module eight), by *Reminding* if the ball is dropped on a commitment (module nine), and by constructively *Confronting* ongoing accountability problems (module ten).

Flaw #1: Expecting Others to Be Mind Readers

The comic strip character Pogo exclaims, "We have met the enemy and he is us!" We can be our own worst enemy regarding accountability. We often blow off a Commitment Conversation, assuming others know what we want or what bothers us.

Back in the workshop, I invite your group to generate the differences between "Expectations" and "Commitments." Our lively brainstorm surfaces these flip chart entries:

Expectations	**Commitments/Agreements**
One-Way	Two-Way
Internally Conducted in My Mind	Externally Seen and/or Heard
Covert	Overt
May Be Unrealistic, a Pipe Dream	Reality-Tested with Others
Compliance-Oriented	Commitment-Oriented
Less Likely to Be Met	More Likely to Be Met
Unilateral	Mutual
Monologue	Dialogue
Doesn't Surface Obstacles	Discusses Obstacles
Command and Control	Cooperative and Collaborative ∎

A Moment of Truth. Time for some "fessing up." Look at the people you identified above as stressing you out by *not doing* what you want, doing something you *don't want* them to do, or doing something the *wrong way*. Now, be honest. For how many of these aggravating situations is at least *part* of the problem that you haven't conducted a true Commitment Conversation? Did you really have clear agreement in place that met the above agreement criteria: two-way, seen or heard, overt, achieved through dialogue, addresses obstacles, commitment-oriented, cooperative, and collaborative? ∎

People Aren't Mind Readers. We often need to take greater "response-ability"—the ability to respond—for some of our stress and problems. We walk around with expectations in our head when others can't read our minds!

- *Negative Self-Talk:* "Come on! She should know this. It's part of her job . . ." or "This is clearly stated in our policies and procedures manual."
- *Positive Self-Talk:* "Maybe she should know, but her actions say that she doesn't or that she just forgot. Sure, it's in the policy manual, but that handbook's a bear. After all, *nobody* memorizes every policy and procedure. I need to cut her some slack and forge an agreement." ■

Time-Out for a Time-Out Story! My friends Miyoko and Misha dearly love their wonderful daughters—eight-year-old Alexia and four-year-old Svetla. Alexia is more headstrong, so at times winds up in the "Time-Out Corner" in the hallway away from the family room and kitchen.

One day, Svetla, who is a perfect angel, uncharacteristically acted out so much that for the first time ever, they sternly told her, "Svetla, you march to the Time-Out Corner, sit down, and think about what you've done." Svetla trudged into the hallway and plopped down on the Time-Out chair as the rest of the family returned to preparing dinner.

After the normal ten-minute time-out duration, Misha went to get Svetla for dinner, only to find the Time-Out chair empty. Perplexed, he went to the girls' room where Svetla was quietly flipping through a storybook. "Young lady, what are you doing here when you're supposed to be in time-out?" His distraught little girl sobbed, "I'm sorry, Daddy. I don't know even know what time-out is or what it means."

Dad's heart melted as he realized his baby girl was right. Svetla was such a doll, she'd never earned a time-out! She wasn't a mind reader! He hugged Svetla and reassured her, "I'm sorry, sweetie, you're right. We should have explained that if you're in a time-out, you have to stay until we come to get you. Okay? Now let's get dinner!"

Do You Unwittingly Expect Anyone to Be a Mind Reader? Do *you* ever get mad at your employees, colleagues, boss, friends, or family for not reading your mind to know what you want them to do differently? It's important to identify where our expectations need to be converted into clear *Commitments* that build account-ability, results, and relationships. We need two-way *G.A.I.N. Commitment Conversations* about two categories of needs: (1) New Issues and (2) Preexisting Issues.

New Issues: A Clean Slate. We often need to request newly desired behaviors or results when we're introducing an issue for the first time. We may ask others (e.g., reports, peers, customers, bosses, vendors, etc.) to complete a task, accept a new responsibility, do us a favor, buy into a strategy, commit to new norms or procedures, or accept a change we're announcing. The person has done nothing wrong since we're discussing a totally new area of their work.

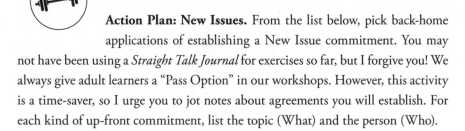

Action Plan: New Issues. From the list below, pick back-home applications of establishing a New Issue commitment. You may not have been using a *Straight Talk Journal* for exercises so far, but I forgive you! We always give adult learners a "Pass Option" in our workshops. However, this activity is a time-saver, so I urge you to jot notes about agreements you will establish. For each kind of up-front commitment, list the topic (What) and the person (Who).

- Getting buy-in for a new strategy, goal, policy, procedure, or project action steps
- Delegating new tasks or assignments
- Clarifying changing roles and responsibilities
- Setting goals, objectives, quotas, or deadlines
- Establishing new team norms for meetings or overall functioning
- Announcing organizational or operational changes
- Making a request or asking a favor ■

Preexisting Issues: "My Bad!" Other times, we need to *G.A.I.N. Commitment* about something someone's already doing that we want to alter. So what "pre-exists" is a behavior we want to change or adjust. We're asking them to modify an aspect of their performance that we haven't really discussed enough. New Issues involve a clean slate, whereas Preexisting Issues involve adjusting something that's off-base.

It's not the person's fault. We've never talked about this area of responsibility, or we did so but the person's actions are prompting us to add to, clarify, or adjust an initial *G.A.I.N. Commitment* Conversation. Other times, we may not have stressed the importance enough, or at least that's what we'll assume out of good will.

It's never too late to go back and adjust or fix someone's behavior, but for Preexisting Issues, it's in the spirit of an initial agreement rather than *Reminding* (module nine) or *Confronting* (module ten). It wouldn't be fair to come down heavy, so we instead *G.A.I.N. Commitment* with a special starting phrase that avoids accusations and reduces defensiveness because it was our own oversight that led to actions we want to tweak. We can begin our discussion by *taking responsibility:*

- "I neglected to explain a detail about equipment setup in the safety training . . ."
- "You documented each new client onboarding as we discussed. There's just one part I should have been clearer about up front . . ."
- "You had no way of knowing this since I didn't explain that our meeting norms include . . ."
- "We talked about this, but I must not have stressed the reasons enough . . ."

Action Plan: Preexisting Issues. For each item below, jot a note about whom to approach and an example for that topic.

- Someone's doing something you requested, but in the wrong way.
- You must correct something the person "should know" that you never discussed.
- New constraints change how someone needs to do a task (budget, staffing, etc.).
- New regulations mean that someone is technically breaking a standard.
- The person is achieving results, but how they achieved them is problematic.
- Quality standards are being met, but you must clarify results that aren't being reached.
- You haven't emphasized certain responsibilities of a job enough and they are lacking. ■

Flaw #2: Expecting Ineffective Conversations to Produce Effective Results

Fixing a Faulty Communication Process. Our vehicle is again the Dialogue Cycle of Speak–*Check Reactions*–Paraphrase–Recycle that we used in the *Solving* stage of *Advising and Guiding*. We've devoted three entire modules to the core interpersonal influence skills of *Assertive Speaking* and *Active Listening*. Your communication traffic signal's green light flashes back and forth between speaking and listening as the focus alternates between your needs and the other person's reactions. Otherwise, your rambling diatribe will go over the receiver's head. I'm a fan of three "Holy Hyphens": two-way, give-and-take, and back-and-forth.

Fixing Faulty Content. You saw how Jared's post-dinner request fell short. Dad can "clean up" the cleanup problem by giving Cory and Cody a clearer and fuller picture of what he wants and the benefits to the boys and the family. He can also invite any questions or concerns and establish how he'll check in, and so on. These elements form a foolproof *G.A.I.N.* agenda format for getting desired results, building trusting relationships, and baking accountability into agreements:

<u>G</u>OALS. What observable actions and outcomes are desired? Performance consists of targeted behaviors and results, so here is where the Commitment Conversation identifies those specifics. We're influencing to gain buy-in to work outcomes we want, or to achieve cooperation and support around an idea we are advancing.

<u>A</u>DVANTAGES. What are the reasons for seeking the commitment? Include benefits to all parties: you, the receiver, your team, the broader organization, customers, clients, friends, family members, and so on. Your purpose is to influence, so "sell" the other on what's in it for them to make the commitment. My friend Cindy McGovern's book title says it all: *Every Job Is a Sales Job*. You're selling your idea or whatever action you seek, so share convincing reasons for the person to commit, even if it's just to help you out of goodwill. An Advantage may include avoiding the negative consequences of *not* agreeing.

<u>I</u>MPEDIMENTS. What are any obstacles to the other's feeling good about making the commitment so that you can address them? You may wonder, "Why ask

about barriers that might stand in the way? That's just giving them an excuse to not do what I want!" Actually, it has the opposite effect. You're taking *away* excuses by surfacing and resolving them. Besides asking the other what might get in the way, you can also build goodwill and cooperation by proactively citing potential challenges that you suspect. Otherwise, the discussion is a setup, because you know the person may hit a particular roadblock and you are withholding it. Why wait until it's too late? Address Impediments *now*.

NEXT STEPS. Good Commitment Conversations end with a summary of the agreement and establishing needed progress-checking steps. In a football game, a player shouldn't spike or drop the ball just before making it to the end zone. You have a higher likelihood of "scoring" commitment follow-through if there is certainty about what agreements have been made and about what else needs to occur for success.

G.A.I.N. Commitment Format Samples

Example #1 (New Issue): Announcing Change (Report)

GOALS: Results and Actions Desired. "Salim, unfortunately we are no longer being given the freedom to work remotely from home Monday through Wednesday; only on Thursdays and Fridays." [*Check Reactions* and listen.]

ADVANTAGES: Benefits and Consequences. "While everyone needs to make the commute on Thursdays now, there's a benefit. That's the day we'll have clients attend the new user seminars on-site. I'm eager to see how they increase client revenue and up-selling." [*Check Reactions* and listen.]

IMPEDIMENTS: Ask About Obstacles and Concerns. "I'm sorry for the extra hours of driving this means. So that your added commute isn't wasted time, I'm happy to budget for a Bluetooth headset or AirPods, so you can listen to weekly product briefings. What other problems might crop up with this policy?" [*Check Reactions*, paraphrase, and respond to problem-solve.]

NEXT STEPS: Summary and Follow-Up. "What's your takeaway understanding, and any thoughts about next steps?" [*Check Reactions* and listen.]

Example #2 (New Issue): Requesting Help (Peer)

GOALS: Results and Actions Desired. "Taylor, I'd really appreciate your IT team's help next week to walk my call contact center reps through the new data entry software." [*Check Reactions* and listen.]

ADVANTAGES: Benefits and Consequences. "My team isn't tech-savvy. If your group coaches us, it'll reduce our call handling time and make a huge difference in customer satisfaction numbers. I'll return the favor by having my guys get yours up to speed with the client relations skills you've said they need to improve. The teambuilding between our groups will be great." [*Check Reactions* and listen.]

IMPEDIMENTS: Ask About Obstacles and Concerns. "What issues might my request create?" [*Check Reactions*, paraphrase, and respond to problem-solve.]

NEXT STEPS: Summary and Follow-Up. "If it works for you, I'd love to do this next Wednesday. We could spend the morning and I'll spring for a nice lunch. [*Check Reactions* and listen.]

Example #3 (New Issue): A Recommendation (Boss)

GOALS: Results and Actions Desired. "I have an idea for enhancing our finance department's identity as a strategic partner. Since we've acquired two new companies, let's assign a comptroller to each one to explain our protocol for reporting monthly P & L numbers." [*Check Reactions* and listen.]

ADVANTAGES: Benefits and Consequences. "We sometimes get the reputation as being out of touch with the line businesses. This is a way to get face time with them and lower resistance to the new system they have to adopt." [*Check Reactions* and listen.]

IMPEDIMENTS: Ask About Obstacles and Concerns. "I know this drains some resources from your team's regular work, and some folks may argue that it's not their job to help the new people assimilate." [*Check Reactions*, paraphrase, and respond to problem-solve.] "My take is that we'll build rapport with our new colleagues and save time later by reducing mistakes. I think your gang will buy into that rationale." [*Check Reactions* and listen.]

NEXT STEPS: Summary and Follow-Up. "Let's discuss this at Tuesday's staff meeting and decide who has the bandwidth to do this for three months." [*Check Reactions* and listen.]

Example #4 (Preexisting Issue): An Oversight (Report)

GOALS: Results and Actions Desired (Remove Blame). "Pierre, I need to tweak something in your meeting management that you had no way of knowing. I forgot to explain that we send out an agenda in advance, and that we include debriefing time for feedback at the end of meetings. [*Check Reactions* and listen.]

ADVANTAGES: Benefits and Consequences. "These team norms have improved team meeting participation, decisions, and outcomes. Because you're new to the division, I want to help you build credibility, so I'm sorry I didn't fully explain this earlier." [*Check Reactions* and listen.]

IMPEDIMENTS: Ask About Obstacles and Concerns. "You missed the *Leading Meetings* course since you just joined the team, but this workbook will ground you in the skills. How's that sound, and do you have other concerns?" [*Check Reactions*, paraphrase, and respond to problem-solve.]

NEXT STEPS: Summary and Follow-Up. "I'd like to check in before next week's meeting. What's your takeaway?" [*Check Reactions* and listen.]

Example #5 (Preexisting Issue): Bad News (Report)

GOALS: Results and Actions Desired (Remove Blame). "Jenna, the head count increases we anticipated have been postponed, due to our sales slump. I need you to stop announcing that the workload crunch will be easing. I'd approved your announcing new-hire good news at regional meetings, so I'm sorry that I jumped the gun. I'm not criticizing you—it's my bad." [Move chair closer and lower voice.]

"I can see this is upsetting you. I was wishing the news would have been better, too." [*Check Reactions* and listen.]

ADVANTAGES: Benefits and Consequences. "I know it's frustrating, but pulling in our purse strings until next quarter's numbers come out is a necessary strategy. This hiring freeze will create funds for future hires, so our longer-range position will be stronger." [*Check Reactions* and listen.]

IMPEDIMENTS: Ask About Obstacles and Concerns. "I know you've previewed to the UK that there will be head-count good news. I don't want you to look bad due to this change. Should I join you on the call to provide rationale?" [*Check Reactions*, paraphrase, and respond to problem-solve.]

NEXT STEPS: Summary and Follow-Up. "I'm sending Jim a letter saying how your team is handling this disappointment with class, and I'll urge him to bolster staffing ASAP. What additional NEXT STEPS would help?" [*Check Reactions* and listen.]

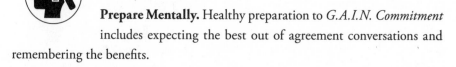

Prepare Mentally. Healthy preparation to *G.A.I.N. Commitment* includes expecting the best out of agreement conversations and remembering the benefits.

- *Negative Self-Talk:* "I'm sick and tired of having to beg my direct reports and sell them on the benefits of this new system when it's their job to do what I say because I'm their manager. I know they'll resist. I should just announce the change in an email, like it or not, no discussion."
- *Positive Self-Talk:* "I know that relying on my position power only gets me compliance when what I really want is true commitment. My team deserves two-way discussion about changes and a chance to voice their concerns. I'd want the same if the shoe were on the other foot and they managed me. Besides, they'll be more reasonable if I show respect and give a rationale for this new direction." ■

Your G.A.I.N. Examples. Pick a few back-home agreements it'd be helpful to forge. Try to target at least one for New Issues and one for Preexisting Issues. For each Conversation, prepare some *G.A.I.N. Commitment* notes in your *Straight Talk Journal* for the G̲ (Goals: results and Behaviors Desired) and the A̲ (Advantages) parts of your G.A.I.N. message content. During the actual Conversations, you'll also inquire about I̲ (Impediments) and arrange for N̲ (Next Steps), so you might jot ideas for how you'll conduct that part of the discussion. ■

Demonstration: *G.A.I.N. Commitment*

You now understand the *G.A.I.N.* Conversation's purpose, three Flawed Commitment Expectations, two categories of topics (New and Preexisting Issues), and the *G.A.I.N.* structure. Let's use the *Straight Talk Mindset, Assertive Speaking, Active Listening,* and the *G.A.I.N.* agenda in the full Conversation Format depicted in diagram 7.1.

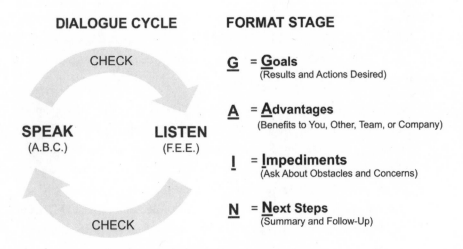

Diagram 7.1 | The *G.A.I.N. Commitment* Conversation Format

Back in the *Straight Talk* workshop, I pull my chair to the center of the room and ask the group to gather around me. I dramatically announce, "It's time for 'Shakespeare in the Round!' I've invited a friend of mine to help me for a demonstration, a famous Oscar-winning actress you've all seen in movies!" A buzz goes through the group as the suspense builds. "And now, ladies and gentlemen, would you please give a warm welcome to . . . my co-trainer, Keisha!" The group cracks up and bursts into applause as Keisha joins me in the center. (I beg forgiveness.)

Join the group in tracking my demonstration of implementing the Dialogue Cycle and the *G.A.I.N.* format's steps. In your *Straight Talk Journal*, list my skill strengths and any areas for improvement, whatever you'd do differently. In reading the script below, you'll miss my body language and voice, but imagine them from my words.

I set up the demo: "In this scene, I am a corporation's chief learning officer (not a stretch for my acting chops!). Keisha is one of my training program managers. This scenario takes place after the pandemic, so in-person training has roared back, with employees traveling to headquarters for courses. However, a new financial crunch means that our executive team is restricting some nonessential travel, necessitating returning to virtual delivery. Ready? ACTION!"

You may perceive this Commitment Conversation as demanding more time than you'd ever devote. In real workshop time, it only takes seven minutes. If this hypothetical situation were real, it would deserve that investment to achieve true, lasting commitment. (Besides, the length is needed to clearly show the skills.)

OPEN

Rick: [*Speaks while maintaining strong eye contact*] Keisha, thanks again for coming in. I need ten minutes. Cool?

Keisha: No worries, Rick. What's up?

GOALS

Rick: [*Speaks*] You may have heard that three of our largest clients just suspended their orders indefinitely due to losses during the pandemic, so we're hurting financially. The executive team just told me that they are putting a freeze on nonessential travel. This will temporarily decrease in-person training except for employees located here at corporate. Management wants Learning and Development to stay active for remote employees, too, so we're being asked to transition half of our face-to-face programs to virtual delivery. [*Keisha is rolling her eyes and scowling.*]

Rick: [*Paraphrases and Checks Reactions*] I can tell you're upset. What's up?

IMPEDIMENTS (Unexpectedly Early)

Keisha: No kidding I'm upset, Rick! [*Rick acknowledges: "Okay . . ."*] I've heard the rumor, and now it's true! [*Keisha shakes her head and sighs with exasperation.*]

Rick: [*Paraphrases*] You're really bummed . . .

Keisha: [*Loudly*] Of course! This is shortsighted! How can we overcome a company crisis if employee development withers away for the sake of dollars? This strategy is idiotic!

Rick: [*Rick uses Focusing body language, an acknowledgment, and a paraphrase.*] Wow. You're really disgusted at what you see as totally misplaced priorities. It's like, "Hello, what ever happened to helping our people to succeed?"

Keisha: Exactly! It's a silly idea! Everybody knows virtual training is crappy.

Rick: [*Rick acknowledges, paraphrases, and encourages.*] Gotcha. I know you're angry. Remote learning strikes you as inferior to the energy and impact of being in the room with people. Say more, Keisha.

Keisha: Well, you know it's true. And, thanks for nothing, Rick! Why can't you ever stand up for L&D to the executive team?

Rick: [*Paraphrases*]: You're steamed at me, too. From your perspective, I don't do a good job as a boundary manager to advocate on our behalf.

Keisha: Exactly!

Rick: [*Calmly paraphrases feelings*] Okay, I get that you're disillusioned with me. Actually, pretty resentful. [*Rick pauses and Checks.*] Am I tracking you?

Keisha: [*She crosses her arms, leans back, and softens, realizing she's dumped a lot on Rick.*] Well, maybe not resentful, to be fair. But really disappointed.

Rick: [*Lowers his voice*] Sure. Let me respond . . . Keisha, I have to weigh which top management battles to fight, and which ones to let go. Remember how last year I prevented our budget from being slashed? [*Keisha nods.*] For this issue, I didn't make a big fuss, because the exec team is disappointed, too. They agree that virtual training is a last resort, like it was during the pandemic. That's why we're only shifting 50 percent of the curriculum. They want our current courses to still all be available to every employee, no matter where they live. Virtual programs will keep our department relevant during the crunch. [*Checks*] Does this help at all?

Keisha: [*Softens and sighs*] Yeah, I understand. I'm just deflated because remote courses are so inferior. I know that you do stand up for us.

Rick: [*Acknowledges and paraphrases*] Sure. You're just really skeptical about virtual training's level of engagement and the stick factor.

Keisha: Yeah, that's it.

Rick: Well, you're preaching to the choir! And top management agrees. That's why they're keeping half of our programs in person. You can select which ones will be impacted the least by virtual delivery. Certainly not Selling Skills because it has role-plays. [*Checks*] How does that strike you?

Keisha: [*Calming down*] I get it. This is better than trashing all training.

ADVANTAGES

Rick: Right. Besides addressing the budget crisis and keeping our function relevant, maintaining your sales courses will increase revenue to hopefully end the travel freeze sooner. Also, this might raise attendance by people who have resisted traveling to headquarters. [*Checks*] Make sense?

Keisha: [*Nodding, understanding*] For sure. Hadn't thought of that.

GOALS (Returning to Provide Details)

Rick: Sounds like you're on board with the "why" of this project. [*Pauses to Check Reactions and Keisha nods*] The "how" is by next Friday for each program manager to submit virtual course macro-designs for half of their programs. For you, that's three of your six courses. I'll email you this macro-design template. It's not to outline content—only to summarize a big picture of content with module titles and lengths, learning objectives, and activities named. This took me two hours apiece for my executive programs. [*Checks*] Whaddya think?

Keisha: I think it's doable, Rick.

Rick: One additional activity is to meet this Thursday for a lunch-time tutorial with Harry Leary, who's developed a cheaper virtual platform. He'll get us up to speed on the bells and whistles of his technology. [*Checks*] How does that sound?

Keisha: [*Nodding*] That's key. I have to know what virtual activities I can include.

Rick: [*Acknowledges and paraphrases*] Right. We can't be blindfolded about what interaction is possible. [*Keisha gives a thumbs-up.*]

IMPEDIMENTS

Rick: [*Asks for IMPEDIMENTS*] Super. Now, Keisha, is there anything that might make it tough to deliver by the end of the business day next Friday?

Keisha: I'm glad you asked. I do teach three in-person half-day classes next week.

Rick: [*Acknowledges*] I see.

Keisha: So, to pull together three macro-designs, I'll need some external delivery support.

Rick: [*Paraphrases*] Your plate's full, but having a contract trainer substitute for you would do the trick?

Keisha: Yep, if Raj takes my New Managers and Onboarding classes Tuesday and Wednesday, that'll free me up to get this done.

Rick: Cool. Exec team knows we're jammed. I can tap into discretionary funds.

Keisha: Super. Thanks for running interference for me on that, Captain.

Rick: No sweat. But you might be surprised, because it only took me two hours per program. [*Checks*] OK?

Keisha: All good.

Rick: [*Checks*] What else could prevent you from pulling off this task?

Keisha: Nothing, really. And sorry about snapping before. I was just bummed. But I'm on board, Rick.

Rick: [*Rick paraphrases and reassures Keisha.*] You're worried you ruffled my feathers . . . [*Keisha meekly smiles.*] . . . Hey, I know that was just your commitment to quality training coming through. Besides, my skin isn't that thin!

Keisha: Well, I was a little over the top, so thanks for understanding.

<u>N</u>EXT STEPS

Rick: Of course. Listen, we both know I sometimes get wordy and dilute my message. [*Checks*] What's your takeaway of our agreement?

Keisha: Well, I'll pick three courses that are best for virtual delivery, attend Harry's Thursday tutorial, and create macro-design plans using the template you'll send . . . [*Rick nods. "Bingo."*] . . . and by a week from Friday, I'll submit module goals, activities, and timing . . . [*Rick gives a thumbs-up signal and jokes, "You're a wizard."*] . . . and I'll include rough content scripting and a few bullet points for each slide.

Rick: [*Gives a time-out gesture and speaks*] Time-out. Forget about that last part. You do not need to include slides or specific content beyond the objectives. That's more work than needed. [*Checks Reactions*] How's that clarification ring for you?

Keisha: It lowers the bar. I may not even need Raj to take any of my workload.

Rick: [*Paraphrases and speaks*] Your call. Tell you what. I'll check in next Tuesday, to be sure there's no unforeseen obstacles. [*Checks*] Does that work?

Keisha: Perfect!

Rick: [*Smiling*] Great. Thanks for partnering with me on this, Keisha.

CUT!

Unpacking the Demo

As the demonstration ends, I point to Keisha and implore the group, "Please give it up for Oscar-winner Keisha Johnson, with thunderous applause!" I ask the group to tell me what positive skills they observed in the demo. "I need the strokes, folks! But we don't have all day, so just give me my first forty strengths!" ■

Big Picture. I gained Keisha's commitment, and that's the bottom line. I met the two litmus test goals of *Straight Talk*—to get the work results desired and to build a trusting relationship. I avoided *Aggressive* or *Passive* communication and hung out in the *Assertive* zone. My frequent *Checking Reactions* and paraphrasing ensured that it was dialogue rather than a monologue.

Core Skills. You couldn't see my body language (*Focusing*), but you will when the movie comes out! I used *Exploring* skills of acknowledgments and encouragements. I was generous with *Empathizing,* including validations and a bonanza of paraphrases (*eleven* times, and they included emotions, since that's where the action is). When Keisha attacked me about not standing up for the team, I stayed calm, didn't convey upset, and paraphrased her emotions. You couldn't *see* my Self-Talk, but I controlled my internal dialogue.

***G.A.I.N.* Format Flexibility.** I followed the *G.A.I.N.* agenda. An interesting wrinkle is that I didn't go in linear fashion from the GOALS into the ADVANTAGES and then IMPEDIMENTS, because Keisha raised objections right away. She interrupted my GOALS piece, so I paraphrased her body language of upset, *Checked Reactions*, paraphrased more, and then responded to her objection. Only then could I loop back to the GOALS and ADVANTAGES steps. Life isn't a PowerPoint slide! The *G.A.I.N.* steps can move around as long as you cover all of them.

ADVANTAGES. The *G.A.I.N.* Conversation is an influence vehicle. I cited these benefits: (1) to meet the executive team's request, (2) to cope with the travel freeze, (3) to keep Learning and Development relevant, (4) to "skill up" salespeople so our revenue dip ends sooner, and (5) to increase course attendance due to reduced travel demands.

IMPEDIMENTS. Even though *obstacles* erupted up front, I returned to this step twice after mapping out the GOAL step's needed behaviors and results. This showed my desire to support Keisha and remove barriers that could create problems.

NEXT STEPS. Did you catch how I made sure the commitment was summarized? I asked Keisha to summarize, because *I* already *knew* the desired takeaway! I wanted to make sure *she* had the commitment internalized, so I asked her to paraphrase the agreement. It's a good thing I did, because she misunderstood. She included more work than required, so I corrected her misinterpretation. The "Subjectivity Sunglasses" had popped up and distorted her understanding. Luckily, her inaccurate summary paraphrase allowed me to prevent a mistake.

One downside of asking the receiver to summarize the commitment is that it risks sounding condescending or parental (e.g., "Now, to make sure you were listening, tell Daddy what we just agreed."). Yuck. That's why I used a little self-deprecation ("I sometimes get wordy and dilute the message. What's your takeaway of our agreement today?"). Here are some ways you can ask the other person to paraphrase in a quick, non-insulting way:

- "Would you mind summarizing our conversation?"
- "Just to make sure we're aligned, what's your takeaway?"
- "So, what are your action steps?"
- "Please feed back to me your understanding of our agreement."
- "Can you recap?"
- "Sometimes I leave a discussion and realize we weren't on the same page, so please review our commitment."
- "Can you do that paraphrasing thing from that great *Straight Talk* book"?

What in the demo did you *not* like—my mistakes? I'll give you some thought time. OK, two seconds have gone by, so I guess there are none. Let's move on.

As if! Of course, there's always fine-tuning. Review the demonstration script above to guess potential tweaks that some groups surface. Take a minute . . . Come on, please play! Because unlike Jack Nicholson's famous line from the movie *A Few Good Men*, I *can* "handle the truth"! Here are possible adjustments:

- *Her Attack:* My paraphrase of Keisha's attack ("Why can't you ever stand up for the Learning department . . .") was solid. But was my *Assertive Speaking* turn a bit too long? As a result, did I sound a bit defensive? Perhaps less is more.

- *Design Task Timing:* I said *twice* that the task only took me two hours per design. Maybe once was enough. Keisha could have interpreted that as, "If you take longer, something's wrong with you."

- *Pacing:* My speaking speed is too fast for some people. You can't see that in print. I spent years in New York, and I drink waaayyy too much coffee in workshops! It's important for me to buffer my speed-rapping by *Checking Reactions* lots. ∎

Mutual Benefit Conflict Resolution

I've made things look easy, haven't I? Rest assured, I'm not *that* naïve. (Okay, I am with car mechanics, but not about *this* stuff.) Your good-faith efforts to *G.A.I.N. Commitment* won't always be Smooth Sailing. You've laid out your GOALS and ADVANTAGES, used skilled *Active Listening* to hear the person's IMPEDI-MENTS, and made good-faith efforts to address questions or obstacles, but you still hit a brick wall. No matter how reasonable and skilled you are, all you get is a broken record refusal.

When "Getting to Yes" Is Tough

This dilemma may mean there's a conflict of incompatible genuine needs. A legitimate, valid reason is driving the resistance. If the person rejects your "ask," then you lose, and they win. If they acquiesce and say "yes," then they lose, and you win. These win/lose and lose/win scenarios are really lose/lose due to lingering resentment. Compromise is better as a last resort, but it's a mini-lose/mini-lose outcome, because neither of you are fully satisfied. That's what I call "living life in the gray zone." By contrast, Mutual Benefit Problem-Solving transforms impasses into win/win cooperative and elegant agreements.

Mutual Benefit Problem-Solving Strategies

Adopt a Win/Win Mindset. When your *GAIN-ing Commitment* efforts devolve into an intransigent stalemate, you might be defining the problem in ways that make win/win impossible. We often approach conflicts in black-or-white terms of "my solution" versus "your solution." This pits us as adversaries fighting for our respective rigid demands.

We can't even see one another much less empathize, because our mutually exclusive either-or, win/lose "solutions" block our line of sight. A win/win mindset transforms seeing each other as opponents into seeing the conflict as our common opponent. We now can direct win/win solutions at the problem, instead of lobbing win/lose solutions at one another.

Identify the Driving Needs. Keep paraphrasing, *Checking*, stressing the ADVANTAGES, and sincerely expressing your desire for win/win agreement. Use *Active Listening* in the same empathic spirit as you do when *Advising and Guiding*. It's harder now because you have strong underlying needs. Strive to redefine the conflict in terms of underlying "Driving Needs" rather than surface-level, myopic "Win/Win Solutions." This refreshing, liberating way of reframing the conflict points to far more creative and numerous win/win solution options.

Example 1: Top Management Presentation Conflict. One of module five's Listening Lab scenarios involved a monthly executive briefing where you present and your colleague Grant handles the Q&A session from his seat. You must travel to a China division, so you want Grant to handle the top management meeting by himself. He refuses.

- *Your Win/Lose Solution:* Grant must present alone at the briefing.
- *Grant's Win/Lose Solution:* Grant refuses to present alone.

Defined this way, the conflict is at an unsolvable win/lose impasse. Grant can't both present and *not* present. But if you use *Active Listening* and search for the Driving Needs underlying each of these rigid Win/Lose "Solutions," you can reframe the conflict:

- *Your Driving Need:* To be in China without canceling the briefing.
- *Grant's Driving Need:* To avoid panic in public that could hurt his career.

You don't *really* need Grant to both present and field questions without you, do you? That's just one solution for handling your absence. And Grant's rigid "no way" stance camouflages *his* deeper need—avoiding a presentation anxiety meltdown. Once these deeper, true Driving Needs are surfaced, there are many ways to resolve the conflict (e.g., conduct a Zoom meeting as you present and Grant fields Q&A in person, reschedule, send a written or recorded presentation and elicit emailed questions, get Grant presentation skills coaching and anxiety management help, have Grant practice with you to calm his nerves, etc.).

Example 2: A Demanding Client's Request. A big client's IT Director is pressuring Stellar Training to teach all of a 1-day program's content in half a day. The salesperson insists on only offering the full-day course.

- *Client's Win/Lose Solution:* Teach all the skills in half a day.
- *Sales Exec's Win/Lose Solution:* Take a full day or cut half the content.

Defined in this way, the conflict becomes a win/lose logjam. It's impossible to both jam all the material into a condensed session and also retain the high-quality design that the full-day course allows. The client is afraid that pulling all IT employees offline all day will mean customers calling for troubleshooting will be angry, but he also really wants his team to learn the full set of skills. The salesperson fears that caving in to the client's demands will result in a low-quality, lecture-only session that will hurt the workshop's outcomes and reputation. Fortunately, the client and sales exec used a win/win mindset, open questions, and paraphrasing to crystallize deeper Driving Needs:

- *Client's Driving Need:* To ensure IT coverage to avoid upsetting customers needing assistance.
- *Stellar Training's Driving Need:* To meet client's timing need to have no one off the job for more than a half-day and to maintain the program's positive reputation.

The IT client and training firm sales exec saw that their Driving Needs weren't incompatible. Both wanted full material coverage *and* full office coverage by the IT team. It's their initial rigid, either-or, win/lose solutions that caused the deadlock. The client's need wasn't to lower training costs, just to ensure office coverage and provide all the skills. So they split the full-day training into two half-days and also split the IT team into two groups. On Monday, Group 1 attended Part 1 in the morning and Group 2 attended Part 1 in the afternoon. On Tuesday, the same strategy was used for Part 2. They delivered all the skills well, while ensuring no angry IT customers.

When defining a conflict in terms of Driving Needs versus competing Win/Lose Solutions, rely on *Active Listening* and honest self-disclosure of your own deeper needs more than questions. If you do ask questions, make them open-ended ones, avoiding "*Why* are you being so insistent on that solution?" "Why" may spark defensiveness, so rephrase it as, "Please help me understand what deeper needs are driving that particular solution."

Virtual Variations: *G.A.I.N.-ing Commitments*

A *G.A.I.N.* Mensa Society Test

If you're like me, you love challenging yourself with those IQ tests in airplane magazines. Let's go sky-high to gauge your astuteness about virtual *G.A.I.N.* Conversations. Think of responses to the following questions.

Phone Calls and Video Conferencing

1. How can you use the *G.A.I.N.* skills over the phone or on a video call?
2. How is *G.A.I.N.-ing Commitments* more challenging over the phone?

Emails and Other Written *G.A.I.N.s* (Texting and Messaging)

1. When should you and shouldn't you try to *G.A.I.N. Commitment* via email, text, or typed messages?
2. What are the pros and cons of forging agreements, assigning tasks, announcing changes, or requesting assistance via email or written messages?
3. How can you avoid the "cons"?

Virtual Meetings with Video

1. How should you adapt *G.A.I.N.-ing Commitments* in a group-based video call?

Think through your answers before jumping ahead!

G.A.I.N. Mensa Society Test Answer Guide

Below are ideas that past participants and yours truly have generated.

Phone Calls and Video Conferencing

1. How can I use the *G.A.I.N.* steps over the phone or on a video call?
ANSWER: G.A.I.N. Commitment over the phone and in video calls just as you do in person. Use the same "Speak-Check-Listen" Dialogue Cycle to move through the *G.A.I.N.* agenda. You're freer to make notes. Email a follow-up summary.

2. How is *G.A.I.N.-ing Commitments* more challenging over the phone?
ANSWER: You can't see body language, so read vocal tone. Use more *Exploring* open-ended questions, encouragements, and acknowledgments along with para-phrasing. People multitask on the phone, so ask more *Checking Questions*.

Emails and Other Written *G.A.I.N.s* (Text and Messaging)

1. When should you and shouldn't you try to *G.A.I.N. Commitment* via email, text, or typed messages?
ANSWER: Factors influencing your selection of in-person, telephone, or written agreements are: complexity, emotional impact, urgency, and time zone challenges. For multidimensional, new, and/or potentially resistance-laden topics, if at all possible, *G.A.I.N. Commitment* by telephone or video chat. This is especially helpful for working through the IMPEDIMENTS. Some topics are so straightforward or routine that they don't warrant actual conversation.

2. What are the pros and cons of forging commitments, assigning tasks, announcing changes, or requesting assistance via email or written messaging?
ANSWER: PROS: It saves time up front (but can take more time if you trigger reactions); there's a digital track record so that nothing slips between the cracks; and writing things forces you to be clearer, so your GOAL step is more objective.

    ANSWER: CONS: You lose body language and voice tone for gauging reactions; there is less sense of connection, so defensiveness may be higher; any written *Aggressive* behaviors (CAPS, loaded language, etc.) can come back to bite you when others simply forward your email noting that it's a shame you cannot be more professional; and longer *G.A.I.N.* content is cumbersome in writing.

3. How can you overcome the "cons"?
ANSWER: Everything can seem more loaded due to lack of vocal tone, body language, and other cues. Paraphrase written replies to show respect and simulate a conversation versus a court mandate. With written speaking turns, use phrasing that softens without becoming *Passive*. Use clear subject lines: "Action Needed," "Update," "Input Requested," and so on.

    For long GOAL *Assertive Speaking* turns, some people employ multiple speaking and *Checking* emails interspersed with listening emails that paraphrase the recipient's reactions and then add the next piece of their GOAL speaking turn. This process is admittedly cumbersome, since you're covering the *G.A.I.N.* agenda over several emails, but it approximates a voice-to-voice dialogue better than sending one long email and only checking for buy-in at the end of it.

Even for simpler, less involved topics, you can use multiple emails, laying out your request in a first email. Then, before inquiring about possible IMPED-IMENTS, ask the recipient to paraphrase (e.g., "Donna, I've laid out the general GOALS and ADVANTAGES in this email, but before I send a second email with the exact steps I need, please shoot me a quick email letting me know your under-standing of the overall project and my reasons for picking you [ADVANTAGES]. Also, please share your reactions so far. Thanks!"). You can see why a voice-to-voice interaction is preferable, but time zones, poor phone service, or other factors may make written *G.A.I.N.* exchanges necessary.

G.A.I.N. Email Examples.
Example #1: A G.A.I.N. *Commitment over Multiple Emails*

Dear Rasheed,

[Rapport Builder and Preview:] I hope you're well and thanks again for the super briefing you gave my team last month. I have a new project [idea/proposal/task] that I'd like your help in implementing.

[GOALS:] I'd like to ask you to . . . [desired results and behaviors].

[ADVANTAGES:] I'm excited about this . . . [topic] and your pivotal role in it, since I think this will really benefit us/you by . . . [Inquire about IMPEDIMENTS:] I have further details to share about the steps you would need to take. I'd rather share these in my next email since I don't want to be presumptuous about your buy-in. Therefore, please email me your understanding of my request, your initial reactions, and any obstacles making it tough to commit to helping.

[ADANTAGES:] Rasheed, I'm confident that the following payoffs will offset your concerns and any barriers you see, which I hope to problem-solve. [List concerns.]

[NEXT STEPS:]. Please reply here or, preferably, let me know a time next week I can call you to discuss any concerns. If you do agree, I'll walk you through NEXT STEPS. Thanks so much, Rasheed!

Warm regards,
Giselle

Example #2: A Full G.A.I.N. Conversation in One Email

Hi, Marcos,

[ADVANTAGES:] In order to effectively update the appropriate systems and prevent a negative client experience with the closing of ABC Company's account by October 31, [GOAL:] we in Client Ops need the following documents verified and signed by the client no later than EOB next Tuesday:

- Updated W-9
- Beneficial Ownership Certification
- Articles of Incorporation

[IMPEDIMENTS:] Please let me know of any questions or concerns about meeting these requirements. [NEXT STEPS:] Once Client Fulfillment receives this material, I'll send a follow-up confirmation that all is in order and verification of positive account status.

Thank you in advance for your continued support. Have a great weekend, Marcos.

Best,
Lawson

Virtual Meetings with Video

1. How can you adapt *G.A.I.N.-ing Commitments* in a group-based video call?
ANSWER: You'll rely on the same format steps and Dialogue Cycle skills as when you're one-on-one: *Assertive Speaking* about the GOALS and ADVANTAGES clearly and crisply, with plenty of *Checking* and paraphrasing of responses, especially when inquiring about perceived IMPEDIMENTS.

Group *G.A.I.N.* work, especially virtually, demands stellar presentation skills, like more authoritative, assertive body language, projecting your voice, strong gestures, standing at times to convey energy, and knowing your materials so well that you can often look directly into your computer's camera.

Prepare a range of ADVANTAGES, since having a variety of benefits in your back pocket will help you appeal to more people (e.g., "Those of you in manufacturing will find this new system cuts line downtime by a third, you in sales will like its reduced paperwork, and for human resources . . .").

Catch signals of resistance, since people may be silently resistant. Pick up on body language clues (e.g., eye rolls, sighs, etc.) even though video gallery views are thumbnail-sized. Ask an ally to alert you whenever they see signs of discontent via the chat function. If you do detect resistance, invite reactions, concerns, and questions (IMPEDIMENTS). For nonverbal resistance, paraphrase what you see and hear: "I'm seeing lots of frowns on camera and there's silence when I ask for implementation ideas. Seems like some of us may have reservations. To be aligned, let's get your concerns on the table. What's up?" Then be nondefensive as you paraphrase, respond, and *Check* again.

Remember that paraphrasing questions prevents answering them before fully understanding, defuses the question, and gives you time to think of an answer. Assess what kind of question is being asked and paraphrase different types accordingly:

- *States an Opinion:* "You're convinced that . . . You're skeptical about . . ."
- *Requests Information or Clarity:* "You're wondering whether . . . You're unclear about . . ."
- *Expresses Agreement:* "So a benefit you see is . . . You plan to apply this by . . ."
- *Expresses Disagreement:* You're unhappy that . . . The policy strikes you as . . ."

Mix up your response techniques after paraphrasing questions:

- Give a straight answer.
- Create a "parking lot" whiteboard.
- Ask the person if their question actually states an opinion.
- Ask the group to offer reactions.
- Refer the questioner to a resource, reading, or person for further answers.
- Use module eleven's Conversational Aikido to tactfully disagree.
- Admit you don't know but will find out.

Managing resistance is a special hurdle in virtual meetings. If a participant hurls hostility, select one of these two deft tactics.

- *Paraphrase to the Individual:* Paraphrase challenging comments using less provocative emotion words. Let's say I'm teaching at CYM Corporation. "Atilla Adam" clicks his Hand Raise icon and says, "This is a crock. You're totally naïve about our world without a shred of experience in our company. You're just spouting pop psychology ideas that don't relate to our company culture." Yikes! Breathe and paraphrase with less inflammatory words: "Adam, you have concerns about my qualifications to teach communication skills here at CYM Corporation and you doubt their applicability." [Adam drips sarcasm: "How perceptive."] I respond: "I hope it helps to know that while I'm not a CYM employee, I've taught thirty groups across three divisions, and that participants report that they appreciate hearing examples from other companies. Adam, that doesn't erase your need to see how the skills link to your world. That's why I often ask for the group's ideas for adapting the skills. Does this help?" Adam finally cools his jets. I recall a similar dust-up, after which "Attila" admitted that his resentment was really aimed at management who sent him to the course at a busy time.

- *Shift Your Paraphrase to the Group:* Normally, we Paraphrase Reactions directly to the challenger. Sometimes it's better *not* to do that if you worry it will open a bottomless pit of venting. After all, paraphrasing encourages further expression of emotions. Let's say that after my paraphrase and sincere *Assertive* response, Adam piles on with *another* hostile remark. I could again paraphrase to him and respond, *or* I can redirect my paraphrase from Adam to the group: "There's real energy around my credibility as a non-employee and whether these skills are relevant to your jobs. Do others share this understandable concern?" I might respond, "I hope over these two days you all find the skills useful. The only way to know that is to practice them and decide, so let's move into trios to try on the *G.A.I.N.* format." This shifting of energy from the hard-nosed person to paraphrasing to the entire group in less loaded terms works well in face-to-face groups, especially as you break eye contact with "Atilla."

Module Wrap-Up

We forge clear, accountability-oriented commitments for two situations: New Issues and Preexisting Issues (when we can often remove blame). We avoid three Flawed Commitment Expectations: (1) Expecting Others to Be Mind Readers, (2) Expecting Ineffective Conversations to Produce Effective Results, and (3) Expecting Without Inspecting. To fix the problems in ineffective conversations of a Faulty Communication Process and Faulty Content, plug the *Straight Talk* Dialogue Cycle of *Assertive Speaking–Checking Reactions–Active Listening* into the *G.A.I.N. Commitment* Conversation Format: GOALS, ADVANTAGES, IMPEDIMENTS, NEXT STEPS.

A key challenge is to not lapse into back-and-forth trading of speaking turns when a person raises an objection or concern. We paraphrase thoughts and feelings to clarify the nature of the push-back response, to demonstrate understanding, and to "earn the right to respond." If we meet immovable resistance, we enter Mutual Benefit Problem-Solving, relying on the Dialogue Cycle to uncover Driving Needs versus Win/Lose Solutions, paving the way to win/win resolution.

Onward to learning how to follow up Commitment Conversations by "Inspecting What We're Expecting."

Module Eight | *Recognizing*

Catch 'Em Doing It Right

> There is more hunger for love and appreciation
> in this world than for bread.
> —Mother Teresa

> There are two things people want more than sex
> and money . . . recognition and praise.
> —Mary Kay Ash, Founder of Mary Kay Cosmetics

> I've yet to find the man, however exalted his station, who
> did not do better work and put forth a greater effort under
> a spirit of approval than under a spirit of criticism.
> —Charles Schwab, Founder and CEO

A Fork in the Road

Flawed Commitment Expectation #3 is "Expecting Without Inspecting." After conducting a *G.A.I.N. Commitment* Conversation, it's crucial to follow up on the agreement to "*in*-spect what you *ex*-pect." You'll take one of two paths. If someone fulfills their commitment, you'll celebrate success and express appreciation by *Recognizing* (this module). When the fork in the commitment road points to difficulties, you'll hold the individual accountable by *Reminding* once or twice (next module). If that falls short, you'll resort to *Confronting* (module ten). Omitting these follow-up strategies after a *Commitment Conversation* leaves accountability to chance.

You'll be well served in your work and personal relationships to be as magnanimous as possible with this module's *Recognizing* Message and format to:

- appreciate commitments that are met,
- reinforce any other constructive behavior or result, and
- express belief in someone's potential for achievement of a tough task.

The Carrot or the Stick?

When dealing with disciplinary challenges, teachers and parents often try to reduce unwanted behavior through negative reinforcement and punishment (i.e., the "stick"). Proponents validate this approach as a deterrent by referencing the "one-trial learning" example of a child touching a hot stove, or the criminal justice system's reliance on incarceration and fines. However, the efficacy of negative motivational methods is debatable given the rates of recidivism for ex-convicts. Often, more favorable results are achieved through rehabilitation, underlining positive reinforcement's value.

The potency of rewarding positive behavior (i.e., the "carrot") is proven in psychology, behavior modification, and parenting research and practice. Ever train a new puppy? Recognize, praise, and reward wanted behavior, and you'll maintain it while avoiding the fear and resentment stemming from punishment.

Robert McNamara, former US secretary of defense, said, "Brains, like hearts, go where they are appreciated." According to *Forbes*, 43 percent of employees cite a lack of recognition as their reason for quitting. In a *USA Today* survey on "Why Good Workers Leave," 25 percent pointed to lack of recognition. PeopleMedia

Research found that 80 percent of employees want their manager's recognition more than money.

If you manage and lead others, *Recognizing* is a principal motivational resource. Catching someone "doing it right" after they agree to do something—telling them you notice and appreciate it—raises the odds of continued performance. *Recognizing* is powerful for maintaining commitments, as well as for reversing problematic behavior or results by stroking the opposite behavior when you see it. Classroom teachers learn to alter unruly behavior this way.

Positive recognition shapes desired behavior and cultivates a fruitful, thriving work atmosphere. It pours vitamins into someone's emotional and motivational life. Other motivators, like compensation, job stability, or work conditions, are tougher to control. You have complete influence over recognition, and it doesn't cost one penny.

Be a Strengths Finder, Not a Fault Finder

A Self-Strengths Bombardment. We can only see other people's positive behaviors, strengths, and talents to the extent that we can see our own. Please jot down notes in your *Straight Talk Journal*:

- *Round One: Strengths (One Minute):* List your positive traits, talents, and attributes.
- *Round Two: Weaknesses (One Minute):* List your negative traits, deficits, and weaknesses.

Which list is longer? Which was easier? What was your Self-Talk in each round? In Round One, did you mentally block yourself from listing any strength by qualifying it, questioning it, or discounting it? Whichever list is longer, you probably censored your strengths to some degree—omitting or denying positives that others might say about you. Even Meryl Streep, arguably the greatest living actress, admitted, "I say to myself, 'I don't know how to act, and why does anyone want to look at me on-screen anymore?'" ■

What Is Your "Strengths Vision Acuity"?

Aggressive people are "strengths-myopic," only seeing their own positives and remaining blind to other people's. Uber-*Passive* people are instead "strengths-farsighted," only seeing other people's strengths and being "strengths-blind" to their own assets. The majority of us fall far short of "20/20 Strengths Vision" for seeing our own talents, skills, aptitudes, and positive traits.

Discounting Our Strengths and Contributions. The tendency to blur our own strengths focus is evident in how we receive positive feedback. Here's how many people react when others compliment them, verbalize a strength, or express appreciation:

1. *Modesty:* "It wasn't that big of a deal."
2. *Disowning Credit:* "I couldn't have done it without Lorraine. She deserves the kudos."
3. *Minimizing:* "Just part of the job."
4. *Comparing:* "You should see Tim's speech. He's the real superstar."
5. *Self-criticism:* "I played a lousy game. Sure, I scored lots, but my defense sucked."
6. *Returning the Compliment:* "Me? It's *you* that's indispensable to the team."
7. *Disagreeing:* "Nah, the workshop wasn't *that* good."
8. *A Rare Reaction:* "Thanks for noticing! I was excited about what I was able to do for the customer."

The first seven common reactions are discounts, even telling the compli-menter that they have lousy taste (#5) or that they're lying (#7). Do you use such self-discounts? How about #8? Surprise! I threw you a curveball, didn't I? It's a rare response to accept positive feedback and feel good about receiving recognition. Do you have "pockets for compliments"?

We often deflect, deny, counter, or downgrade compliments. Often, self-discounts are admirable acts of humility. But this virtue goes overboard if we can never feel appreciation's glow—as receiver and giver. Some people think accepting recognition isn't macho or, sadly, they live in such a desert of recognition that they honestly don't believe it.

Sharpen Your Strengths Vision Acuity. When Gallup asked American workers to identify their strengths, one-third couldn't name any or only listed ones unconnected to their careers. Let's improve your Strengths Vision Acuity by revisiting your earlier Self-Strengths Bombardment list. Remember any strengths you self-censored or hesitated in jotting down. For any reluctantly written or omitted strength, ask yourself:

- *Is it a strength if you were born with it?* YES! If you were born with a talent or gift, it still counts. Harry Potter's powers to cast spells, talk to snakes, ride broomsticks, and transform into animals are God-given, but does that make his wizardry any less of a marvel? NO WAY!
- *Is it a strength if you don't always have it?* YES! You don't have to be perfect and never-faltering for a positive trait to be valid.
- *Is it a strength if others have it more, or are better?* YES! It's not a competition!
- *Is it a strength if you sometimes misuse it?* YES! The flip side of any strength is a weakness. Take humor: Carlos is at a meeting where sales are reported as down for yet another quarter. He slaps his tablemate on the back and blurts, "No place to go but up!" An inappropriate joke. But Carlos's sense of humor is still a gift. He just needs to monitor it.

Return to your strengths list and add any that you censored. Which strengths did you reluctantly include?

Widen Your "Peripheral Strengths Vision." Next, broaden your strengths field of vision beyond its narrow range. Appreciate the full expanse of your positive assets, talents, skills, personality traits, and aptitudes. Think of your strengths across categories like interpersonal, leadership, cognitive, writing, creative, mechanical, learning, athletic, knowledge, values, physical, task prowess, and so on. Blast out of a job-constraining box to also think of your strengths as a parent, child, friend, teammate, volunteer, hobbyist, volunteer, little league coach, religious group member, nonprofit volunteer—whatever. The sky's the limit! Then explode each category. For instance, for intelligence alone, researcher J. P. Guilford's "Structure of Intellect" model theorized 150 types!

Return to your strengths list with expanded peripheral vision and add lots more.

The Crap-Detecting Disease

It's Conditioning. Our "Self-Strengths Vision" is blurred by our discounts, a narrow view of our strengths, and "crap detecting" tinted glasses that darken otherwise positive traits. When we become "Fault Finders" rather than "Strengths Finders," we fall into the pessimistic habit of taking our own and others' positive assets for granted. Many of us grew up in a red pencil environment where teachers told us what we got *wrong* and parents said "no" countless times, so we inherited that mentality. Much of the news we receive about the world is negative. Supreme Court Chief Justice Earl Warren said, "I always turn to the sports page first, which records people's accomplishments. The front page has nothing but man's failures."

The High-Risk Road of Crap-Detecting. A cynic driving a sports car barrels down a windy, treacherous mountain road without guardrails. A puttering old jalopy car comes around a curve, forcing the cynic to jam on his brakes. As they pass, the jalopy driver honks his horn feverishly, sticks his head out his window, and hollers, "PIG!" In a heartbeat, the cynic leans on his own horn and screams back, "SWINE!" The livid speed demon zooms around the next curve and slams into a truckload of pigs being taken to the local slaughterhouse.

Sundials in the Shade. The ingrained reluctance to embrace our own positive attributes was highlighted by Ben Franklin: "Hide not your talents; they for use were made. What's a sundial in the shade?" We need to exercise our strengths vision muscle so that it doesn't atrophy. We can stretch our peripheral vision and sharpen our visual acuity to be Strengths Finders instead of Fault Finders—for ourselves and others. This improved capability, which is a talent itself, develops our proficiency for *Recognizing* others.

Recognizing Skillfully

Avoid Baloney Sandwiches

Make times solely for *Recognizing*, and let it stand alone. Don't sandwich appreciation between negative comments or use *Recognizing* as a bridge to corrective feedback (e.g., "You're doing a super job with timeliness of credit consolidations, but you need to work more on your dividend upgrades."). What does the recipient hear when your recognition is only a springboard into negative input?

A sales rep showed our instructor a memo from her manager. The first part was complimentary, recognizing great monthly revenues. The last part said, "However, we need to work on Credit Protector product revenues, since those numbers have been abysmal." The rep tore off the top part of the memo, crumpled it up, and held up the negative part. "Here's what the memo really says. I hate when he does that."

> This is NOT to say coaching and performance reviews should only include kudos and exclude corrective feedback. It's just that sometimes—even lots of times—it's great to deliver purely positive recognition, especially when reinforcing a commitment being met.

Descriptive *Recognizing* vs. Global Praise

Don't confuse praising with *Recognizing*. They are *not* the same. Praise is evaluative, nonspecific, and general. *Recognizing* is descriptive, concrete, and specific about the exact behavior or result that you're applauding. The difference harkens back to *Assertive Speaking*'s B of *Bias-Free Language*.

In your workshop, I exemplify the difference by saying, "I want you to know you're a great group, just super." When I debrief reactions to this kind of global and nonspecific feedback, responses are: "It fell flat . . . wasn't believable . . . didn't sound genuine . . . kind of 'blah,' since it could be said to any group . . . we don't know what you like or what to replicate . . . sounded insincere . . ." Global praise says, "In my almighty power as the Supreme Evaluator, I deem you to be . . . a super group!"

Next, I give an alternative *Recognizing* Message: "I really appreciate how intensively you worked with me today. I'm grateful for how you returned promptly from breaks, since groups often float in late. We got so much accomplished. Many of you volunteered for activities, helping the material to come alive in dramatic ways. I also enjoy how you're letting me shift from humor into dedicated work, making the day productive *and* fun. Thank you." This time, the participants report that the recognition is more believable, clearer, and more likely to encourage repeated positive behavior. All I did was ask myself what I objectively observed—using *Bias-Free Language's* "Just the Facts" Test. ■

Ineffective Praise Is Better Than Nothing! Once, a participant reported, "I *never* hear positive appreciation from my boss, so even if he would do it poorly with B.S. global and insincere praise, I'd welcome it. Hey, halitosis is better than no breath at all!" Funny, but also sad.

The *Recognizing* Message

The *Recognizing* Message Template for appreciating someone's fulfilled commitment or other positive behavior is called the "Three-Part 'I' Message" because it gives *my* frame of reference versus the receiver's and discloses *my* positive emotions.

POSITIVE BEHAVIOR ("When you . . ."). State the fulfilled commitment or other behavior that you value and want to reinforce. EXAMPLE: "Dana, when you finished reviewing the resumes for the marketing candidates earlier than we'd discussed . . ."

POSITIVE FEELINGS ("I feel/felt . . ."). Disclose your emotions about the positive behavior that you're *Recognizing*. EXAMPLE: "I was relieved . . ."

POSITIVE IMPACT ("Because the result was/is . . ."). Describe the desirable results of the person's positive behavior. EXAMPLE: ". . . because we got a head start on staffing for the new marketing initiative. None of us planned on the curveball we were thrown with the extra marketing needed for the product revision's early release. Now, thanks to you, we'll have the manpower to pull it off. We're going to look like heroes. Thanks!"

Generously describe the cause-and-effect relationship between the appreciated actions and their tangible outcomes. Vividly identify *actual* positive consequences and/or *potential* favorable outcomes, as long as they're believable, so that the receiver isn't thinking, "Well, thanks, but that's a stretch."

Mix It Up. Feel free to vary the order of the *Recognizing* Message's three parts as I did in my appreciation to the workshop group: "I really appreciate . . . [positive feelings first] . . . how intensively you've worked with me over such a long day. [positive behavior] I'm really grateful [positive feelings] for how you return promptly from breaks, since many groups float in late. Many of you volunteered for demos and activities [positive behavior], making the material come alive in dramatic ways. [positive impact] I've also enjoyed [positive feelings] how you're letting me shift from humor breaks to getting back down to work [positive behavior], making the day productive *and* fun. [positive impact] Thank you."

Back in our *Straight Talk* workshop, I ask the group to write two *Recognizing* Messages, preferably for someone in the room, or it can be for someone at work or home. Next, I give directions: "Please mill around the room reading your messages to the two or three people you've targeted for appreciation. If you receive someone's recognition, it might feel awkward, but don't discount it. The only two things you're allowed to say are, 'Thank you' or 'How perceptive of you for noticing!' If the person you're *Recognizing* isn't in the room, tell your partner who the recipient is."

After ten minutes of milling, I reassemble the group and debrief the activity: "What emotion words describe the atmosphere in the room?" The group responds:

"warm . . . positive . . . glowing . . . appreciative . . . affection . . . grateful . . . relaxing . . . liberating . . . loving . . . bonding . . . teambuilding . . . trusting."

I kneel and share, "You have the power to cultivate this kind of work climate. *Recognizing* doesn't have to be a grand declaration. It says, 'You matter to me, plain and simple.' Do people in your life know they matter to you and others? Think of Bette Midler's 'Wind Beneath My Wings' hit and ask yourself who is the wind beneath your wings. Tell them! *Recognize* little acts that aren't monumental but matter to you." ∎

Write Some *Recognizing* Messages. Who in your professional or personal life deserves *Recognizing*? A direct report? A task-force member who's an unsung hero? A supplier who delivers above and beyond the call of duty? Your children or significant other? Your bestie? YOU? Jot down some *Recognizing* Messages. Remember the format ("positive behavior . . . positive feelings . . . positive impact . . ."). ∎

The *Recognizing* Conversation Process

If you make a self-commitment to deliver these appreciation messages to the people in your "village" who make a difference in *your* life, it will make a difference in *theirs*. They may deflect or minimize your appreciation out of humility or slight discomfort with warm emotions. But you can pierce the veil of their self-discount by paraphrasing the dismissal, gently countering it, and repeating your *Recognizing* Message.

Imagine you're debriefing a joint sales visit with Javier and you give him positive behavioral feedback about his presentation to the customer. Javier discounts your input: "Well, they couldn't have been that great since I didn't land the contract." You paraphrase, "You're disappointed in the meeting outcome, so you don't think your skills mattered much. [Javier nods, so you continue.] Javier, I still think you did a great job of empathizing with Cloe's budget objection. You responded professionally and she said she'll keep the door open for meeting again next quarter when funding unfreezes. That's great!"

Other times, you don't need to paraphrase the receiver's self-discount. Just reply that you're still appreciative or admire the strength or contribution. An example is when I deplane from flights. I once read that President Gerald Ford thanked the Air Force One pilot each time he disembarked. This inspired me to regularly call out to the cockpit as I pass, "Thanks for the safe flight!" The pilot often answers, "You're quite welcome," or "Thank *you!*" At times the reaction is "Just doing my job . . ." which is when I smile and reply, "Well, I assure you that my family back home is glad you do it . . ." or "No big deal to you, but massive to me. Thanks again." I bet my second *Recognizing* attempt gets put into the pilot's self-esteem pocket.

Recognizing Potential in Others

So far, we've recognized people's strengths and positive behaviors (especially keeping a commitment). Now we'll recognize someone's potential for performing and/ or for coping with a challenge. When you express belief and faith in someone, the impact can be monumental, especially when they're hurting, in a slump, or lacking confidence about tackling a new challenge.

Positive Expectations in Your Life. Think of a time when someone you respected expressed belief in you, and it made a positive impact. It could be a parent, manager, colleague, coach, teacher, uncle or aunt, friend—whatever. Maybe they cited a talent or potential they saw in you that you didn't see, or were only dimly aware of, and it made a difference in your life. Who was it? What did they say? What was the result? How'd you feel about you, the other, and your life? ■

Self-fulfilling Prophecy

Besides in your own life, the power of positive expectations to shape reality has been illustrated in various fields, a phenomenon psychologists call "self-fulfilling prophecy."

- *Literature:* Greek mythology's Pygmalion was a sculptor who carved a statue of a lady. He fell in love with the statue and deeply believed it could be real, so it turned into a woman.
- *In Education:* The famous "Pygmalion in the Classroom" study randomly selected certain kids and told teachers that they would be "late bloomers" making tremendous intellectual and academic strides. The teachers expected this and conveyed their belief to the kids, who in turn excelled far more than would be expected by chance.
- *In Sports:* Venus and Serena Williams ruled Wimbledon, the French Open, and the US Open for a decade. There were many newspaper stories of how their father told them since they were very young that this would happen.
- *In Medicine:* Steve Martin once joked that his doctor totally cured his allergies with an incredible new drug called "place-bo"! Mere positive expectations have been shown to be curative. The healing power of the belief for managing cancer is used when patients visualize cancer cells being killed by white blood cells. Half the battle in counseling is getting a person to believe they can change. Hence the joke "How many psychologists does it take to change a light bulb? . . . None, but the light bulb REALLY has to believe it can be changed!"

The "B.O.S.S." Format

You have a powerful ability to impact people's motivation and results by expressing real, non-B.S. belief and faith in their capabilities, talents, or future potential. By now, you know I'm into acronyms for remembering skills, so here are the steps for you to "B.O.S.S." people around!

Belief. Express the specific accomplishment you have faith in the person's achieving. EXAMPLE: "I see you as having what it takes to be successful in outbound sales, so I hope you apply for that position you're considering."

Obstacles. You'll express *believable* belief if you acknowledge, rather than ignore, any challenges. EXAMPLE: "I'm not saying it'll be easy. There will be lots to learn about selling that's different from your current inbound customer service job, and you'll need to handle tough objections."

<u>S</u>pecific <u>S</u>trengths. Cite concrete, objective examples of related strengths or accomplishments as evidence for your belief in the person. EXAMPLE: "I've seen you handle so many angry callers in your service role, and you field tough problem escalations when I'm not around, right? You're a quick study, like when you learned the new systems technology faster than the rest of the team and tutored us, remember?"

Module Wrap-Up

This module's *Recognizing* skill is simple yet spectacular in its impact on rapport, performance, morale, and team spirit. It's 100 percent within your control, doesn't cost a cent, and requires no one's permission. The Three-Part "I" Message ("When you . . . I felt . . . because it . . .") super-charges motivation.

Positive recognition lasts longer than you may think. France recognized the United States when they commemorated the one-hundredth anniversary of our Declaration of Independence with their gift of the Statue of Liberty. We were so proud of their recognition, we placed it in New York Harbor for all to see as they enter the gateway to America. It serves as a continuing motivator for us to strive for the ideals of freedom and liberty that it represents. So, remember the enduring power you have for placing a "Statue of Liberty" in someone's harbor.

There may be someone on your team who is starving for appreciation and gets it too rarely in their lives. You stand in a position of tremendous positive influence. *Recognizing* is your superpower for enriching lives, so don't wait to use it until it's too late. Make someone's day. Catch 'em doing it right, especially to reinforce someone's keeping a *G.A.I.N. Commitment*. You'll keep accountability percolating. Go for it!

Part III

Rough Sailing
Conversations

Module Nine | *Reminding*

Tap 'Em on the Shoulder

> To err is human, to forgive, divine.
> —ALEXANDER POPE

Back to the Fork in the Road

Recognizing corrects the Flawed Commitment Expectation #3 of "Expecting Without Inspecting" by thanking people for keeping their agreement. Another follow-up opportunity arises if someone *doesn't* keep a commitment. *Passive* people neglect addressing the issue for fear of offending or triggering tension. Others jump straight to *Confronting* the culprit, which is *Aggressive* if the situation isn't urgent or doesn't have critical consequences.

Cut 'Em Some Slack, but Don't Ignore It. Some broken commitments or problem behaviors demand swift and serious *Confronting*, but many deserve the *Assertive* choice of giving the benefit of the doubt by first *Reminding* the errant party. Haven't *you* ever dropped the ball on a commitment? You ran into unforeseen obstacles, lost track of time, didn't realize an agreement's importance, or just plain forgot. You wouldn't appreciate being angrily cornered. You'd want your boss, peer, or family member to respectfully bring the lapse to your attention by *Reminding* you.

To Err Is Human. Mae West adapted the above Alexander Pope adage to read, "To err is human, but it feels divine." This module's version is, "To err is human, to remind, divine."

The *Reminding* Conversation Format underscores accountability when you need to:

- reconfirm commitments that have faltered, or
- manage your stress about project milestones.

The *Reminding* Message

You're unsure of a commitment's status and want to check in without being overly parental *or* you know that follow-through has fallen through the cracks. If you *don't* know whether the person is on track with an agreed-upon task, simply check in (e.g., "I'm wondering how it's going with the new wireless installation announcement we'd agreed would be ready for next week?"). As soon as you *do* know that someone has faltered on some aspect of a commitment or has fallen so far behind that it's unlikely that they can deliver, use the following *Reminding* Message that covers the *G.A.I.N.* agenda with a new kickoff:

GOALS: Reference the Gap. Begin the interaction with a non-accusatory spirit of checking in: "What we'd discussed was/What you committed to was . . . and what's happened/been happening is . . ."

ADVANTAGES: Reemphasize the Importance. Reiterate the ADVANTAGES from your initial *G.A.I.N.* Conversation. Add new benefits to build even greater buy-in, since it's apparently needed. Use the Dialogue Cycle to *Check Reactions*, paraphrase, respond, rinse, and repeat! A caveat is that you don't want to nag or insult someone's intelligence, so pare back ADVANTAGES if you sense that they already "get it" and simply spaced out the commitment.

IMPEDIMENTS: Ask for Obstacles, Problem-Solve, and Support. Since a difficulty arose that derailed the commitment, return to the IMPEDIMENT step of the original *G.A.I.N.* Conversation. Ask in your own style, "Since you ran into unforeseen obstacles this time, is there anything else that might stand in the way of meeting the commitment moving forward?" Any guesses what you do next? You guessed it. Paraphrase! Then address concerns, provide support, and problem-solve to remove any barriers.

NEXT STEPS: Discuss Next Steps and Close Appreciatively. Just as you did in the up-front *G.A.I.N.* Conversation, one of you should summarize the reestablished agreement. Since your check-in was needed this time, the person won't feel offended if you arrange another one. Your Smooth Sailing demeanor will usually achieve goodwill, contriteness in the other, and cooperative recommitment. Why not express appreciation for their good-faith accountability efforts?

A *Reminding* Message Example

We'll soon see the *Reminding* Conversation in action. For now, let's review the Message.

GOALS: Reference the Gap: "What We Discussed . . . What's Happening." EXAMPLE: "Karl, you committed to reviewing the resumes from staffing and start interviewing likely candidates. Charles mentioned today that Alphonse and Sunita haven't been contacted." [*Check Reactions*, paraphrase, and discuss.]

ADVANTAGES: Reemphasize Commitment's Benefits. EXAMPLE: "Your following through is important, since this hiring is pivotal to our new marketing initiative. Also, corporate is tracking this project loosely and we want to be heroes at budget time." [*Check Reactions*, paraphrase, and discuss.]

IMPEDIMENTS: Ask for Obstacles, Problem-Solve, and Support. EXAMPLE: "With all you have on your plate, this slipped through the cracks. Is there any barrier we didn't foresee that we can remove?" [*Check Reactions*, paraphrase, and discuss.]

NEXT STEPS: Discuss Next Steps and Close with Appreciation. EXAMPLE: "What's your understanding of where we stand on NEXT STEPS, and when can I check in to make sure we're back on track?" [*Check Reactions*, paraphrase, and discuss.]

Your *Reminding* Message. In your *Straight Talk Journal*, make notes for a back-home discussion. The first two agenda steps are the main ingredients of your planning.

G̲OALS: Reference the Gap: "What we'd discussed/You committed to . . . What's Happening." Write an opening statement to invite a recommitment.

A̲DVANTAGES: Reemphasize Commitment's Benefits. What reasons for reestablishing the original commitment can you stress so the person senses its importance at a deeper level?

I̲MPEDIMENTS: Ask for Obstacles, Problem-Solve, and Support. How can you non-blamefully ask about further obstacles or factors threatening the commitment? You'll paraphrase and problem-solve to remove them once and for all.

N̲EXT STEPS: Discuss Next Steps and Close with Appreciation. Remember that you'll offer your support, summarize or ask the person to do so, set up follow-up steps as needed, and close appreciatively. ∎

Demonstrations: The *Reminding* Conversation

You've prepared a *Reminding* Message of "What we'd discussed was that you'd [or what you'd committed to was that] . . . and what's happening is . . ." Loop back through your *G.A.I.N.* agenda steps to lock in recommitment.

The following *Reminding* interactions follow up on Keisha's commitment about showing up (she didn't!) for the meeting with Harry to learn about his virtual delivery platform's features before completing her virtual training macrodesigns. We'll see *Passive* and *Aggressive* horror stories before a more effective, *Assertive* version.

Reminding Conversation: *Passive* Demo

ACTION!

[*Keisha and Rick pass each other in the hallway.*]

Rick: [*Looking timid*] Hey, uh . . . hey, Keisha . . .

Keisha: [*Hurriedly*] Oh. Hi, Rick.

Rick: [*Shoulders slumped*] Hi, um, I'm glad I ran into you, and I . . . I don't mean to bother you, but if . . . uh, I can talk to you at another time if this isn't . . .

Keisha: [*Looks at watch impatiently*] No, I guess it's OK. What's up?

Rick: Well, you know the project thing with the . . . with the, um, virtual training design templates? Well, no offense, but weren't we gonna [*gestures tentatively and shrugs his shoulders, glancing away*] . . . meet with Harry today to learn his technology platform? I dunno, but . . . you know . . . I noticed you weren't there, so I'm just . . .

Keisha: Oh, yeah . . . [*Rolls her eyes, taps her foot impatiently, and looks at her watch.*]

Rick: [*Gesturing anxiously*] It's OK if you were too busy. I'm just a little worried. I mean, I know something might have come up, and that's okay, but . . .

Keisha: [*Rigid body tensing up and with a sharp, rat-a-tat voice*] Rick. I had a fire to put out today in my department . . .

Rick: Ohhhh. Okay . . .

Keisha: [*Curtly snaps*] So, I just couldn't make it. Sorry about that. [*Looks at her watch.*] I'll take care of it.

Rick: Okay, okay, no worries, and . . . and, you know, I'd just . . . [*looks down*] . . . hate to see us not meet the . . . you know . . . [*Voice breaking and pausing*] the Friday deadline, but if you can't do it, I guess it's . . .

Keisha: [*With annoyance*] No, Rick. I didn't say that, did I? I'll talk to Harry and set up a make-up session with him. I'll handle it myself . . . [*Rolls her eyes, showing disdain.*] . . . You know, as usual.

Rick: Oh, OK. [*Keisha briskly departs. Rick shrugs and shuffles away . . . yes, pathetically.*]

CUT!

Debriefing the *Passive* Demo. Do we really need to? Hopefully, the above Aaron Sorkin–like screenplay is clear enough, isn't it?!

Reminding Conversation: *Aggressive* Demo

ACTION!

Rick: [*Sharply*] Keisha! [*Struts up, then places his hands on his hips*]

Keisha: [*Startled, taken aback*] Hi, Rick.

Rick: [*Loudly*] Thanks a lot!!

Keisha: [*Rattled, defensively retorts with hands on her hips, facing off*] For what??

Rick: [*Sarcastically*] For nothing!

Keisha: [*Rolls her eyes and matches his caustic, loud voice*] What are you talking about?

Rick: Oh, so you're playing stupid again on me, huh? I'm talking about—

Keisha: [*Indignantly interrupts, and we're off to the races!*] I'm not playing stupid!

Rick: [*Glaring, aggressively gesturing and enunciating in a staccato way*] I'm. Talking. About. The. PROJECT! The virtual training designs! Hello???

Keisha: [*Remembering*] Ohhhh, OK.

Rick: [*Sarcastically, mocking Keisha*] Ohhhh . . . What the hell happened to you with the meeting to learn Harry's platform?

Keisha: I'm really sorry. I had a fire to put out in my team.

Rick: [*Dismissively*] We all have fires.

Keisha: I should have called you. My people bailed on me on a separate project. I had them getting speakers for the offsite customer convention—

Rick: [*Cutting her off*] It's always something with you. Get out the violins. It's not my job to manage your people, it's yours.

Keisha: I get it. I'll take care of this. Maybe I can talk to Harry . . .

Rick: [*Still escalating unnecessarily, overlapping*] Well, find a solution. And fast, 'cause if you don't, then . . . well, just get it done. Look, can I count on you or not? Are you willing to do what it takes?

Keisha: [*Angrily*] YES! You can count on me. I said I'll handle it!

Rick: All right. Good. That's what I like to hear. [*Turns. Storms away.*]

Keisha: [*Puts hand on hip, ticked off*] Fine! Peachy keen!

CUT!

Debriefing the *Aggressive* Demo. Go purchase a thicker notebook to write notes on the hundred ways I screwed up!

Reminding Conversation: *Assertive* Demonstration

As opposed to a more serious *Confronting* Conversation, *Reminding* can be casual and spontaneous, but *do* still give it advanced thought, consistent with Mark Twain's attitude: "I never spend less than two weeks on a good impromptu speech." *Reminding* someone, of course, isn't a speech, but Twain's point about preparation applies.

ACTION!

Rick: [*Stopping Keisha with a wave*] Oh, hi, Keisha! I'm glad I ran into you . . .

Keisha: [*Smiling*] Oh, hi, Rick.

Rick: [*Speaks, facing Keisha assertively with a relaxed eye contact and even, non-accusatory voice*] I was going to give you a call. [*GOALS*] We had discussed that as part of our webinar planning by next Friday you were going to attend today's meeting with Harry . . . [*Keisha grimaces.*] . . . and you weren't there this morning to learn about his new virtual technology platform. [*Checks, expressing compassionate concern*] That's not like you. What's up?

Keisha: [*Looks to the ceiling and rolls her eyes*] Rick, I'm so sorry! I totally spaced! My team and I have been planning the customer off-site for Monday. [*Rick nods, listening.*] I'd tasked two team members with getting speakers and they completely dropped the ball. I've been scrambling to fill in those spots, and I missed the meeting. I probably looked pretty sloppy with everyone sitting waiting for me.

Rick: [*Paraphrases*] You were really frazzled when your people dropped the ball on another time-sensitive commitment. You seem embarrassed this happened.

Keisha: Totally. It's humiliating to know I stood up Harry. Now I'm behind on the platform's bells and whistles. I hate to take more of Harry's time. He was already doing us a favor. Crap!

Rick: [*Paraphrases*] So you're still on board with the design project but are upset with yourself about not being up to speed on Harry's technology. You're apprehensive about imposing on him to re-teach you.

Keisha: Plus, I'm already behind, and I'm clueless on possible activities for my designs. [*Sarcastically, mad at herself*] Way to go, Keisha!

Rick: [*Speaks with a soft, reassuring voice*] Keisha, this is salvageable. I'm actually relieved to know your absence was unintended—you were thrown a curve ball. Neither of us are glad it happened, but we'll work it out. [*Keisha sags down, relieved and appreciative. Rick paraphrases.*] I get how things were frantic and pressured. You couldn't deliver if your people didn't deliver for you.

Keisha: Wow, thanks for understanding, Rick. I'm a hundred percent on board for Friday. But it's a drag that Harry, you, or another program manager has to catch me up.

Rick: [*Paraphrases*] You're anxious about how to get some tutoring.

Keisha: I'm gonna be a stranger in a strange land.

Rick: [*Speaks to resolve the unforeseen variable*] Yeah, the new platform is unique, as we learned in the meeting. Tell you what, though. I recorded today's meeting for you and any future designers. I'll send it over in an hour.

Keisha: [*Relieved*] Fantastic!

Rick: [*Comforting*] Yep. Call me with any questions, since I want to respect Harry's time.

Keisha: Perfect, Rick. I'll listen to it tonight. Thanks so much.

Rick: Sure. [*Inquires about IMPEDIMENTS.*] Now, since this came up today and I want to be sure we stay on track, I'm wondering . . . [*Expresses concern*] . . . is there anything else that could bubble up before next Friday?

Keisha: I don't think so. My off-site meeting planning will be done tomorrow morning. My guys know I wasn't pleased. They're back on track, too.

Rick: Great.

Keisha: I'm full speed ahead for my finished designs.

Rick: [*ADVANTAGES, speaks enthusiastically*] Super. I'm confident this project will keep training alive, get new salespeople skilled up to boost revenue, and address people's not wanting to schlep here from remote sites.

Keisha: And more revenue will translate to a shorter travel freeze.

Rick: [*NEXT STEPS*] Bingo. OK, when I get your designs by Friday, I'll consolidate them with everyone else's for the exec team's review. And how about shooting Harry a note—not to grovel, but to apologize? [*Keisha gives a thumbs-up, smiling.*] Hey, thanks a lot, Keisha.

Keisha: No, thank *you*, Rick.

CUT!

Module Wrap-Up

See how easy that was? La-dee-da! Everyone lived happily ever after, Keisha won the state lottery the next day, the company exceeded sales projections by 300 percent, and world peace ensued. Well, maybe not! *Reminding* won't always do the trick. Sometimes, correcting the "Expecting Without Inspecting" Flawed Commitment Expectation requires constructively *Confronting*. Stay tuned for that action-packed, challenging journey in the next module.

Module Ten | *Confronting*

The Lion, Scarecrow, and Tin Man

> I like straight talking. I think transparency is important.
> Authenticity is important. I always imagine myself as
> the other side of the audience and how would I like
> to hear things. So, I have learned the courage to talk
> straight, but if you do it with empathy, you can be a
> straight talker without being an unpleasant person.
> —JANE FRASER, CITIGROUP CEO,
> CNN INTERVIEW WITH POPPY HARLOW, 2020

Uh-Oh, Toto, We're Not in Kansas Anymore

The *G.A.I.N. Commitment* follow-up fork in the road now doesn't point to a yellow brick road leading to a magical land of enchantment called Oz. However, *Confronting* demands the courage of the Lion, the brains of the Scarecrow, and the heart of the Tin Man.

You've conducted a *G.A.I.N. Commitment* Conversation, and the person's dropped the ball. Everyone else is keeping the needed agreement, but this person is not. You tried *Reminding* the person, at least once, maybe twice. How many times will you give them the "benefit of the doubt" before *they're* getting all the benefit and *you're* getting all the doubt? It's reckoning time—a serious you-and-me discussion is necessary. Other times, you must hold a person accountable even though there wasn't prior discussion about the behavior, because it's way out of line and bugs you.

Constructive *Confronting* Conversations help us stay poised, firm, and fair when we need to:

- improve problem behaviors and accountability, or
- change patterns of broken commitments.

Confronting Blunders

If You're *Not* the Boss. *Reminding* and *Confronting* are powerful whether or not you possess position power over someone that you're holding accountable. When you aren't the manager, don't *Passively* hesitate or bail out. Avoid getting *Aggressive* if the other person reacts defensively, allowing your own volatile emotional juices to flow. *Straight Talk* help is on the way!

If You *Are* the Boss. When you manage the offender, you have other disciplinary resources at your disposal: official verbal warnings, written warnings, or termination. However, first try *Confronting* since it's a serious step that will save you time, hassle, and maybe a relationship. Some managers' aggravation triggers them to impulsively resort to termination. Later, they realize they've omitted due diligence steps of an up-front *G.A.I.N.* discussion, appropriate *Reminding*, and *Confronting*. Then they work backward to document transgressions that justify axing the person. NOT COOL! *Straight Talk's Confronting* skills provide an alternative pathway.

A Vital Premise

You're 100% Justified. The skills you'll learn will help you to handle defensive reactions in many other interactions besides *Confronting*—whenever you're hit with an emotional response. In this module, we are applying the de-escalating skills to *Confronting* situations where you have the right and responsibility to correct a wrong. You are totally justified in *Confronting*, either because the person is way out of line or because the person is breaking a commitment. You've cut them slack by *Reminding* them when they faltered. Everyone else is keeping the commitment. You have a legitimate beef!

Don't Get Sucked In! Whatever defensive response the person lobs at you when you *Confront*, please assume that it's pure, unadulterated cow cookies! Don't get manipulated into letting them off the hook. They are in the wrong and they probably know it. Any excuse for dropping the ball was dealt with in your original *G.A.I.N.* discussion or while *Reminding*. You secured a recommitment that removed any excuses for not complying with the fair agreement (you thought). Clear? Do *not* feel sheepish about *Confronting*.

Other times, you won't have had a prior Commitment Conversation, but the person has done something so disagreeable that you must call "foul." If *Confronting* someone the first time that their actions bother you would be too punitive, approach the conversation as a nonconfrontational *G.A.I.N. Commitment* Conversation about a Preexisting Issue (module seven). However, if the misdeed is so upsetting that anyone from planet Earth would think it's out of bounds enough to deserve *Confronting*, go for it. Just be sure you're not being overly reactive.

Your Survival Kit. Besides the vital premise of being totally justified, this module gives you another gift-wrapped package—this survival kit for *Confronting*:

- *The Confronting Message:* You'll learn to craft this potent kickoff.
- *Understanding Defensive Reactions:* You'll get derailed if you lack perspective on the true, psychological nature of emotional responses.
- *Defusing Skills:* Your friend the Dialogue Cycle will be your salvation when blended with the artful steps of the *Confronting* Conversation Format.
- *Tips for the Tough Ones:* You'll even learn to handle volatile reactions such as fake crying, stubborn silence, threats, guilt trips, and stomping out.

Confronting: Flip the *Recognizing* Message

The *Confronting* Conversation uses a potent Message followed by the Dialogue Cycle and procedures for securing recommitment. The *Confronting* Message repurposes *Recognizing*'s Three-Part "I" Message to express our displeasure.

Recognizing Message	*Confronting* Message
• Positive Behavior	• Negative Behavior
• Positive Feelings	• Negative Feelings
• Positive Impact	• Negative Impact

As with the *G.A.I.N.* agenda and *Recognizing* Message, the *Confronting* Message's three parts below can be re-sequenced. The second piece, Negative Feelings, can even be omitted if you have a rationale (beyond chickening out!).

Negative Behavior ("When you commit to . . . and don't . . ."). State the broken commitment in clear, *Bias-Free Language* terms citing a specific instance. Be clean, clear, and focused. EXAMPLE: "Hayden, when you agree to attend our task force status update meetings and don't, like happened this morning . . ."

Describe the transgression without labels (e.g., "unprofessional behavior"), evaluations (e.g., "lousy report"), or exaggerated language (e.g., "you never . . ."). Avoid the temptation to list everything the person has done wrong since before they were born! That dilutes the *Confronting* Message's focus and sounds like nagging (which I define as using a long, weak message).

(Optional) Negative Feelings ("I feel/felt/get . . ."). Tell the person how you feel about the broken commitment. You've already discussed the problem during your original *G.A.I.N.* discussion and possibly while *Reminding*, so you're *not* in the "happy zone"! EXAMPLE: "I feel inconvenienced and frustrated . . ."

Use a feeling word (e.g., "furious . . . upset . . . undermined . . .") or a feeling-*laden* phrase (i.e., "at the end of my rope"). Avoid the lead-in of "I feel *that* . . ." since this articulates an opinion rather than your actual emotion (e.g., "I feel that you're not adhering to our core values . . .").

As with *Active Listening*, don't *over*shoot or *under*shoot your own emotions. If you're furious, express it in a way that *reports* it rather than over-expressively *acts it out* with polluted anger. Use straightforward anger statements rather than sarcasm (sideways anger), snide comments (disguised name-calling), or spewed expletives. To ensure "clean anger," blow off steam to a friend before *Confronting*, vent your emotions as you edit your Three-Part "I" Message, and use Self-Talk that helps you stay calm.

Why share feelings at all? Because *Straight Talk* is a *relationship*-based versus *position*-based model. If you possess position power over someone, that isn't as influential as relationship power. *Straight Talk's* potency rests upon "power *with*" rather than "power *over*."

The impact of *Confronting* stems partly from the other person experiencing you as a full human being—including your emotional life. Your *Active Listening, Advising and Guiding, Recognizing,* and *Reminding* have earned you goodwill, relationship strength, credibility, rapport, and the right to "tell it like it is." Most people will respect you for being candid, and you'll respect *yourself* for having the courage of your convictions. Some people think it's inappropriate to share upset feelings when *Confronting* a boss, unless you enjoy an egalitarian relationship. You decide.

Negative Impact ("Because the result was/is . . ."). Describe the adverse effects of the other person's lack of follow-through (or whatever the Negative Behavior is). Be precise and persuasive in depicting the tangible fallout. EXAMPLE: "Because you miss vital information to act on, others (including me) have to take time updating you, and the team's composite report is delayed."

Vividly identify the observable negative consequences on productivity, time, stress, money, and morale. The unfavorable repercussions may be for you, the team, other departments, the broader enterprise, internal or external clients or customers, and/or the person you're *Confronting.* If you can't honestly cite outcomes that have already occurred, foretell potential future negative results. These must be believable and realistic rather than a stretch, or the defender will dispute, "Aw, come on, really?"

This critical third piece of the Three-Part "I" Message is less effective if you fall into these mistakes:

- *Looping Back:* Don't merely expand on Negative Behavior you've already stated (e.g., "Because you weren't keeping your commitment . . ." or "Because you didn't submit the report with a good format"). These ideas were already conveyed in the first part of your Message (e.g., "When you commit to . . . and don't . . ."). Push beyond redundancy by asking yourself, "So what? What's the resulting Negative Impact of the problematic behavior?"
- *Evaluative Name-Calling:* Judgmental labels for the Negative Impact are just your interpretation versus what a camera would see (remember the "Just the Facts" Test?). Don't ignite defensive responses and demotivate the person from recommitting (e.g., "Because it is incredibly immature . . ." or "Because it's lousy team management.").

- *Mind Reading:* Diagnosing the person's inner intent or feelings plays psychologist and is presumptuous (e.g., "Because you don't respect me . . ." or "Because you have issues with authority and were trying to undermine me"). The receiver can just deny your analysis and say, "Who the hell are you to play shrink or tell me what I feel?" If anything, embed your hunches about intent into the Negative Feelings (part two) without assuming the other's inner world (e.g., "When you . . . I felt *undermined*, because . . .").

Sample *Confronting* Messages

Read these examples. What qualities characterize them all? Some Messages are longer, some are shorter, some rearrange the pieces, and some omit the feelings. But what adjectives can describe them all?

Example #1 (To an IT Call Center Direct Report): "Dori, when you commit to responding to emails and voicemails within twenty-four hours, at least to acknowledge receipt, and then you don't, like happened this week with three calls from Supply Chain [Negative Behavior], I get annoyed [Negative Feelings], because I end up spending time troubleshooting problems and soothing upset managers, and our reputation suffers." [Negative Impact]

Example #2 (To a Boss After Reminding, *No Feelings Piece):* "Toby, you had kindly committed to giving me more complete specifications for new projects to save us both time. Your email assigning me the beta project report left out which template to use, omitted milestone dates, and didn't provide project decision criteria. [Negative Behavior] As a result, we risk the project delays while I track down these details, or I'll have to guess what you want. I don't want to frustrate you with an inaccurate, delayed, or incomplete analysis." [Negative Impact]

Example #3 (To a Report, Starting with the Feelings Piece, No Prior Conversation): "Farid, I'm surprised and upset. [Negative Feelings] In today's meeting, you gossiped to Diane, our new client, that our customer Talia is 'a pain who's never satisfied.' [Negative Behavior] This violates our stated Customer Focus Credo, and Diane said she hopes we don't talk about all our clients behind their backs. You jeopardized her trust, and if Diane tells Talia, it's bye-bye to both accounts." [Actual and Potential Negative Impact]

Example #4 (To a Boss, Beginning with the Negative Impact and Omitting the Feelings Piece): "Genevieve, my HR group had three exit interviews this quarter, and our division's latest engagement survey showed 'Workload Fairness' in the 15 percent category. [Negative Impact] I wonder if one reason is that we didn't follow through on your April promise about outsourcing tedious administrative HR compliance tasks so that we can spend more rewarding time as business consultants. [Negative Behavior]

Example #5 (To a Peer, Referencing a Previous Agreement): "Dez, we've discussed the need to control your emotional and disruptive behavior. I'm disappointed and upset [Negative Feelings] about how you again behaved in yesterday's staff meeting. You slammed down your notes, pounded the table, and loudly complained about the new hires' long learning curve. [Negative Behavior] As a veteran supervisor, you could trigger other managers to adopt a command-and-control, *Aggressive* mode. Your outbursts hurt team morale. In fact, one of the new folks quit today." [Potential and Actual Negative Impact]

Can you rattle off adjectives, traits, or characteristics that the above *Confronting* Messages have in common? Think of at least three descriptors. Participants often say: "powerful . . . honest . . . concise . . . behavioral . . . objective (other than the Feelings piece) . . . accountability-oriented . . . firm but fair . . . doesn't pull punches . . . descriptive versus evaluative. . . brave . . . noninflammatory . . ."

Your *Confronting* Message. Think of a commitment that isn't being kept. If you need to go back and *G.A.I.N. Commitment* or *Remind*, do so. However, for this drill, imagine you've conducted those prerequisite steps. Your scenario might instead involve a problematic behavior pattern or incident that's bothersome enough to warrant *Confronting* without a prior commitment. Use your *Straight Talk Journal* or the one you've downloaded from www.BrandonPartners.com/StraightTalkBook to write a *Confronting* Message. Edit and fine-tune your Message: Is the Negative Behavior wording objective versus judgmental or fuzzy? Do the Negative Feelings overshoot or undershoot? Is the Negative Impact a convincing actual one or believable potential one? ∎

Be Straight with Yourself. Hold yourself accountable for appropriate *Con-fronting*. Do you really have the right to call out the other person, or are you overreacting? Does the person's Negative Behavior really have a concrete Negative Impact on you? Is your upset more about your own style-based pet peeve, so that *Confronting* actually intrudes on the other's space? Have you earned the right to *Confront* because the person's actions were egregious or because you had a prior give-and-take *G.A.I.N. Commitment* Conversation? If you met with resistance, did you invite Mutual Benefit Problem-Solving to address concerns? Did you try *Reminding* before *Confronting*?

Don't Squeeze the Trigger! The *Confronting* Message is potent, so expect a defensive reaction. That's why, before delivering it, we must adjust our mindset about the true nature of volatile emotional reactions, prepare for the meeting, and learn defusing skills. Please do NOT go deliver your *Confronting* Message right now. Do you trust me? Do NOT conduct a *Confronting* Conversation until you finish reading this module!

The Overeager Learner. I always warn groups *not* to deliver their Three-Part "I" Message before learning how to handle the predictable defensiveness it triggers. Otherwise, it's like a glad-iator jumping into the arena to face the lion without a sword or armor. Once, after this Day One caution, an overeager attendee arrived the next day in tears. "Rick, you were right! I should have trusted you! I sent my husband my Three-Part 'I' Message and he sent me back a Two-Part 'F' Message!"

Preparing for the *Confronting* Conversation

Crafting your *Confronting* Message is a key part of your preliminary work, but also: (1) learn your Message, (2) strategize the setting, (3) invite the receiver, and (4) visualize the conversation.

Learn Your Message

Read your *Confronting* Message aloud to sense how it will land. Hearing the words help you know whether to tweak it further. Once it's perfected, recite it many times to memorize it. As you do so, try to "drain your anger." Vent any polluted anger and "clean out your pipes" before *Confronting* the person. Slash their tires in your mind if it helps you to exorcise *Aggressive* anger! You're less likely to lose your cool and dump during the meeting. Practice your delivery in front of a mirror or with another person.

Strategize the Setting

Strategize where to meet, preferably in person. Some people invite the person to their own office, but this can make it awkward at the end to have to ask the other to leave. Other confronters prefer going to the offender's office, to be in control of when to depart and to help the other feel safer.

Invite the Receiver

When you contact the receiver, reveal little about your reason for meeting. This isn't to catch someone off guard, although it does prevent them from preparing defenses or gearing up for a fight. It just prevents getting sucked into the *Confronting* Conversation before you're ready, stealing the thunder of your Message, or conducting the meeting in an inopportune location.

Visualize the Conversation

Mark Twain quipped, "My life has been a series of horrible misfortunes, most of which never happened." Actors have dress rehearsals. Some of us have "dread rehearsals." The lesser-known Muppet character Worry Wart walks around with a wastebasket on his head in case the sky falls on him, and he never wears a red hat because a bird might think he is a cherry and eat him. Are you like Worry Wart?

Imagining a blowup when *Confronting* conditions your brain to expect a negative outcome, initiating a self-fulfilling prophecy. Instead, train your brain to expect positive outcomes by visualizing the discussion going well. Olympic skiers and gymnasts mentally rehearse routines. Basketball free throw studies found that pairing physical practice with mental practice improves performance—imagining the arc of the ball . . . nothing but net! I've given presentations and taught seminars for decades, but I still visualize myself teaching. I sometimes visit the meeting room the night before so that I can visualize my session more distinctly.

Visualizing Practice. Give it a whirl, creating a mental movie of the *Confronting* Conversation using your drafted Message. Or internally practice any presentation, personal exchange, or other scenario that's anxiety-producing.

Visualize the scene unfolding on the back of your eyelids. See yourself *Confronting* as vividly as you can. Notice the exact surroundings, sights, and sounds. Picture each step of the Conversation—opening, stating your "I" Message, using *Assertive* body language and voice, handling defensive reactions, and closing with recommitment. Play out the interaction and feel the high of achieving a positive outcome.

Make sure to include seeing yourself overcoming a problem spot. Visualize getting triggered by the person's defensive reaction and then recovering by breathing, relaxing, shifting your Self-Talk, regaining calm self-control, and successfully completing the discussion. ■

Understanding Defensiveness

The Chamber of Horrors

Even if your Three-Part "I" Message is objective, you prepare for the meeting, and your delivery is *Assertively* firm yet fair, you'll likely encounter a defensive, volatile "fight" or "flight" reaction:

FIGHT	FLIGHT
Blaming Others	Distracting, Changing the Topic
Blaming You	Making Excuses
Turning the Tables, Confronting You	Denying, Lying
Verbal Attacks and Insults	Playing "Poor Me" Victim
Mocking You	Guilt Tripping
Sarcasm	Minimizing the Situation
Yelling	Silence
Stomping Out	Crying "Crocodile Tears"
Pulling Rank, Threatening	Trying to Postpone

We're *Confronting* in this module, but defensiveness can erupt at other times:

- *Checking Reactions* in a *G.A.I.N.* Conversation and you get stony silence.
- *Reminding* someone goes south (e.g., "Wow, Big Brother is watching!").
- Meeting resistance to an announcement (e.g., "Typical silly policy!").
- An employee cries during an appraisal (e.g., "There goes my bonus!").
- A co-trainer snaps (e.g., "I don't need your nitpicking feedback. I'm more experienced!").
- A peer attacks you (e.g., "Save your breath with the advice. You're not my boss!").

Nice. Fun. Sign me up! No worries, though, because the defusing skills you're about to learn are portable to other situations besides *Confronting*.

Scan Your World for Defensive Reactions. Peruse the above emotional reactions. Which ones have you encountered? Which ones do *you* employ yourself, even when you know you're wrong? Which emotional responses might "hook you," provoking you to lose control of your poise, professionalism, and *Straight Talk* skills? ■

Reframing Defensiveness

A prerequisite for coping with strong emotional reactions is to understand the true nature of defensiveness. Psychological insight will help you to cool down the interaction rather than escalate it. Your *Straight Talk Mindset*'s Self-Talk will come in handy, big-time.

Mentally transport yourself back into our group as I guarantee a volunteer thunderous applause. Matt, a buff 250-pound ex-college linebacker jumps up. I ask him to stand and face me, putting his two hands up with his palms gently touching mine. I say, "OK, Matt, now do whatever comes naturally." Then I push against Matt's outstretched hands, which immediately elicits his push-back reaction.

As we each exert more and more pressure, the group eggs on Matt: "Go Matt! . . . You got him, man!" Matt easily prevents me from backing him up. I'm tilting like the Leaning Tower of Pisa with all my weight and force, but he's standing straight up, keeping us at a stalemate. I mutter, "Crap, I used the wrong volunteer." After thirty seconds, I gradually let up the amount of pushing pressure I'm exerting, and Matt reflexively reduces his resisting force until we are back in our initial stationary relaxed stance. I goad on the group to give Matt raucous, soccer-cheering applause by yelling, "Woo, woo, woo!" Matt takes a bow.

I ask Matt what he did when I pushed him and he replies, "I pushed back." I follow up by playacting dumb: "Oh, so you consciously strategized how you'd respond and thought, 'Hmmm, Rick is pushing me, so I'll tense all of the muscles in my legs and arms in order to exert a resisting force equal to or greater than the force with which Rick is pressing against my palms'? Is *that* what you did?" The group chuckles as Matt says, "Duh, no. It was just an automatic reaction that came naturally." I say, "Of course. Next, your fans here couldn't feel it, but I started letting up my pressure against you. What did you do?" He acknowledges that he also pushed less and less. I thank Matt and invite a final round of applause—this time with the "golf cheer" (fast and soft). ∎

The True Nature of Defensiveness. The dynamics of defensiveness are embedded in its definition.

> **Defensiveness:** The automatic physiological, emotional, and behavioral response to protect oneself from perceived threat, attack, or loss.

Let's unpack the key elements of this definition.

- *Automatically triggered:* The moment I pushed against Matt's hands, he didn't calculate or plan his response. His "push-back" was a reflexive reaction. When I gradually stopped pushing, Matt's reaction to stop pushing was also reflexive.

- *... physiological, emotional, and behavioral reactions:* Don't expect defensiveness to be rational. It's not about logic! It's a purely visceral, emotional reaction. When someone claims they don't remember making a commitment, they are technically lying. Their "alternative facts" are untrue if we just interpret them literally. But defensiveness is not only about the *literal truth* of what a person is saying. It's about their *psychological truth.* We need to treat defensive responses with greater interpersonal astuteness than merely assessing the facts. Their chemical, emotional reactions fuel behavioral reactions of "Flight" (e.g., denial, crying, trying to leave, etc.) or "Fight" (e.g., blaming you, sarcasm, yelling). When *Confronting,* cut people slack on what they initially say before calming down, because they are literally "out of their minds" in the sense that they're having a purely visceral, gut-level, emotional response.

- *... to protect from perceived or actual threat, attack, or loss:* Matt felt pushed when I pressed against his palms, so he pushed back. Analogously, your receiver experiences your *Confronting Message* as a "push" psychologically, so may have a "push-back" defensive reaction. Consciously or unconsciously, validly or not, they experience your *Confronting* as a threat, attack, or potential loss (e.g., their job, money, reputation, dignity, self-esteem, etc.).

We Are Kids with Bigger Feet. All parents have seen these dynamics of defensiveness at work. "No, Daddy, I wasn't running into the living room. The lamp broke 'cause it just fell off the table." Do me a favor. Lean over and look at your shoes . . . You're now looking at the only difference between you and a five-year-old when it comes to feeling triggered when being confronted. It's the size of your feet! Even as a well-meaning adult, don't you sometimes react defensively?

The Physiology of Emotional Reactions

Brain Physiology. The *amygdala* is the older, involuntary part of the brain's limbic system. It's where we process strong emotions like fear and pleasure. The *frontal lobes* comprise our newer and advanced brain system where reasoning, decision-making, planning, and rational responses originate during conflict. Prehistoric cavemen faced threats from saber-toothed tigers and other tribes, so the amygdala's automatic survival response kicked in—releasing cortisol and adrenaline that pumped oxygen to their arms and legs for Fight or Flight. Feet and fists, do your stuff! Blood flow to their muscles increased for speed and strength, blood sugar amped up for energy, and pupils dilated for sharpened vision. Physiological responses included rapid heartbeat, sweaty palms, accelerated breathing, a rise in body heat, and an increase in galvanic skin response.

We're No Different! Today, when a threat is mild or moderate, our frontal lobes override the amygdala, so we respond in helpful, rational, and appropriate ways. When the perceived threat is stronger, our amygdala kicks in to overpower our frontal lobes. Our Fight or Flight physiological responses are activated, resulting in sudden, illogical, and irrational overreactions like denial, sarcasm, verbal attacks, or manipulative tears. We don't *intend* this escalation and emotionality. It's just our amygdala cookin' on high flame!

Oxygen is flowing to our extremities. What's the one place it's not flowing? Our brains! So, we're well suited for brawling or bailing, but poorly equipped for constructive dialogue and rational problem-solving. When threat-induced emotions clog someone's pipes, you already know that the cure is defusing through *Active Listening*.

Conducting the *Confronting* Conversation

You've kept yourself honest while writing your *Confronting* Message. You've prepared for the meeting and adjusted your attitude about defensive reactions. It's now time for the actual *Confronting* Conversation. As diagram 10.1 shows, it's just our old friend, the Dialogue Cycle, with some twists and bookended by opening and closing.

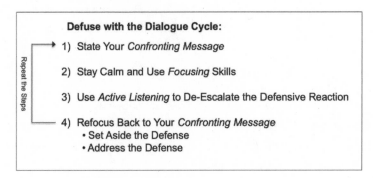

Diagram 10.1 | The *Confronting* Conversation Format

Open *Assertively*

Set the Right Tone. Don't shoot yourself in the foot right out of the gate. Don't begin *Aggressively,* but do *set* a serious tone. Get down to business instead of *Passively* slipping into excessive small talk. After all, the other person has likely guessed the purpose of the meeting, especially if you've already *Reminded* them about the targeted issue. Why pretend or delay?

Don't try to soften the blow with positive feedback before stating your *Confronting* Message. This backfires since the receiver suspects that *Recognizing* isn't your real purpose. They won't even hear your positive input as they wait for the other shoe to drop. Or, if they don't suspect your true purpose, the receiver will feel sucker-punched by your eventual *Confronting.*

Convey a Balanced Perspective. "Hi, Yuki. I need to talk about an issue we've discussed before. It's not about the rest of your overall performance—just this one, but it's an important one. When you agree to . . ." Without citing specifics, this opening puts the meeting into proper context so that Yuki doesn't think you're ignoring all the ways she contributes.

Anticipate a Good Outcome. Try to convey goodwill, create readiness for dialogue versus "duel-logue," and express faith that the two of you *will* resolve the matter. For example, say, "Willa, I'm confident that our good relationship will help us to work this out and move on. When you commit to . . ." or "Calib, we've worked through conflicts before, so I know we'll resolve this one. When you agree . . ."

Defuse: State Your *Confronting* Message

You've carefully constructed, edited, and memorized your Three Part "I" Message to be clear, non-loaded, and potent. Everything you need to say is embedded in your well-crafted *Confronting* Message. So stay true to it. Just say it. Don't improvise or elaborate, or you might muddy it.

Your Message wording is noninflammatory and *Assertive* rather than *Passive* or *Aggressive*, so make sure your delivery is as well. You've memorized it, so try not to sound rote or mechanical. Sit up, lean forward, and look the person in the eyes without glaring. Firmly deliver your *Straight Talk* Message. PAUSE. Let it sink in.

Defuse: *Stay Calm and Use Focusing Skills*

Use Focusing skills' attentive body language. This demands staying calm with your Self-Talk. Confucius said, "He who conquers himself is the mightiest warrior." This ancient wisdom means that we can't prevent adversity, but we can control our reactions. This applies to our mental state for handling defensiveness. Self-monitor, self-regulate, and change that little voice in your head when you're hit with a defensive reaction.

Reframing. We've redefined defensiveness from being calculated lies or attacks, to being automatic emotional reactions to protect oneself when feeling unsafe. This mental shift is called "reframing." Any painting looks better or worse with a different frame. Reframing views any experience as having multiple meanings and choosing one that serves us best.

George Carlin observed how environmentalists decided to reframe "swamps and jungles" as "wetlands and rain forests" and the donations came rolling in! Thomas Edison was a master of reframing. A reporter asked him how it felt to have failed ten thousand times in trying to invent the light bulb. He retorted that he didn't fail, rather had succeeded in discovering how *not* to invent the light bulb. You don't need to be a brilliant inventor to reinvent your Self-Talk so that you're in control of your own reactions to the other person's reaction.

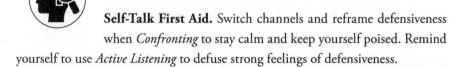

Self-Talk First Aid. Switch channels and reframe defensiveness when *Confronting* to stay calm and keep yourself poised. Remind yourself to use *Active Listening* to defuse strong feelings of defensiveness.

- *Negative Self-Talk:* "Whoa! Where is this coming from, out of the blue! I didn't expect or deserve this kind of treatment! I can't believe this!
- *Positive Self-Talk:* "OK. There's his predictable reaction to perceived threat. I knew to expect it. I remain calm under heat. I've got this."

- *Negative Self-Talk:* "Who the hell does she think she is? If she wants a fight, she's got one. She'll regret messing with me."
- *Positive Self-Talk:* "Easy does it. These attacks aren't about *me*. They're about her perceived threat. I can only control my own half of the relationship. I can keep this professional and she'll thank me later."

- *Negative Self-Talk:* "He's lying! We DID talk about this!"
- *Positive Self-Talk:* "I have notes on our meeting that I can pull out once I calm him down by paraphrasing. Defensiveness isn't supposed to be rational. It's about emotions, not logic. It's cool. I won't get triggered." ■

Defuse: Use *Active Listening* to De-Escalate the Defensive Reaction

You'll defuse volatile emotions more quickly by empathically paraphrasing. Speaking more (pushing back) doesn't calm a defender's anger as much as paraphrasing, "Wow, you're ticked at me for even bringing this up." I guarantee that the defender won't yell, "Stop trying to understand my feelings!" To keep fighting as you paraphrase would be like punching fog. It takes two to tango (*and* two to tangle).

Defensiveness Deafness. Until you de-escalate the other's defensiveness, their emotions will block them from hearing your *Confronting* Message. They may be able to repeat your words verbatim, but they don't "get it" at a gut level. They can't feel *your* emotions, because theirs prevent yours from registering. *Active Listening* clears the path for your *Confronting* Message to resonate when you recycle it.

How Long? Patiently paraphrase the person's first blast of defensive emotions until they confirm you've understood their "push-back" defense. This doesn't mean they agree with your *Confronting* Message. They're just saying, "Yes, you've understood my emotional reaction." They're signaling that you've accurately and empathically paraphrased their defense. They feel heard and expect your response. Some tips:

- *Unclog Their Emotional Pipes:* It may take several paraphrases before they are ready to hear your response to their defensive reaction.
- *When Silence Is Golden:* Their confirmation may be verbal (e.g., "Yes . . . damn right . . .") or nonverbal. Crossed arms and an expectant look after you paraphrase means their vitriol is drained for the moment. There may be more rounds of emotionality after you then respond to their first push-back.
- *Pause After Confirmation:* When the defender says, "Yes" to your para-phrase, PAUSE. This makes sure the person isn't saying, "That's right, and *furthermore* . . ." with more venting. Pausing after the "Yes" conveys, "I'm carefully considering what you've said and letting it sink in." It also gives you time to decide how to address their defensive reaction.
- *Give Up Control to Stay In Control:* It may feel like you're giving up control, but you're not. When fishing and hooking a big one, you don't jerk the rod and fight to reel it in. You'll lose it. You give it line, giving *up* control to stay *in* control. When I tamed wild horses, I didn't first throw on the bit and reins. I rode bareback, blended in my energy, and gradually took control. (Okay, I never actually did that. I grew up in St. Louis, not Texas!)

Refocus Back to Your *Confronting* Message

You surrendered the steering wheel of the "communication car" to the other for their defensive reaction to your *Confronting* Message. They've signaled with a verbal or nonverbal "Yes" that you've empathically understood their defensive response. You've earned the right to take back the wheel and again drive the con-versation. You'll segue back to your *Confronting* Message either by *Setting Aside the Defense* or by briefly *Addressing the Defense*.

Set Aside the Defense. When the defensive response is irrelevant or off-track, it doesn't erase or diminish the point of your *Confronting* Message. So just

Don't worry that by paraphrasing, the other person will think you agree with their defense. NO WAY! They may think that at first, but not as soon as you pause and refocus back to your *Confronting* Message. To convey that your empathy is *not* agreement, use paraphrasing lead-ins like "From your perspective . . ." or "So, from your side of the fence, you're upset that . . ."

paraphrase the defense and return to your Message (almost like ignoring it). Let's say the person is whining about their workload, which doesn't excuse their broken commitment. Others are overworked and still keeping the agreement. After paraphrasing to the "Yes," you'd Refocus by *Setting Aside the Defense*: "We still have the issue of . . ." "At the same time, I hope you'll see . . ." or "Our challenge remains . . ."

Imagine you're *Confronting* someone about breaking your team meeting norm to avoid distracting side conversations. The person changes the subject by insulting your competence at leading the meetings. You paraphrase, "Sounds like you also have a beef about our meetings. You get bored by my briefing detail and monotone voice." [Defender: "You got it."] You Refocus, saying, "Lorraine, that still leaves us with the issue of our team's agreed-upon ground rules, so when you agree . . ."

Address the Defense. Other times, the only way to get the person off of a defensive reaction is to speak to it before moving on, or else the person will return to it like a broken record. In fact, if you try *Setting Aside the Defense* (e.g., "The issue remains . . ."), you may pour gasoline on the fire. Your method of *Addressing the Defense* depends on the type of defensive reaction you've gotten:

- *Clarify the Facts or Background:* "You don't remember our agreement. You're surprised that this is coming out of left field." [Defender: "Right."] "You must have forgotten our April meeting and this follow-up email. Riley, when you agree to . . ."
- *Postpone Side Issues:* "You resent never getting enough positive feedback from me." [Defender: "Exactly."] "Tito, I'm glad to tell you what I appreciate about your work after we finish this discussion. Right now, the issue is how you treat your people. When you . . ."

- *Reassure with Self-disclosure:* "You're distraught and worried that this could get you fired." [Defender: "Yes" (sobbing).] "Jax, that's the last thing that I want. This is serious, but I don't believe that will happen, since I'm confident you'll take care of this once and for all. What I need you to hear is the impact on the team when you . . ."

- *Call the Bluff:* "You feel discriminated against as an older employee, and you might complain to HR about ageism." [Defender: "Damn straight."] "Erin, I'm sorry to hear that. I don't see it that way. In fact, I just assigned Levi and JoEllen [two tenured associates] to a prestigious project that other divisions give to new MBA graduates. My diversity record will speak for itself if I need to meet with HR. Meanwhile, I still need to say that when you . . ."

Demonstration: Refocusing

Let's see how Cesar *Addresses the Defense* when he confronts Thea about a salesperson standard practice. ACTION!

Cesar: [*States the Confronting Message*] Thea, when you don't visit customers at least once a quarter like our sales standard practices require, I get upset because it breaks our published Customer Commitment Credo and risks losing an account if a client figures, "Out of sight, out of mind."

Thea: I can't believe you're laying into me when we're friends! We used to make fun of supervisors being so uptight about policies. You sold out once you got promoted to a big-shot supervisor.

Cesar: [*Paraphrases*] I hear you, Thea. You're mad because it seems like I care more about my business role than our relationship, and that hurts.

Thea: [*Leans forward accusingly and snaps*] Yeah!

Cesar: [*Pauses to absorb Thea's upset before Addressing the Defense*] Thea, from my perspective, it's because I care about you that I'm talking this out instead of just writing you up. My being responsible for team results will never erase our friendship. I care about our relationship. At the same time, I do think friends keep their commitments to each other, so [*Restates Confronting Message*] when you do agree you'll visit customers at least once a quarter and don't . . .

CUT!

Thea might bring up other defensive excuses like too many competing demands, but she's unlikely to continue hitting Cesar with the friendship guilt trip. If Cesar had tried *Setting Aside the Defense* with a segue like, "The problem remains . . ." then Thea might say, "See? You're not even responding to my hurt feelings now, which proves you don't care!"

Don't Adapt the *Confronting* Message. As you Refocus to restate your Message, don't adjust it too much, since you might add "loaded" words, or become long-winded instead of short and sweet (well, maybe not so sweet, but you get the idea!). Some people worry that repeating the same *Confronting* Message sounds like a broken record. Remember that the receiver didn't fully hear it the first time, due to their clogged-up emotions. It's fine to embellish your Message with a few words, condense it, or vary your vocal tone, but beware of weakening or polluting it.

Don't Send Solutions. Often, impatience lures people into abandoning their Message and just telling the person what to do. The template of "When you agree to . . . and don't, I feel . . . because . . ." is less parental or militaristic than saying, "I need you to keep your agreement to . . ." or "Just stop . . ." or "You have to . . ." Your *Confronting* Message has the embedded implied solution of simply keeping their original commitment or to cease the problem behavior. Therefore, try not to lecture or infantilize the person by ordering the solution. They know it anyway from the *G.A.I.N.* and *Reminding* Conversations. Simply restating your *Confronting* Message and pausing allows the receiver to offer the solution. They'll feel better as an adult than they would by sheepishly acquiescing to your demand.

Repeat the Dialogue Cycle

One Dialogue Cycle May Do the Trick . . . When you first *Confront* someone, they're not likely to say, "Thanks, I needed that!" They'll give you at least one round of defensiveness before coming around to take responsibility for their actions (or nonaction). You'll "listen down" the Fight or Flight defense, no matter how zany or in the Land of Make-Believe it is, and then you'll reassert your same basic Message. Often, your skillful handling of the emotional reaction and Refocusing will prompt the person to apologize and recommit to constructive behavior.

. . . Or Not. Other times, you'll need to repeat the Dialogue Cycle once, twice, or more if the person is a tough cookie. Sooner or later, the person will grasp that your persistent *Confronting* Message means you're not going away and that your empathic, dedicated *Active Listening* means you're being more than fair. They'll gradually soften and offer a solution for keeping the agreement or modifying whatever the out-of-line behavior was. The exception is if a new, legitimate conflicting need has surfaced, one that necessitates Mutual Benefit Problem-Solving (see module seven).

Trust the Process. When you Refocus back to your *Confronting* Message, the receiver often moves to a *different* defensive reaction. Don't be discouraged or think the process isn't working. It's actually working beautifully. You've so successfully handled the first defense, restating your *Confronting* Message has triggered a second kind of defensiveness. They're still in the resistance, excuse, and ploy mode, but at least they've moved off of their first line of defense.

The Next Punch May Be Spiked! Don't be alarmed if the second round of defensiveness is stronger than the first, just like an earthquake's initial shaking may be followed by aftershocks. Don't let this dynamic shock you! When the defender realizes that you're not backing off and that their first tactic didn't work, they may panic and become more desperate with a more explosive defense.

This isn't surprising. The cop-out coping mechanism they used as a little kid hasn't worked. They consciously or unconsciously dig deeper into their pocketful of defenses and get more emotional. Here are analogies for a defensive person becoming even more emotional as they fear that you are prevailing in your goal of holding them accountable:

- *Cornered Animals:* Ethan Chandler in the *Penny Dreadful* horror movie says, "Cornered animals are the most dangerous." This line may stem from the Chinese proverb, "Corner a dog in a dead-end street and it will turn and bite."
- *Boxing:* A boxer knocks down his foe and thinks the fight's in the bag, but his bloodied opponent rises to unleash a flurry of fury.

No worries. You've got this! Just breathe. Trust the Dialogue Cycle, alternating *between Active Listening* and *Assertive Speaking*, and use artful Refocusing segues to either *Set Aside* or *Address* their maneuvers.

Close with Accountability

Voila! You made it! You've looped back through the Dialogue Cycle enough— probably one or two times (or maybe a dozen with The Wicked Witch of the West, Thanos, or other meanies of the world!). You've whittled down the person's resistance and they stop being defensive. They're ready to resolve the issue.

End the meeting with the same *N* for NEXT STEPS you used to *G.A.I.N. Commitment* and when *Reminding.* Elicit the person's takeaway intent and action steps for fixing the problem (aka, keeping the agreement). Paraphrase and appreciatively accept the promise to change their behavior, and preview any needed follow-up. By now you're relieved and genuinely grateful for their cooperation, so offer thanks and close. Then treat yourself to a nice dinner or whatever your celebration pleasure is. You've earned it!

Closing a *Confronting* Conversation with accountability sometimes requires handling "Thin Ice" solutions. When gingerly walking across a frozen lake, the ice is thinnest and most precarious at the edge, where land's edge warms the waters. You see safe ground, so you're tempted to run off the ice, but that's dangerous. Similarly, at the edge of a *Straight Talk* conversation, don't blow it by hurriedly accepting a soft solution.

Empty Commitments. If you believe "I'll try" or "I'll make a better effort" is genuine, then accept it. But if you sniff a brush-off—that "trying" isn't a true commitment—don't take the bait. Paraphrase the effort, offer thanks, say why "trying" won't suffice, and elicit other ideas: "Dina, I appreciate that you'll try to arrive on time. Unfortunately, 'trying' hasn't worked in the past, so what specific steps can you take this time? We don't want to be back here again when it's not comfortable for either of us." Yoda, the wise Jedi mentor in the *Star Wars* movies, says, "Do or do not. There is no try."

Trying Doesn't Cut It. I often prank on a good sport volunteer. Let's call him "Rafael." I say, "OK, here's the activity. Please try to stand up." Rafael eagerly stands up. I say, "No, Rafael. You're not listening. Sit down." My poor victim sits as I say, "Now, Rafael, *please* follow my directions. Try to stand up." Rafael catches on and stoops halfway between sitting and standing, or he stays seated but clenches his fists and grunts, mock-*trying* to stand. I lead a cheer for Rafael. "*Now* you're trying! Good listening! Rafael, now stand up." He does, and I deadpan, "Isn't Rafael brilliant?"

Negotiating. The person says, "If you call me on Monday mornings to remind me, I'll get to the meetings by ten o'clock." Uh, thanks, but no thanks! It doesn't matter whether it's a good-faith or bad-faith offer. What matters is whether the offer is acceptable. Can you live with it? If not, paraphrase the "solution," graciously decline it, and invite other ones: "You see the need for punctuality, so you'd like me to remind you. [Pause] I can see where my nudging you would help. Thanks for working toward a solution. That one doesn't work, since it makes me responsible for fixing the problem, not you. Any other ideas?" Once you get an acceptable answer, paraphrase it, express gratitude, arrange NEXT STEPS, and end the conversation appreciatively.

Bailing. "No sweat. Got it covered. I'm late to a meeting. Anything else?" Whoa. I don't trust that resolution, do you? Unless the person is sincere and truly rushed, you are knee-deep in a Flight tactic. Either way, paraphrase and offer to reschedule: "You're saying you'll handle this, so thanks. You seem pressured right now. I'm not comfortable rushing closure, so let's finish after your appointment when we're both less stressed." If the rushed recommitment is sincere, the person will agree. If the feigned recommitment is a defensive ruse, the person may bark in a huff, "Fine! I guess you just won't let this go! Let's deal with this B.S. now!" You know what to do. Paraphrase your tail off to scoop out obvious unexpressed emotion: "Sounds like you're still really angry that I'm holding you accountable." This overlaps with the next "Thin Ice" situation.

Lingering Defensiveness. Don't be fooled by resentful acquiescence. False-positive recommitments like "If you say so . . . Whatever . . . You're the boss . . ." are kisses of death signaling residual upset about your persistence. Paraphrase and ask an open-ended question to unearth true feelings, or else you'll wind up with compliance rather than true recommitment: "You're saying you'll address the problem. It seems like you're just giving in, resenting it, and feeling under my thumb."

Similarly, if the person claims they'll keep the agreement, but their nonverbals are screaming at you, paraphrase that mismatch: "Jake, I appreciate your recommitting. At the same time, you're rolling your eyes and clenching your fists, so I can't help feeling that you're still pissed off." Another style is, "Your words say 'yes' while your eye rolls seem to say 'up yours, Rick.'"

Defusing Tougher Defenses

General Guidelines

Rough Sailing *Straight Talk* skills are pushed to the max when Fight or Flight defenses are especially strong. Before sharing tactics for coping with silence, crying, or stomping out of the room (the other person, not you!), here are overall tips for managing heavy feelings:

- *The Straight Talk Mindset:* Remember your noble mission of being *Assertive* rather than *Passive* or *Aggressive*, and your self-commitment to being part of the communication solution rather than part of the problem.
- *Self-Talk:* Rely on mental self-discipline to expect heavy-duty defensiveness, to not take it personally, and to reframe "lies" or "insults" as

emotional reactions to perceived threat. Defensiveness isn't *supposed* to be fair or sensible!

- *Feelings Focus:* Paraphrase the person's emotions and the reasons for them, or at least for *claiming* to have them (since at times the defender manufactures a feeling to manipulate you). Either way, paraphrasing the *feelings* is where the action is and will elicit the "yes" confirmation that you've understood more quickly than by only rephrasing *thoughts*.

- *"Clean Anger" Nonverbals:* Curb accusatory, doubting, or vengeful body language or vocal tones that sabotage empathy. This doesn't mean to deny being upset, since "clean anger" is warranted and impactful.

- *Don't Taint Your Listening:* Don't conflate your listening and speaking turns by adding your own viewpoint to your paraphrases. Check out this loser: "You felt helpless when IT didn't get you the data to complete your analysis, and that's why you didn't get me the report even though you *knew* it was due today and still *failed* to meet your commitment." Sorry, but close is only good in horseshoes and hand grenades! This "paraphrase" (uh, NOT!) adds on the confronter's own agenda as a caboose, which opens Pandora's box, letting polluted anger flow (e.g., "you *knew* was due . . . *failed* . . .").

The Tough Ones

Extremely volatile defenses might make you feel like a minor league baseball rookie called up to the majors and thrown into a playoff game. I'm your Guardian Angel coach to help you defuse silence, crying, or stomping out of the room.

Silence. "The Sound of Silence" is a great Simon and Garfunkel song, but it's not a welcome melody when you state your *Confronting* Message and get nothing back. Nada. Zilch. Zippo. Options for handling silence depend on its duration and flavor:

- *Return the Silence:* If someone goes mute, return the favor. Calmly gaze at the person and wait. The person being held accountable feels more on the spot. They'll likely eventually mumble something. Paraphrase and move on.

- *Offer an Open-Ended Question or Encouragement:* However, don't lapse into an absurd game of "Chicken" to see who blinks first and speaks! Explore what's going on (e.g., "What's up for you, Maggie?") or offer encouragement (e.g., "Ollie, it's OK to tell me what you're thinking.").

- *Paraphrase Body Language:* Try to name the emotion being nonverbally expressed:
  - *Hurt.* With eyes to the floor, the person looks disheartened: "Maria, I get the sense this is coming as a real surprise to you, and that I've discouraged you—a real kick in the stomach. [Open question] What's up?"
  - *Anger.* No words, just steam coming out of their nostrils: "Chang, you look really ticked off at me. [Empathic question] Is your silence saying you'll get back at me by shutting down? [Open question] Come on, Chang, what are you thinking?"
  - *Confusion.* Furrowed brow and perplexed grimace: "Uri, if I were in your shoes, I might feel baffled by what my boss was saying, or helpless about how to respond—at a loss for words. [*Check*] Is any of that on target?"

- *Self-disclose:* Nothing has worked so far. Make a sincere person-to-person appeal to help the person be more forthcoming: "I've hesitated approaching you about this because it's stressful for me, too. I'm not trying to hurt you, Francois. I just want to talk this out person to person. OK?"

- *Paraphrase Stubborn Resistance:* If the person's *still* silently digging in their heels, reflect their fury: "Wow, Tanya, I get it. You are mad as hell. You must be thinking, 'Screw you, Rick. I'll show you. You can't make me talk.'" This may prompt her to blurt, "No kidding I'm livid! You always . . ."). You may not get a verbal "yes" that you're on target, but her eyes may confirm your spot-on paraphrase. That's your cue to say, "Tanya, your eyes are shouting, 'Damn right.' I still need you to know that I get steamed when you . . . [*Confronting* Message]."

- *Raise the Stakes:* If these good-faith efforts still fall short, it's blatant defiance. A rarely needed last resort is *Confronting* this refusal to engage. *Passive-Aggressive* obstinance is unacceptable and more serious than the original *Confronting* topic. A working relationship can't exist without communication. If you're the manager, you might escalate this situation, issue a written warning, bring in your boss, or contact HR. But first try a last-ditch *Confronting* Message. Maintain eye contact, slow down, and firmly say, "Lawrence, when I come to you in good faith after *Reminding* you twice about a performance concern and all I get is stonewalling silence, I'm at the end of my rope and furious [Negative Feeling], because it means we can't talk things out and I'm forced to take more serious steps." [Negative Impact]

Crying. Cory crumbles into tears before you finish your *Confronting* Message. RED ALERT! These crocodile tears are "weapons of mass distraction." Remember, your gift for this module is that this sobbing is a manipulative ploy, one he used as a kid to not get grounded. Don't get sidetracked. He's playing victim so that you'll feel sorry for him and back off. Don't take the bait! Paraphrase more gently than you would for blame or attacks. Move closer, use a softer voice, and pick feeling words that capture sadness, pain, angst, or anxiety. Then Refocus to your *Confronting* Message.

Naturally, if Cory never cries and seems genuinely sad or overwhelmed, you'd respond in a supportive, caring way. It'd be callous to keep *Confronting* if some distressful new variable has cropped up since your *G.A.I.N.* or *Reminding* conversations. You'd treat Cory compassionately, as if he'd despondently approached you for *Advising and Guiding*.

Stomping Out. Groups often ask, "What if the person gets so angry that you won't let them off the hook that they stomp out?"

- *Use Stronger Feeling Words:* Accurately and empathically capture the person's emotions with strong feeling words (e.g., "fuming . . . incredibly mad . . . enraged . . .") or feeling-laden phrases (e.g., "You want to throw in the towel . . . you've had it . . . you're fed up . . . you're not going to take this B.S.").
- *Use the Person's Name:* Use their name as you paraphrase (e.g., "Manny, you're so disgusted by our talk that you're out of here . . ."). Manny may

turn around and confirm your paraphrase, "No s***, Sherlock! I'm pissed off, and furthermore . . ." Manny's not saying "yes, *period*," since he's still spewing. But he's remaining engaged at the door. Refocus by *Addressing the Defense*: "I get how upset you are, Manny, and that wasn't my goal. I'm not happy either. Let's work this out so it's off both of our plates." Manny, still standing, at least is staying and facing the music as you restate your *Confronting* Message.

- *Adjust Your Voice:* Just as you would paraphrase softly to match the mood of downer emotions, now empathize with Manny's anger by raising your voice slightly (not as loud as his). Paraphrasing someone's rant too softly can sound over-logical, unfeeling, or condescending. Do *not* amp up your volume during your speaking turn—only while paraphrasing his upset feelings.

- *Stand Up:* Only if you're physically smaller and not a male *Confronting* a female, consider standing yourself when the defender stands to leave. Paraphrase with the person's name and *slowly* follow them partway toward the door. This must not seem like a threat or provocation—just engaging. As you "listen down" their venom, "wean" the venter from the door, edging slowly back toward the chairs.

- *Preview Accountability:* Your attempts to draw the hothead back into conversation may not work. As the person storms out, clarify that they may go away, but the issue won't. As the avoider reaches for the doorknob, calmly but firmly say, "Manny, I understand if you need to gather yourself. We do need to finish this conversation. I'll be here tomorrow at nine o'clock. I'd rather not leave it hanging, but if you need to, we can." You've made it crystal clear in a nonthreatening way that you are not letting this go. Manny knows that he needs to deal with you . . . *this* century!

No Hall Hell! If the person leaves, never follow. It'd look pretty silly walking down the hall paraphrasing Manny as you pass people: "Manny, you're so mad you want to throw in the towel . . . (Hi, Elena, how's your new consultant?) . . . Anyway, Manny, I know you're fed up with this rule . . . (Hey, Mary! Sorry about the pricing changes.) . . . As I was saying, Manny, I know you're tempted to quit because . . ."

Virtual Variations: *Confronting*

Confronting virtually is high-risk. Make every effort to hold someone accountable in person or at least by video conferencing. The temptation is to hide with email *Confronting* (e.g., "It lets me cool off and choose my words more carefully"). Trust me. If at all possible, don't go there.

Fallback Position: Video Call or Telephone

In our global world, more and more conversations—including emotional ones—happen virtually. For *Confronting*, email or text that you need a phone video call about an important issue. On the call, open like you would in person, setting the serious tone while also expressing optimism that you'll get to the other side together. Paraphrase like crazy, carefully document, and send a follow-up email thanking the person for recommitting.

Last Resort: Email

If a telephone or video conversation isn't possible, only then resort to email. Use extra care, due to lacking nonverbal cues or instant feedback. Email *Confronting* may come across as more *Aggressive* and "loaded" than intended. Counteract these dangers with the following guidelines.

- *Avoid CAPS, Red Fonts, and Exclamation Points (!!!):* Unless your colleague and you always use these to convey excitement versus anger, it's standard practice in business to avoid them.
- *State Your Intent:* Set a positive spirit like in face-to-face *Confronting*: "Hi, John. I have some real concerns about your performance at the off-site meeting. I care about your success, so please don't read this as an unfriendly tone." Avoid clichés like "Not to sound mean, *but* . . . I hate to say so, *but* . . . with all due respect . . ." since they may put people on the defensive.
- *Use "Feeling Words" Versus Judging Words:* "I felt upset when you . . ." sounds better than "I can't believe that you . . ."

- *Avoid Orders:* "Don't send the reports to Jason anymore" or "Stack the boxes only twenty-five feet high" may seem efficient to you. Without tone of voice to help, these sound overly bossy. Effective *Confronting* Messages avoid sending solutions. They state the problem behavior, your feelings (maybe), and the Negative Impact, leaving it to the other person to offer the solution or recommit. If you *must* send a solution, avoid commands or mandates by using respectful statements (e.g., "I'd prefer . . . I'd like . . . I need you to . . .") or questions (e.g., "Could you . . . May I ask you to . . . ?"). *Please* and *thank you* go a long way when *Confronting* via email.

- *Be Careful About Copying:* Be wary of inviting others to your *Confronting* party. If others are bcc-ed, say why they're being included, since they may otherwise think you're inappropriately calling out someone or wasting time with irrelevant emails.

- *Paraphrase Abundantly:* If the other person is upset in their email reply or text, paraphrase in writing before expressing your own point of view. You *can* "listen" via email or text.

- *Use a Back-and-Forth Process:* Some people prefer text threads or an exchange of multiple shorter emails that simulates a telephone or face-to-face conversation. This method strives for a *dialogue* in writing rather than one-way communication of an intense message. Instead of one long email and one response, an exchange allows for immediate clarifications. A single long email may set off reactivity. Misunderstanding can "spin out" of control before you can say, "Wait. Sorry, that's not what I meant."

Module Wrap-Up

This module tackled the toughest Rough Sailing situation, constructively *Confronting* people who break commitments or exhibit behavior we can't tolerate. We've leveraged all of your skills to tackle this cliff-edge conversation's perilous twists and turns.

Remember that the skills can be adapted to other difficult interactions. Just replace the Three-Part "I" *Confronting* Message with whatever content your *Assertive Speaking* agenda entails (e.g., announcements, poor appraisal ratings, bad news about a promotion, tough *G.A.I.N.* requests, etc.). Then use Self-Talk, paraphrasing, refocusing, *Bias-Free Language*, and closing for accountability.

As you read about *Confronting* Conversation skills, you may have felt lost or overwhelmed by the various steps, nuances, and examples. Remember that you're really using the same core skills of the *Straight Talk Mindset*, *Assertive Speaking*, and *Active Listening*. Admittedly, there's lots more going on (e.g., using a behavioral message, understanding the nature of defensiveness, managing your Self-Talk, Refocusing with artful segues, and sandwiching all this between the bookends of opening assertively and closing with accountability). You can do it!

Module Eleven | *Disagreeing Agreeably*

Using Conversational Aikido

> A spoonful of sugar helps the medicine go down.
> —MARY POPPINS

Disagreeing Without Being Disagreeable

Your boss tells you to implement a new idea or policy that you believe will cause problems (because it's a boneheaded idea!). You'd be out of integrity not to raise your concerns or tactfully disagree. Still, you don't want to commit a career-limiting move. Or, you're comfortable with the overall idea, but you want to foster deeper thinking about potential obstacles, and oh, yeah . . . you want to live to talk about it!

You'll *Disagree Agreeably* by using the Conversational Aikido Technique with managers, associates, clients, vendors, friends, family (especially kids), and others in order to:

- tactfully disagree, express misgivings, or say "no" to someone's idea, and
- invite others to consider factors they haven't.

Aikido Philosophy. The Eastern martial art of aikido is about harmony, not conflict, and equates well to *Disagreeing Agreeably*. Western boxing involves over-powering a foe—force against force. Aikido isn't about striking, overpowering, or forcing an opponent to comply. It entails moving with and aligning with the other's energy to remain in control. Conversational Aikido involves understanding their viewpoint and finding its merit before expressing your differing point of view.

Using Political Savvy. Conversational Aikido is interpersonally savvy *and* politically savvy. When power, politics, and ego are involved, this tool helps you to fly under the radar of a superior's "hyperactive ego gland." Your well-intentioned feedback may be interpreted by ego-trippers as unwarranted criticism or an implied threat. Politically naïve people put their foot in their mouth so much they contract Athlete's Tongue. They could floss with shoelaces!

The Conversational Aikido Technique prevents you from wounding the king or queen. The king or queen is still alive. Your head may get chopped off! Don't let your intellectual "rightness" or subject matter expertise lure you into criticizing an idea in an overly zealous way, even if the egotist doesn't possess position power. Being in someone's doghouse is unwise regardless of their status.

The Conversational Aikido Technique: Step-by-Step

Influence adeptness requires awareness of the impact of your behavior. You already know that direct but respectful wording and tone must supplant inflammatory (*Aggressive*) language or weak (*Passive*) language. Let's plug *Assertive Speaking, Active Listening,* and the *Straight Talk Mindset* into the steps of the Conversational Aikido Technique for *Disagreeing Agreeably*:

1. *Listen* Nonjudgmentally and Empathically to the Idea
2. Generously State the *Merits* of the Idea
3. Tactfully Surface Your *Concerns*
4. Give Your *Conclusion*

1. *Listen* Nonjudgmentally and Empathically to the Idea. *Focus* your body in order to pay empathic, nonjudgmental attention to the person's idea or request, regardless of what you're thinking. Paraphrase thoughts and feelings to capture the idea's essence, rationale, and emotions behind it. This demonstrates respect for the person, proves that you've understood their idea, and conveys that you accept its validity for that person. You're absorbing the idea instead of prematurely reacting, evaluating, or dismissing it. This is akin to aikido's aligning philosophy, as is the next step.

2. Generously State the *Merits* of the Idea. Before expressing negative reactions, first show that you see the pluses of the idea or proposed action. Genuinely say everything you like about the idea, and not just in a token way. Really lean into this step with multiple, specific, and sincere positive comments about the idea's redeeming qualities and benefits. Like Mary Poppins sings in the movie, "A spoonful of sugar helps the medicine go down." You're helping the person consider their idea's downsides by first being in harmony with its upsides (acknowledging). This "spoonful of sugar" does NOT mean you are BS-ing or sugar-coating your viewpoint about the idea's cons or drawbacks.

Most ideas have some merit, even if it's just the passion that the person has for it or the energy they invested into developing it. If you can't find anything positive to say, can you spell r-i-g-i-d? Aren't you being a crap-detector? Show good faith by digging deeper to find some aspect of the person's idea that you respect. It'll pave the way for what comes next—your concerns or disagreement. Lead-in phrases for this merits step include: "What I like about your idea is . . . I can appreciate . . . You've done your homework . . . What's admirable is how you . . . The upsides are clear, like . . . I support your goal of . . . Some merits I see are . . . We're really aligned on . . ."

3. Tactfully Surface Your *Concerns*. You've earned the right to candidly share the idea's variables they haven't considered, or missing pieces. You've generously shared the pros, so don't be shy about voicing the cons. This step's lead-in phrases include: "Let's also consider the possibility that . . . An issue might be . . . One concern is . . . A major challenge could be . . . I'm not as confident as you since . . . How will we respond to . . . A downside I see is . . ."

When bridging from acknowledging the idea's positives to voicing reservations, steer clear of the word *but* or its cousins *however* and *nevertheless*. They erase everything you said before them. The person will only hear the "but," not the merits you've cited. You know what I mean if a romantic interest has ever said to you, "I really like you as a friend, *but* I'm not interested in dating you." Ugh. "But" risks your "likes" about an idea coming across as merely going through the motions because some book told you to do so. Worse, the "but" might make your genuine accolades sound like you're spouting condescending B.S. to placate the person.

Instead of saying "but" after sharing merits, just insert a beat of silence before surfacing your concerns. Other options are to replace the "B" word (!) with "and" or the phrase "at the same time . . ." Interpersonal skills courses are often too absolutist about the "but" taboo. If everything else you do shows that you sincerely do see an idea's assets, then banishing "but" need not be a court mandate. The world won't end if you do say "but," so just keep this pointer in mind.

4. Give Your *Conclusion*. You've conveyed both sides of the coin—the idea's pros (merits) and cons (concerns)—acknowledging that they can stand side by side in the universe. Now, give your bottom-line conclusion, which might be to problem-solve around your concerns and move forward, to withhold support until later, or to graciously decline supporting the idea. You still can convey respect for the person. You're not rejecting *them*, just their idea.

But It Really IS a Bogus Idea! One workshop group marveled at a participant's creativity in handling a colleague's pretty ridiculous ideas—one from the land of the bizarre. Lynn described how, once, her team member's suggestion was so weirdly unrealistic, people sat stunned in awkward silence. No one could come up with a single merit. Lynn broke the discomfort by saying, "You know, Kim, we can always count on you to think outside of the box!"

Back after a break, I blow a fanfare on my trumpet to introduce Darryl, who rehearsed a script with me during lunch. I set up a demo saying, "My boss, Darryl, is the finance director and I'm his finance manager. Darryl wants to change our monthly consolidation process so that newly acquired businesses can submit monthly numbers using their legacy company's reporting format. I'm worried about how labor intensive this will be."

Demonstration: ***Disagreeing Agreeably.*** In our demo, as participants take notes, I *Disagree Agreeably* with the Conversational Aikido Technique. Ready? ACTION!

LISTEN NONJUDGMENTALLY AND EMPATHICALLY

[Rick Focuses with his body and uses Explore skills as Darryl lays out his idea.]

Darryl: I've been thinking about our Corporate Buzz reputation with our four newly acquired businesses. I'd like you to announce that new companies aren't required to use our uniform month-end financial reporting template until Q4. They can submit numbers however they want—using their old company's format. This will send the message we're adapting to them rather than vice versa. It'll build trust and raise our political stock with them.

Rick: Darryl, you sound pumped about building stronger networking relationships with new business units by letting them use their own reporting template. You're optimistic that this will help us avoid our usual negative buzz as force-fitting functions into our way of doing business, and that it'll improve our rapport with them.

Darryl: That's a great summary. You're tracking me. What do you think?

GENEROUSLY STATE MERITS OF THE IDEA

Rick: Well, we're on the same page as far as wanting to change perceptions of Finance. The new business heads will appreciate your goal of adapting to their unique needs. Even our existing businesses sometimes complain that we're out of touch with the line businesses. *[Darryl responds*

*affirmatively, "Exactly . . ." so Rick continues with more
merits.*] Your idea also seems savvy about the politics of
acquisitions, since it'll reduce resentment about being
swallowed up by a larger corporation. Plus, I'll learn about
each new business as I sit with them to understand their
report formats. You've obviously thought this through . . .

Darryl: Right. I'm glad you're on board, so can you announce
this next week?

SURFACE CONCERNS TACTFULLY

Rick: Darryl, I can tell you're eager to get returns on this innovation, and I want to support it full steam. I do have one
concern to resolve to ensure our success. [*Darryl expresses
openness: "Sure, I want to reality test my idea."*] You've
probably already considered how it'll take extra time to
compile, process, and send our monthly consolidation up
the ladder since we're integrating multiple reporting formats. You might not realize just how much time. I worry
the plan could backfire, since even an extra day's delay in
assembling our composite numbers for Jim as CFO might
rattle him. We don't want him to take it out on the new
businesses and mandate using the usual uniform template. That could lower our credibility with Jim and with
the new folks.

Darryl: Well, what do you suggest other than scrapping the plan?

Rick: What if we give the new business groups a choice? They
can use our current corporate format and submit reports as
usual on the last Wednesday of the month. If they'd rather
use their legacy reporting format, they have to submit it on
Monday, two days early. That will give my team adequate
time for integration by Friday.

Darryl: That's a great idea, now that you bring it up. They'll still appreciate the added flexibility. I'll sleep on it and let's revisit the idea first thing tomorrow morning, OK?

GIVE YOUR CONCLUSION

Rick: Sure thing. And don't get me wrong. I love the goal behind your idea. We just don't want to disappoint Jim because he can get antsy about summary report timeliness.

Darryl: For sure, I get that. OK, so let's meet tomorrow at ten.

CUT!

As we applaud Darryl and debrief the demonstration, I explain, "You may worry that others might see you as weak or kissing up when you state merits of an idea. Not so. You're just preventing defensiveness and resentment that you'd set off by jumping all over someone's idea (e.g., 'Aw, no way! My team will throw a fit!'). You're *not* backing off, and the person will know it when you surface concerns. After you gently *Disagree Agreeably* with Gary (your boss) in a group meeting, you might later explain, 'Gary, I actually have even stronger reservations than I shared publicly, and here's why . . .' Gary will respect and appreciate your verbal discipline of not trashing his idea in the group." ■

The Tactful "No"

A slight variation on *Disagreeing Agreeably* involves turning down someone's request for you to take on a project. We've all been there. Someone approaches you to *G.A.I.N. Commitment.* You can't comply with the request, because you'd regret or resent it later. You want to build a positive, trusting relationship, so you use Conversational Aikido to express positive energy before expressing your concern or, in this case, before saying "no."

1. Listen Nonjudgmentally and Empathically. You know how to *Focus* your body, so combine nodding, a forward-leaning posture, facial reactions, and eye contact with plenty of *Exploring* skills' acknowledgments and encouragements. Paraphrase the request to show you're carefully considering it. Capture the speaker's eagerness, enthusiasm, or other emotions around the request (e.g., "Dora, you sound excited about the employee engagement survey initiative and the role you're hoping I can play.").

2. Generously State the Merits of the Request. Don't hold back on genuine compliments and the idea's benefits (e.g., "I admire the mission of the engagement survey project, since we can't address our retention challenge without identifying people's dissatisfactions. Your work on survey design and rollout is really impressive.").

3. Tactfully Say "No" with Reasons. Apologetically yet *Assertively* explain why you are declining (e.g., "Unfortunately, I need to decline serving on your task force. Tara has me starting clinical trials and this quarter is the key start-up time. I don't want to only deliver halfway on both commitments.").

4. Offer Alternative Support. Be clear that "no" means "no," instead of waffling or leaving the door open. You're doing the person no favors by providing false hope. Offer any alternative support that you *are* comfortable providing (e.g., "Tell you what, Dora. I *can* support you by making sure my team promptly completes the survey, and by talking it up with other directors, so they get their people on board. You mentioned that there is a monthly advisory council. I'm happy to participate that way.").

Module Wrap-Up

Regardless of how adamant someone is about their idea or how much you'd like to accommodate their entreaty for help, there are times you need to express concerns or simply decline. The Conversational Aikido Technique is a recipe for

Disagreeing Agreeably or saying "no" tactfully and amicably. It's also useful when responding to appeals by voicemail or email. You don't just send a reply that kills someone's idea; you paraphrase the idea in writing, share its merits, and then tactfully surface your concerns (especially if you copy others). Now, think about your key insights and possible changes you can benefit from making when *Disagreeing Agreeably*.

Epilogue

Weaving the Skills into Your Life

> Success is the process of moving from failure to
> failure without losing your enthusiasm.
> —WINSTON CHURCHILL

Straight Talk Is an Art

Sorry about bringing up the "F" word in the above Churchill quote. You'll make mistakes and falter at times, but you can't *really* fail as long as you're *Taking the Straight Talk Challenge* of giving the skills a try. Still, let's not be naïve about the challenges of implementing the interpersonal best practices you've learned. Holding yourself accountable for positive communication in today's "brave new world" of work is a daunting mission fraught with obstacles. So is mastering any competency, discipline, or art. And interpersonal influence is all three: an applied behavioral sciences competency, a demanding discipline, and an admirable art.

The groundbreaking social philosopher Erich Fromm wrote *The Art of Loving*, in which he postulates that love is an art that can be learned, versus some magical and mysterious construct. Although "love" isn't this book's topic, Fromm prescribes these relevant five elements for mastering *any* art so that it's less ethereal and less subject to chance: Concentration, Patience, Discipline, Practice, and my favorite . . . "Supreme Concern with Mastery of the Art" (I love that one!).

These same ingredients are needed to master the art of *Straight Talk*. They will keep you on track toward world-class communication skills and sustain you as you encounter four inevitable challenges along your path to more productive, harmonious relationships: (1) faltering Self-Talk, (2) people you dislike, (3) the skills' "fade-out factor" over time, and (4) a back-home organizational culture that doesn't support *Straight Talk* skills. Let's address and overcome these hurdles.

Challenge #1: Faltering Self-Talk

Our journey began with *Straight Talk Mindset*'s inner game—vigilant awareness of your Self-Talk. Implementing *Straight Talk* will demand taking heed of your Self-Talk with each person before, during, and after various interactions. If you find yourself embroiled in counterproductive thoughts about any of the skills, just remember the adage "Garbage in, garbage out." You *can* reprogram yourself for more constructive attitudes as we've explored throughout this book.

Challenge #2: People You Dislike

The comedian George Burns once quipped, "Sincerity. If you can fake that, you've got it made." We *can't* fake sincere, genuine affection. We've all worked with someone who was just tough to like. They reminded us of someone, had an annoying mannerism, or rubbed us the wrong way. It's hard to use *Straight Talk* skills to treat someone with respect (e.g., *Active Listening*), honesty (e.g., *Assertive Speaking*), and positive regard (e.g., *Recognizing*) if we don't care for them! Let's gain perspective on people we seem to involuntarily dislike with a final *Straight Talk* concept called the *"A" Stairway*.

A Final Self-Talk Shift: The *"A" Stairway*

This last *Straight Talk* model is a mental map for transcending involuntary either/or feelings of "I like this person" or "I don't like this person." While we can't *make* ourselves like someone, the *"A" Stairway* offers behavioral options that we can *decide* to implement. Each *Stairway* step entails a beneficial quality and *Straight Talk* skill that we can extend to an "unlikable" person without faking affection. Each step feeds into and makes it easier to reach the next one. As we climb the *Stairway*, we may gradually find ourselves at the last stairstep, genuinely liking the person.

The diagram below doesn't guarantee a "Stairway to Heaven" like the Led Zeppelin song, but at least you won't be trapped in a forced choice between *Avoidance* and *Affection*. I find this model liberating and uplifting, so I hope you do, too.

A̲voidance ("I Dislike You"). This first step is involuntary. If we simply don't like someone, we tend to steer clear of them. We often hear that hate is the opposite of love. In truth, the opposite of love is the isolation of *Avoidance*. We can decide to ascend the *Stairway*.

A̲ttention. Without liking someone, we can still decide to pay *Attention* to them, to look at them, to merely acknowledge their existence. One participant commented on the loneliness of workmates not even establishing eye contact, "Those can be mighty long hallways." Researcher René Spitz found that institutionalized babies who didn't receive enough human contact had higher rates of illness and mortality. We can nudge ourselves to at least *see* the "unlikable" person with our *Focusing* skills, fulfilling a basic human need.

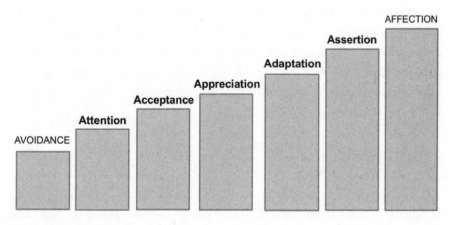

Epilogue Diagram 1 | *The "A" Stairway"*

Acceptance. After *Attention*, we can intentionally offer *Acceptance* of a person's right to have their own opinions and feelings. Whether or not we like them or agree with their thinking, we can still show them respect by affirming their frame of reference and their place in the world as an inalienable right. The best way to offer *Acceptance* is through *Active Listening*.

Appreciation. This next *A* step and quality is kindled by *Recognizing* strengths. You now realize its power and motivational magic. Without liking someone, we can acknowledge and applaud their positive behaviors, traits, and strengths. The previous steps of *Attention* (*Focusing* skills) and *Acceptance* (*Active Listening*) allow us to see others' assets and positive attributes.

Adaptation. The Golden Rule says, "Treat others as you would have them treat you" (Respect, Honesty, Fairness). The Platinum Rule says, "Treat others as *they* would have you treat them." *Adapting* to someone respects their communication style, comfort zone, ethnicity, culture, gender, interests, and so on. We can show sensitivity to their uniqueness. If they're into sports, we can talk sports. If music is their thing, we can relate to that. Models that teach flexing to different communication styles (e.g., Myers-Briggs, Social Styles, and D.I.S.C.) honor others as individuals. After all, everyone is unique—just like everyone else!

Assertion. Climbing the *"A" Stairway*, we've reached the point where we can hold the other person accountable. We now have the right and even the responsibility to assertively *G.A.I.N. Commitment*s to meet our work needs, *Remind* people if they drop the ball, *Challenge Ideas*, and *Confront* ways that they're out of line. *Confronting* broken agreements can cultivate positive working relationships. Aren't some of your richest relationships on the other side of conflict? Remember, anger is not the opposite of love. *Avoidance* is far more hurtful.

Affection ("I like you"). As we will ourselves to climb the *"A" Stairway*, each step dovetails into the next. Before we know it, we may experience spontaneous *Affection*. It's not a conscious decision, rather an outgrowth of our previous acts of volition. If we don't reach this step, the *"A" Stairway* still helps us to climb further from dislike and *Avoidance*.

Wee Wisdom. My son was philosophical at an early age. When Eric was aged five, he was listening to my wife, Cheryl, reading a bedtime story to two-year-old Carrie. As Mommy read about a boy's jealousy of his baby sister, Eric murmured, "Yeah, sometimes your anger can block your love." Later, while tucking Eric in, Cheryl and I repeated Eric's wise line and asked him if he'd learned it from his kindergarten teacher. "No, I figured it out myself. Sometimes your anger can block your love. You know, like clouds can block the sun . . . The sun is still there." What?? Who is this kid's real father? Confucius, Sartre, Hegel, or Kierkegaard?

Challenge #3: Fighting the Fade-Out Factor

Thank you for investing time, energy, and vulnerability into your interpersonal performance development. I respect and admire your dedication and "Supreme Concern with Mastery of the Art." But sorry. *Taking the Straight Talk Challenge* as we invited in module two requires some additional integration work: practicing, implementing, reinforcing, and teaching the

What reactions do you have to the *"A" Stairway*? While at first it may seem naïve about the difficulty of some relationships, its alternatives to only liking or disliking someone are freeing. May you earn "Straight As" on the *Stairway* and become a valedictorian of *Straight Talk*! Seriously, I hope this twist on your influence skills further inspires resolve to apply them.

Straight Talk skills. These steps are "the price of the dream" of retaining your skills and fighting the fade-out factor that plagues learning programs.

Practicing and Implementing

As the saying goes, "Use it or lose it." Any value you've derived from this book will wither away if you don't apply your *Straight Talk* skills ASAP. Don't implement them in the toughest situations right off the bat. Start small. Notice the lack of *Focusing* in social situations (but don't lecture people about it!). Mentally paraphrase people on TV. Empathically paraphrase a hurting friend's feelings. *G.A.I.N. Commitment* on lower-stakes topics. Use *Recognizing* skills with various people (no need to hug the grocery store clerk!). Be cognizant of your Self-Talk and notice which *"A" Stairway* step you've reached with different people.

Next, gradually put your foot in the water with the Rough Sailing applications of *Reminding, Confronting,* and *Disagreeing Agreeably.* For any situation that will be challenging, practice with a friend. Explain who you want them to role-play and elicit feedback. Ask about what you did that was *Assertive* and any *Borderline Passive* or *Borderline Aggressive* behaviors that leaked into your practice.

Reinforcing

At the conclusion of *Straight Talk* courses, I often whip out my trumpet to play "Pomp and Circumstance." Graduations bring out the Hallmark Card in me! I want you to sustain your *Straight Talk* skills, so please visit my training company's website (www.BrandonPartners.com/StraightTalkBook). You'll find some graduation presents for keeping your learning alive, your skills growing, and your mission enduring: the *Straight Talk Self-Assessment,* action planning tools, a *Straight Talk Meeting Toolbox* for weaving the skills into meetings, the *Blocks to Skill Use* screening tool, and links to video clips to see me discussing the skills (if you aren't sick of me).

Teaching *Straight Talk*

> If you can't explain it to a six-year-old,
> you don't understand it yourself.
> —ALBERT EINSTEIN

The best way to learn a skill is to teach it, so I urge you to share *Straight Talk* concepts with others. National Training Laboratories' (NTL) research found that while lecture, reading, audiovisual, and demonstration modes positively impact learner retention, the best grounding comes from group discussions (50 percent retention), practice (75 percent retention) and teaching (90 percent retention). Therefore, discuss and drill *Straight Talk* skills with others. Find ways to teach the skills: briefing your team on this book, tutoring someone, spearheading a *Straight Talk* blog or Google Doc discussion site, setting up a Q&A public forum, or finding other ways to help people learn interpersonal influence skills.

Challenge #4: Back-Home Organizational Culture

Your company or agency may have a communication strategy for improving the work climate, but as the saying goes, "Culture eats strategy for lunch." You won't use your *Straight Talk* skills in a vacuum, rather within your organization's culture, which will present both supportive tailwinds and resistant headwinds. You'll experience both positive and negative inertia for *Straight Talk*'s candor and empathy.

These supporting and restraining forces around positive communication will depend on leadership's modeling and messages, work demands, company norms, people's reactions, and other variables. What can you do to reduce the restraining forces against a *Straight Talk* culture in your organization and leverage the supporting forces for improved interactions? Are you willing to be a change agent for cultivating a more positive communication environment?

A Parting Parable

As you strive to foster a *Straight Talk* culture in your organization, it's important to keep perspective that we can only work on ourselves, rather than tackling the daunting task of transforming an entire company, agency, or institution. Culture change work demands patience, since organizational change is more like a cruise ship's wide arc than a speedboat's sharp turns. And culture change happens one person at a time, as this allegory illustrates.

> A mother is at her desk when her five-year-old son interrupts her to play. Engrossed in her work, Mommy wants to occupy Max. She promises to play together as soon as the eager child tapes together a jigsaw puzzle. Mom grabs a magazine and rips out an advertisement page that has planet Earth on it. She tears the page into thirty pieces. "Honey, Mommy will play with you after you put together this puzzle." She goes back to work confident that she'll have two hours of uninterrupted concentration.
>
> Twenty minutes later, Max hands his mother the puzzle all taped together. Amazed, Mommy asks Max, "Sweetie, how did you put the

world together so fast?" With a twinkle in his eye, the five-year-old-going-on-eighty guru explains, "Silly Mommy. Nobody can put together the whole world. But I turned the puzzle pieces over and on the other side was a picture of just one person. That was a lot easier to work on, and when I put the person together, the whole world just fell into place."

Acknowledgments

I believe that these "Acknowledgments" would be better titled "Gratitude." I view the process getting *Straight Talk* written, published, and promoted as being analogous to a ship's voyage. I am deeply grateful to quite a few people who helped me build the "ship," plot its course, set sail, ensure proper maintenance and operation, navigate the high seas, and arrive safely in the harbor of being in your hands today.

Just as a ship's engine propels it forward, the subject matter expertise I bring to this book forms the "go power" of the *Straight Talk* ship. My content engine has been fueled and tuned by many thought leaders such as Carl Rogers, Thomas Gordon, Herb Otto, Shad Helmstetter, Albert Ellis, Victor Frankl, and many others during my graduate studies. I am humbly indebted to my teachers, mentors, and colleagues, most notably Bob and Dot Bolton, Hugh Gunnison, Jerry Jud, Jerry Jampolsky, and Diane Cirincione. I am ever-thankful to have had Dr. Marty Seldman in my life—as a colleague, teacher, mentor, coauthor, friend, and brother from another mother.

I'm ever-grateful to my early-career fellow training staff, training professionals, and instructional designers for invaluably influencing my thinking about interpersonal skills. More recently, Brandon Partners' training staff and external brokers have been a constant source of pride, fulfillment, and success as my learning partners. Great thanks especially goes to Genevieve Davy, Maryann Rettig-Zucchi, Karen Martz, Diana Gruber, Holly Peck, and Moira Garvey.

Merry Cohen, I bow to the "Diva of Detail" within you. Thank you, first mate, for tirelessly funneling the *Straight Talk* concepts into clear, attractive, and user-friendly courseware and so much more. Your operational and organizational prowess is exceeded only by your devoted friendship.

Great thanks to my agent, John Willig, for your seasoned, practical, on-course navigation of the book proposal and for "docking" with BenBella Books. I salute and admire captain Matt Holt, my managing editor, for your faith, investment, and embodiment of the highest standards for a collaborative, straight talk–based publisher-author partnership.

Heartfelt appreciation goes to BenBella's Katie Dickman for exceptional developmental editing and steady-at-the-helm project management. Jessika Rieck seamlessly integrated Brigid Pearson's wonderfully playful jacket design with an interior book design that was congruent with my vision of a fun, easy-flowing reader journey. Jessika's patience, skill, and team spirit with manuscript revisions and her orchestration of the interior design and production process were world-class. Major kudos go to Mallory Hyde for remarkable marketing acumen, patient coaching of this promotion-naïve author, and unflinching publicity execution. Smith Publicity provided dedicated, skilled partnership with BenBella's marketing team. Tressa Jumps "jump-started" website promotion collateral with good grace and humor.

Thanks to a cadre of savvy, supportive advisors, including Maurice Ghysels for helping me re-sequence my early content, Ellen Seebold for caring social media coaching, and Diana Gruber and Holly Peck for generous help with *Straight Talk*'s virtual applications.

As COVID locked me down, my family's support and encouragement helped me make chicken salad out of chicken poop. To Eric, Scoops, Bob, Lori, and Matt, for your title and book jacket brainstorming feedback. High praise goes to my daughter, Carrie, for "youth-anizing" the manuscript. No words can capture my appreciation for my womb-mate, twin brother Bob, who has witnessed my communication ups and downs since before we were born. "Skip," your emotional support and legal guidance throughout the publishing process has been vital. Your uncanny, sharp mind and endless giving of time, patience, and wisdom can never be repaid (and I know it doesn't need to be—that's who you are). To my beloved sister Carla and dear friend Naomi, while you are no longer with us, your way of being fully present and focused listeners helps you live on as quiet heros and models of *Straight Talk* skills.

To my wife, Cheryl, thank you for helping me clarify my writing goals, clear the decks for my work, and tweak the early manuscript. You helped to infuse the final version with creative stories and metaphors when I was running on fumes. I'm forever indebted to you for being my sounding board, patient counselor, and forgiving friend when I'm not "walking the talk." You keep me accountable, keep me laughing, and keep me going in so many ways. You are the gift that keeps on giving.

Index

Page numbers in italics refer to illustrations.

About the Author

Photo by Michel Edens

Rick Brandon, PhD is the founder and president of the internationally respected training firm Brandon Partners. He has devoted thirty years to designing and delivering leadership and professional development workshops to hundreds of thousands in organizations, including scores of Fortune 500 companies. He coauthored the *Wall Street Journal* bestseller, *Survival of the Savvy: High-Integrity Political Tactics for Career and Company Success* (Simon and Schuster's Free Press), called "the pre-eminent book on organizational and political savvy" by leading experts and that won awards and recognition globally. He is honored to serve as distinguished faculty for the Institute for Management Studies and has taught and guest lectured at eight colleges and universities.

Dr. Brandon earned his PhD in counseling and management at the University of Arizona, his MA in school psychology from St. Lawrence University, and his BA in psychology from Case Western Reserve. Rick lives with his wife in Marin County, California, and has an adult son and daughter. He is lead singer and trumpeter in a popular local R&B cover band, performs in musical theater, and emcees community events. He also regularly volunteers through the non-profit *Bugles Across America* playing live "Taps" at the funerals of veterans. Rick's latest passion is coauthoring a new book with his actor-singer daughter to help performers conquer stage fright.